Nietzsche's Will to Power Naturalized

Nietzsche's Will to Power Naturalized

Translating the Human into Nature and Nature into the Human

Brian Lightbody

LEXINGTON BOOKS
Lanham • Boulder • New York • London

Published by Lexington Books
An imprint of The Rowman & Littlefield Publishing Group, Inc.
4501 Forbes Boulevard, Suite 200, Lanham, Maryland 20706
www.rowman.com

Unit A, Whitacre Mews, 26-34 Stannary Street, London SE11 4AB

Copyright © 2017 by Lexington Books

All rights reserved. No part of this book may be reproduced in any form or by any electronic or mechanical means, including information storage and retrieval systems, without written permission from the publisher, except by a reviewer who may quote passages in a review.

British Library Cataloguing in Publication Information Available

Library of Congress Cataloging-in-Publication Data

Names: Lightbody, Brian, author.
Title: Nietzsche's Will to power naturalized : translating the human into nature and nature into the human / Brian Lightbody.
Description: Lanham : Lexington Books, 2017. | Includes bibliographical references and index.
Identifiers: LCCN 2016050396 (print) | LCCN 2016050971 (ebook) |
 ISBN 9781498515771 (cloth : alk. paper) | ISBN 9781498515788 (Electronic)
Subjects: LCSH: Nietzsche, Friedrich Wilhelm, 1844–1900. Wille zur Macht. |
 Nihilism (Philosophy) | Values. | Will. | Power (Philosophy)
Classification: LCC B3313.W54 L54 2017 (print) | LCC B3313.W54 (ebook) |
 DDC 193—dc23
LC record available at https://lccn.loc.gov/2016050396

∞ ™ The paper used in this publication meets the minimum requirements of American National Standard for Information Sciences—Permanence of Paper for Printed Library Materials, ANSI/NISO Z39.48-1992.

Printed in the United States of America

Contents

Preface		vii
A Note on Sources		ix
Introduction: Nietzsche, Naturalism and Will to Power		xi
1	What is Naturalism? Two Key Aspects	1
2	Interpretations of Nietzsche's Naturalism in the Secondary Literature: Methodological and Substance Naturalism	25
3	Naturalism and Will to Power	55
4	Three Solutions: Clark, Richardson, Williams	89
5	Naturalism and the Human Being: Nietzsche's Naturalized Ontology	125
6	The Human Being and Naturalism: Nietzsche's Naturalized Epistemology	145
7	Homo Natura: Nietzsche's Naturalized Morality	173
Conclusion: Genealogy		189
Bibliography		195
Index		207
About the Author		209

Preface

The aim of the present book is to provide a naturalized account of Nietzsche's will to power. The primary goal then is to distill from Nietzsche's many passages on the subject of will to power in particular and power more generally, a coherent rendering of what will to power is in itself. The attempt to provide a clear, intelligible conceptualization of some idea is a standard approach to philosophical investigation. However, will to power resists easy theorization for several reasons. First, one of the core tenets of will to power is its claim that to conceptualize anything, is to totalize it—it is to strip the thing from the dynamic relationships it has to other things and thus to denature it. Thus, one does an injustice to an object or idea by removing it from the very environment which makes it possible. There is, however, another aspect to this: to totalize something so claims will to power is to constellate it in some new way; it is to reinterpret it according to the agenda of some agent, some will. Thus any attempt to understand the will to power is *ceteris paribus* to falsify and constellate it according to some prior schema. Hence, one cannot get at what anything is in and of itself, the will to power included. Indeed, trying to arrive at something in itself (*Ding-an-Sich*) is breathtakingly incoherent, so Nietzsche avows. Whether, therefore, the above objective of this book proves to be impossible, I leave for the reader to decide.

Notwithstanding these significant philosophical challenges, there are other issues as well. Nietzsche's manner of writing and philosophizing presents further complications to an already difficult task. I have therefore attempted, at times, a charitable reconstruction of Nietzsche insights to explicate them better and to make them stronger, philosophically speaking. The following then is an effort to think along and think through Nietzsche as much as it is a book on Nietzsche's views.

A Note on Sources

I use Nietzsche's *On the Genealogy of Morals* as a touchstone in two key ways: First, I believe that Nietzsche articulates a genealogical method. Underpinning this approach is an epistemic model of inquiry called virtue foundherentism. *The Genealogy of Morals* exemplifies what I take to be the core epistemic schema for all well-warranted empirical investigations. I attempt to extract this method from *The Genealogy*. Second, Nietzsche provides several naturalized examples of the will to power at work in this magnificent book. I take these examples as concrete manifestations of will to power. I then try to extract the properties of will to power, in the abstract, from these examples.

With all that said, I also supplement my account of will to power by using Nietzsche's middle and mature writings. These include *Human All Too Human, Daybreak, The Gay Science, Beyond Good and Evil, Twilight of the Idols, The Anti-Christ, Ecce Homo*, Nietzsche Contra Wagner as well as notes and selections from *Kritische Gesamtausgabe* (KGW) *Kritische Studienausgabe* (KSA), Kaufmann and Holingdale's *The Will to Power* and, where appropriate, Ludovici's translation of the same work. The use of *The Will to Power* may be controversial given the problems with its supposed authenticity as identified by Bernd Magnus and others. However, it is undeniable that there are dozens of profound ideas in this work that, while may not be Nietzsche's thoughts to the letter, are certainly in keeping with his spirit and philosophy.

Introduction

Nietzsche, Naturalism and Will to Power

Nietzsche's will to power has garnered much confusion and puzzlement by scholars over the years. Some, like Martin Heidegger, argue that will to power is a metaphysical principle in that it attempts to ground and explain all things, events and relationships in the universe to the drive for power. According to Heidegger, will to power is Nietzsche's attempt to "permanentise" becoming: Will to power is what remains once becoming is distilled.[1] For Heidegger, Nietzsche is, therefore, the "last metaphysician" because the will to power is an attempt to delineate the formatting of flux itself; "will to power is the word for the Being of beings as such, the *essentia* of beings."[2] It is a theory or perhaps better put an understanding that unlocks the secret, esoteric essence of the world and is, therefore, clearly a piece of metaphysics despite Nietzsche's protestations to the contrary.[3] Others think the position is merely a parable: It warns us to refrain from totalizing things, the world included.[4] Still, another group of scholars, small in number, but vocal, argue that Nietzsche only articulated the theory to reject it out of hand.[5]

When the position is understood and articulated well, it is the subject of savage attack in the secondary literature; even by those who are, by all accounts, scholars of Nietzsche's work.[6] The idea is often considered to be an ill-conceived attempt to narrate absolute becoming or to impose the idea of will, a notion Nietzsche seems to reject clearly, onto reality.

My task in this work is twofold: First, I attempt to articulate will to power in all its many facets. I endeavor to show how we may comprehend will to power—as much as any comprehension is possible—and that it is will to power that ties together and explains Nietzsche's ontology, epistemology, and ethical thinking. Will to power, in brief, is an attempt to understand, explain, and measure reality in all its dynamic fluctuations and permutations and yet for all that does not constitute first philosophy in the Aristotelian sense. It is best understood, as

Nietzsche suggests, from the inside: a channel of our all too human perspectivism.[7] Second, I then show how one can justify will to power by naturalizing it. My desire to naturalize will to power is twofold. First, the naturalizing of will to power demonstrates that the doctrine is not just another species of German metaphysical armchair philosophizing as Heidegger, at least on occasion, holds. Presenting the will to power as a naturalistic teaching is more consistent with Nietzsche's views. Second, one can affirm will to power on all levels of existence—from the cosmological to the zoological to the psychological. We do not need to present minimalistic accounts of the doctrine to save it from absurdity.[8]

Naturalizing any idea is no easy task and will to power is no exception. My plan of naturalizing is to demonstrate that will to power has causal, scientific supports in much the same manner that a spider web has anchor weights where the web is attached to nearby objects lending stability to the interior threads. Nevertheless, this does not entail that will to power is a scientific theory of either substantive or methodological stripe. The threads of will to power are more akin to channels: Scientific research supports them, but science is shot through with power, agenda, and perspective. There is, then, only a perfect holism of force where even the divisions of outside/inside, subject/environment, I/you, breakdown.

My interpretation is nuanced and subtle and open to misinterpretations especially when interpreters are too beholden to traditional epistemic and metaphysical dualisms (e.g., rationalism vs. empiricism, realism vs. antirealism, correspondence theories of truth vs. coherentist theories of truth, foundationalist vs. coherentist theories of justification, natural vs. human kinds of things, etc.). I attempt to address these issues and forestall as much confusion as I can as I proceed.

To begin, I will consider, albeit briefly, the idea of "ground" as a metaphysical term, and the purpose ground serves. The second term that needs to be considered carefully is that of "naturalization." I devote much of the present book, indeed an entire chapter, to examining the "how" and "what" of naturalism—how does one naturalize some entity or idea and what does it mean to naturalize an object or theory in philosophy. Thus I will not examine the idea of naturalism in any detail in this section as I will cover it extensively in the chapters to follow. What I will focus on in this section is the idea of ground. In the subsequent chapters and sections, I signal how will to power is grounded by scientific research without thereby reducing it to a methodology or school of scientific inquiry.

GROUND

Before beginning, I think it is important to understand what I understand by ground and what it means to claim that will to power is a grounding principle in that according to some interpreters, will to power conditions the very dynamism of becoming itself. It is always possible to take up a more traditional and perhaps all too German understanding of ground. However, I choose not to do this given the mysteriousness of such an idea.[9] For clarity's sake, I use ground in a Finean sense and will attempt to fit will to power into Fine's metaphysical schema. As will be demonstrated the results are rather mixed.

Kit Fine in his seminal article entitled, "What Is Metaphysics?" seeks to discover the common components to all metaphysical thinking. He notes that there are five main features: (1) "the aprioricity of its methods; (2) the generality of its subject matter; (3) the transparency or 'non-opacity' of its concepts; (4) its *eidecity* or concern with the nature of things; and (5) its role as a foundation of what there is."[10] Fine's model is illuminating and helpful for the purposes of my project for several reasons. First, Fine's notion of ground assists in articulating the nature of metaphysical claims. "Grounding," in a Finean context, refers to the *eidetic* character of a statement; that is, what the nature of the object or property is, to which the statement refers. In Fine's water example, he claims that stating that water by its very nature is H_2O, is an example of a statement that is *eidetic* regarding its content insofar as it makes an explicit reference to the very essence of water. If we compare this statement to section 1067 of *The Will to Power*: "The world is will to power and nothing else besides!" Or, if we prefer, section 36 of *Beyond Good and Evil*, "The world viewed from the inside, the world defined and determined according to its intelligible character—it would be will to power and nothing else."[11] It becomes clear that these are *eidetic* statements having to do with content along the lines described by Fine.[12] Nietzsche makes two claims in the above quotations: (1) To understand the will to power is to understand the world and, I would argue, all of the things contained therein; this is the universal, abstract conception of will to power with which so many scholars struggle to appreciate and (2) There is no distinction between the nature of the world and will to power; they are one and the same.

Thus, given this brief excursus it would seem that will to power, as exemplified by the two statements above, satisfies some of Fine's criteria. It clearly satisfies condition 4 but it also clearly satisfies condition 2 in that will to power is the most fundamental idea one may use to understand the very nature of reality.

What's more, Nietzsche explains that will to power may be used to understand the intersectional relationships between things within reality. If we confine ourselves to the biological world, for example, Nietzsche tells us that the category of life can be explained in more general terms of the will to power. "Life itself is will to power," Nietzsche declares in section 13 of *Beyond Good and Evil*.[13] Regarding self-preservation, Nietzsche contends that it is merely an indirect form of the will to power. He writes: "Physiologists should think before putting down the instinct of self-preservation as the cardinal instinct of an organic being. A living thing seeks above all to discharge its strength—life itself is will to power; self-preservation is only one of the indirect and most frequent results."[14] If we add additional passages to this initial comprehension, then it becomes even more apparent how Nietzsche's will to power satisfies an additional criterion (condition number 5) on Fine's list. Will to power serves as a "foundation for what there is" by describing why and how things are. Nietzsche argues: "This 'will to power' expresses itself in the interpretation in the manner in which force is used up; the transformation of energy into life, and 'life at its highest potency' thus appears as the goal. The same quantum of energy means different things at different stages of evolution."[15] It is clear that will to power is intended to serve as some ultimate explanation to explain the emergence of life itself and in combination with other passages, noted above, can be used to explain organic life from some new, higher perspective, hitherto not thought. Will to power is a grounding principle because it explains the *telos* of all things as bent on power and following Heidegger is the one common residue of being once all other properties, fluctuations, and essences are stripped away.

Fine's model, however, does collapse. This breakdown becomes clear when one views will to power through the lenses of conditions 1 and 3. Will to power is not, according to Nietzsche, a product of *a priori* hypothesizing; in fact, I will come to argue that the notions of *a priori* and *a posteriori* introduce a false dichotomy once will to power is truly understood. Moreover, the will to power does not satisfy condition number 3 because one can never reveal the essence or expose the depths of a concept, will to power included. Nietzsche writes in this regard: "A fundamental will to knowledge is the root in which . . . our ideas, our values, our yeas and nays, our ifs and buts, grow out of us with the necessity with which a tree bears fruit—related and each with an affinity to each, and evidence of one will, one health, one soil, one sun."[16] Will to knowledge, I will submit at this point, but later show more concretely, is simply a manifestation of power. Every idea and every value grow out of soil that can, in principle, never be fully exposed. Thus any attempt to reveal the conceptual or empirical constituents of the ground necessary to will anything give rise to an investigation of the organic conditions necessary to disclose these constituents and so on *ad infinitum*. Will to power, then, grounds nothing and reveals only a bottomless abyss. Expressing this point beautifully with much clarity Alphonso Lingis writes, "The Will to Power is an abyss (*Abgrund*) the groundless chaos beneath all grounds, all the foundations, and it leaves the whole order of essences groundless."[17]

These further implications of will to power proceed to unravel our attempt to fit Nietzsche's idea into Fine's model. Given the most minimalist construal of the notion, will to power simply denotes the proclivity for things to exercise force within their respective environments. Every bare unit of power,

Nietzsche evinces, "strives to become master over all space and to extend its force," and each encounters "similar efforts on the part of other bodies."[18] More than this all actions undertaken by a creature or thing are nothing more than expressions of force. This notion of force may be construed in different ways but from the above discussion it becomes clearer just how deeply disconcerting and puzzling—at least when understood as a metaphysical concept—will to power is. Fine, if we remember, claims that metaphysics serves as a grounding discipline; the purpose of metaphysics is to provide a foundation for things and to provide the *eidecity* understanding for truth claims. As argued above, the will to power certainly seems to satisfy both of these requirements. However, this reading is superficial for this "ground," as was discovered, is one founded on ever-shifting sands. For the will to power denotes the inherent perspectival nature of those creatures who take up a stance on a confoundedly created reality constructed, in part, by the very perspectives of the things in an environment. Following Muller-Lauter it makes more sense to speak about will to power than the will to power in the nominalized form.[19] "All evaluation," Nietzsche writes, "is made from a definite perspective."[20] Moreover, it is an assessment, after all, that is responsible for the construction of values and indeed as I will show things themselves.

What's more, the perspectives and attitudes we form and adopt are all those that are bent on dominating other persons, creatures, and even inanimate things. If we combine two passages this point becomes clearer: "When we speak of values we do so under the inspiration and from the perspective of life: life itself forces us to posit values; life itself values through us when we posit values."[21] Combining this passage with the following from *The Genealogy,* Nietzsche's full, chilling, unadulterated perspective on life comes into full focus: "To speak of just or unjust *in itself* is quite senseless; *in itself*, of course, no injury, assault, exploitation, destruction can be 'unjust,' since life operates *essentially*, that is in its basic functions, through injury, assault, exploitation, destruction and simply cannot be thought of at all without this character."[22] Nor does Nietzsche restrict his views to the human realm. Indeed, even simple organisms are considered by Nietzsche to be mere conduits of will to power:

> The will-to-power can manifest itself only against resistances, therefore it seeks that which resists it—this is the primeval tendency of the protoplasm when it extends pseudopodia and feels about. Appropriation and assimilation are above all a desire to overwhelm, a forming, shaping and reshaping, until at length that which has been overwhelmed has entirely gone over into the power domain of the aggressor and has increased the same.[23]

It is hoped by now that such passages reveal just how puzzling will to power is when understood as a metaphysical principle. However, such puzzlement becomes even acuter and vertiginous. For if one can reasonably claim that all actions undertaken by a creature are attempts to exert force within its environment, no matter how the notion of force is understood, then the proclamation that "the world is nothing more than "will to power" is itself a clear exertion of strength. Nietzsche's will to power, reflexively understood, seemingly undermines itself because even the idea of truth (as a manifestation of the will to knowledge which is itself an expression of force) becomes nothing more than a mere tool of coercion existing within a determined language game produced by power.

Stranger still is our response to will to power as a metaphysical or, if one prefers a grounding principle. Because embedded within the idea, is a normative component: If we are inclined to resist or even reject will to power, then we are merely expressing our will to power in simply denying it. More appropriately and perspicuously stated, it would be correct to say that will to power denotes nothing more than an aggregate. There are wills to power; perspectives on objects, people, attitudes, beliefs, but that even this view of an aggregate of wills is itself an example and manifestation of the will to power. The position is itself grounded in perspective. If the position, however, is only perspectively true then it does not seem grounded at all; it would be merely one perspective on the world and possibly a false one. So why take it seriously?

With this brief introduction in mind, the problems faced by the project of this book are significant but surmountable. On the surface, the will to power appears to fit nicely into Fine's model of metaphysics. However, as has now been shown, there are significant problems with this "fit." My thesis is that by naturalizing will to power we thereby discover its Finean grounding qualities. My general strategy will be one of pulling apart the various modes through which one can understand the will to power: ontological, epistemological, and ethical and then articulating the problems and paradoxes that emerge from each mode. I argue that we can then naturalize these modes in order, first, to better articulate will to power and second, to solve the most pressing problems in each sphere.

Turning to the second concern of the present book, which is that of naturalism, I think it is clear that to naturalize some object or process is difficult to define. I, therefore, begin by asking and answering the question: "What is naturalism?" Along with its corollary: "What does it mean to naturalize some entity or principle?" As I demonstrate in chapter one, the goals of naturalizing are often not made sufficiently clear nor is it always possible to understand how such a project may be carried out. I begin my investigation by providing, in very broad brushstrokes, a notion of naturalism which I take to be profoundly fruitful yet nontendentious.

In chapter two, I investigate competing interpretations of naturalism to my own, with an eye to demonstrating how these renderings apply to Nietzsche's philosophy. I am not the first to naturalize Nietzsche nor will to power, but I believe that my analysis can save a robust "metaphysical" reading—at least one that would satisfy some of Fine's criteria without turning Nietzsche into a metaphysician. I proceed by articulating two dominant interpretations of naturalism: substance naturalism and methodological naturalism. I show that substance naturalism is problematic on its own merits and demonstrate that in no way can Nietzsche be viewed as a substance naturalist *simpliciter*. I then turn my attention to methodological naturalism again showing that some interpretations of the doctrine are difficult to justify. I then show how various scholars in the secondary literature who have applied these renderings of naturalism to Nietzsche's work as a whole are off base or cannot articulate a position that matches up with many of Nietzsche's claims.

In chapter three, I articulate how the will to power can be understood as a cosmological theory and as a zoological position. However, from this very articulation, a series of problems issues forth. I divide these problems into three main groupings: ontological, epistemological, and ethical. I articulate these problems resolving some of them in the chapter, but leaving the most difficult problems for chapters five, six, and seven.

In chapter four, I examine three contrasting and very different interpretations of will to power from that of my position. The aim here is one of showing that these three positions are either deeply incoherent and/or greatly impoverished in that they either eliminate will to power from Nietzsche's philosophy or significantly reduce the scope, content, and therefore profundity of the claim itself.

In chapters five through seven, I reconstruct will to power along three lines of investigation: the ontological, epistemological, and ethical. I demonstrate that the problems remaining from chapter three are solvable. I articulate the ontological features of will to power by likening it to a kind of non-material emergentism. Will to power is a looping of force. This notion is carefully and methodically explained. I then turn my attention, in chapter six, to explaining the epistemic features of will to power and demonstrate that the non-material emergentist position I outline must be coupled with a non-doxastic perspectivism. Finally, in chapter seven, I face the most difficult challenge: resolving the residual ethical paradoxes remaining from my analysis in chapter three. I demonstrate how the power of self-reflection is an expression of the core drive of will to power itself which is that of envelopment. It is this latent power of envelopment, expressed as self-reflection and more generally by selective cognition, that enables one to uphold the ethical goals of Nietzsche's philosophy, while remaining free and non-determined to do so.

NOTES

1. "In the thought of will to power, what is becoming and is moved in the highest and most proper sense—life itself—is to be thought in its permanence. Certainly, Nietzsche wants Becoming and what becomes, as the fundamental character of beings as a whole; but he wants what becomes precisely and before all else as what remains, as 'being' proper, being in the sense of the Greek thinkers." Martin Heidegger, *Nietzsche* 3 Volumes Trans. Joan Stambaugh, David Farrell Krell, and Frank A Capuzzi (San Francisco: Harper and Row, 1987), 156.

2. See Catherine F. Botha's "Reconsidering the will to power in Heidegger's Nietzsche," *South African Journal of Philosophy*, 35:1 (2016), 111–120, 111. According to Muller-Lauter, Heidegger's interpretation of will to power reduces to "the original assertion of essence. Will to power is a metaphysical principle unfolding out of itself and indeed ultimately returning to its own origin." Wolfgang Muller-Lauter *Nietzsche, His Philosophy of Contradictions and the Contradictions of His Philosophy,* Trans. David J. Parent (Chicago: University of Illinois Press, 1999), 20.

3. Nietzsche is critical of any attempt to reveal a true, Platonic, eternal and static world behind the "false" world of sensation characterized by flux, becoming and impermanency. This can be viewed in several of Nietzsche's later texts but especially in III: 6 of *Twilight* where Nietzsche remarks that the true purpose of the Platonic metaphysical world is to "revenge ourselves on life." See Friedrich Nietzsche, *The Twilight of the Idols*, Trans. R.J. Holingdale (New York: Penguin Books, 1990).

4. See James I. Porter, "Nietzsche's Theory of the Will to Power," in *A Companion to Nietzsche*, edited by Keith Ansell (Pearson, UK: Blackwell Publishers, 2006), 548–565.

5. Maudemarie Clark, *Nietzsche on Truth and Philosophy* (Cambridge University Press, 1990).

6. See Bernard Reginster, *The Affirmation of Life: Nietzsche on the Overcoming of Nihilism* (Harvard University Press, 2006). Reginster argues that many scholars' view of will to power, in its most universalized form as a theory of everything hold it to be "wild-eyed speculation not untypical in nineteenth century German metaphysics, which simply does not merit serious attention." 104.

7. Friedrich Nietzsche, *Beyond Good and Evil*, in *Basic Writings of Nietzsche*, Trans. Walter Kaufmann, Intro by Peter Gay (New York: Random House, 2000), section 36, 237–238.

8. I discuss two minimalist doctrines of will to power in great detail: Christopher Janaway's and John Richardson's. I discuss Janaway's position in Chapter two and Richardson's position in Chapter four.

9. For a very good introduction of German Idealism seen through the lens of Heidegger's understanding of ground, see Rudiger Bubner, *Modern German Philosophy* Trans. Eric Matthews (Cambridge University Press, 1981), especially 20–27.

10. Kit Fine, "What Is Metaphysics?" in *Contemporary Aristotelian Metaphysics* edited by Tuomas E. Tahko (Cambridge University Press, 2012), 8–25.

11. Nietzsche, *Beyond Good and Evil*, in *Basic Writings of Nietzsche*, section 36, 238.

12. Friedrich Nietzsche, *The Will to Power,* trans. Walter Kaufmann and R.J. Holingdale, with an introduction by Walter Kaufmann (New York: Vintage, 1968), sections 1067 and 687. See also Friedrich Nietzsche, *Beyond Good and Evil,* in *Basic Writings of Nietzsche*, section 36, 238.

13. Nietzsche, *Beyond Good and Evil*, in *Basic Writings of Nietzsche*, section 13.

14. Nietzsche, *Beyond Good and Evil*, in *Basic Writings of Nietzsche*, section 13, 211.

15. Nietzsche, *The Will to Power*, section 639.

16. Friedrich Nietzsche, *On/Towards a Genealogy of Morals*, Trans. Walter Kaufmann, in *Basic Writings of Nietzsche*, GM preface 2, 452.

17. Alphonso Lingis, "The Will to Power" in *The New Nietzsche*, edited by David B. Allison (Cambridge, MA: MIT Press, 1977), 37–64, 38.

18. Nietzsche, *The Will to Power*, section 636.

19. Wolfgang Muller-Lauter, *Nietzsche His Philosophy of Contradictions and the Contradictions of His Philosophy,* "Every expression of will to power . . . this already presupposes a multitude of wills to power," 19.

20. Friedrich Nietzsche, *The Will to Power*, section 259, 149.

21. Friedrich Nietzsche, *The Twilight of the Idols*, Trans. R.J. Holingdale, "Morality as Anti-Nature," section 5.

22. Friedrich Nietzsche, *On the Genealogy of Morals: A Polemic*, Trans. Walter Kaufmann and R.J. Holingdale (New York: Vintage Books, 1989), GM II: 11, 76.

23. Nietzsche, *The Will to Power*, sections 656 and 346.

Chapter 1

What is Naturalism? Two Key Aspects

Within the past ten years alone, hundreds of articles and books have been published on the topic of naturalism, broadly construed.[1] It is all too common to find articles on the subjects of "ethical naturalism," "naturalized epistemology," "mind naturalized," and so on. Naturalism, seemingly, has declared war on every area of traditional philosophy. Moreover, with naturalism and its generals, *every area of philosophy has been colonized.*

Even continental philosophers such as Heidegger and Nietzsche are not safe from naturalism's advance.[2] Indeed I would argue that no continental thinker has been more colonized by the forces of naturalism than Nietzsche. The Nietzschean secondary literature is awash with books and articles that interpret Nietzsche's positions on the nature of mind, knowledge, metaphysics, as naturalistic views of one stripe or another.[3]

The intentions behind such endeavors, to my mind, are multifaceted and sometimes but not always work in tandem. Certainly, Nietzschean scholars of all schools agree that Nietzsche intended to give a nonreligious interpretation of the origin of humanity in all its splendor and misery. Moreover, while naturalism is not exactly congruent with non-religious explanations of the above phenomenon, the two have much in common as I will demonstrate shortly. A second reason stems from a concern about legitimacy: The traditional sciences of physics, chemistry, and biology are commonly thought to be the only metric when it comes to revealing the very structures of reality. More broadly, such disciplines study nature in all its many facets; Nietzsche's philosophy is an attempt to study one particular and peculiar object within nature, namely, human being. Thus, if Nietzsche's philosophy is undergirded by such research (whether methodologically or substantively speaking or both), then his philosophy is conferred a similarly exalted status as these sciences. As I acknowledged in the introduction, my project is informed and impelled by these two considerations.

There is a problem with these interpretations, however. Moreover, that problem, succinctly put, has to do with the articulation—or lack thereof—of naturalism itself. For starters, it is not entirely clear what naturalism entails and therefore it is difficult to ascertain what benefit such a qualifier possesses when applied to either a school of thought or a thinker. Also, those scholars who do in fact define naturalism and then proceed to view Nietzsche through their definition either attribute to him a view that is contentious with his other doctrines or defend a position which, when examined on its own merits, is deeply problematic.

Keeping the above points in mind, it is of paramount importance to consider the notion of naturalism itself before applying the term to any philosopher or position; this is especially true when interpreting a philosopher such as Nietzsche. In this chapter, my aim is to scrutinize naturalism from two different, yet, in some cases, complimentary perspectives. First, I discuss naturalism as an activity: a procedure which, in some sense, is applied to some philosopher or theory. Next, I review naturalism as a definite, circumscribed position with a set of either ontological and/or methodological commitments.

To be clear, the above two notions of naturalism are very often closely related, but need not be. In some cases, a scholar might have definite methodological notions regarding what naturalism entails and then apply these insights to naturalize some idea or notion. In many cases, however, the activity of naturalization is implemented without much thought to one of the driving questions of the present book: "What is naturalism?"

Because I am interested in clarifying the notion of naturalism so that I may then naturalize will to power in an attempt to provide causal supports for the theory itself, it is therefore only fitting that I begin my investigation by examining the concept of naturalism in the broadest terms possible. With that aim in mind, I start by thinking about naturalism *via negative*—articulating what naturalism is not before proceeding to articulate a positive, substantive position. The following section identifies several nontendentious aspects common to all forms of naturalism whether of a methodological or substance type. I will then proceed to build on these elements as I begin to identify and explain the key elements of naturalism.

1.1 NATURALISM *VIA NEGATIVA*

When thinking about naturalism as a procedure, to naturalize something is to process a position, philosopher, or idea with the aim of establishing a product that has been purified of its supernatural and/or mysterious elements. Looking at the left-side term that appears on the and/or sentence connective, naturalism, in all forms, or so I contend, entails anti-supernaturalism. Naturalism, at this stage of the inquiry, is parasitic on supernaturalism. Thus, a robust conception of supernaturalism is required to flesh out naturalism. For this study, supernaturalism is the attempt to explain some phenomenon whether empirical or not by relying on some entity or notion that is in principle unknowable. The ground for the position cannot be examined any further—it is beyond investigation and must be accepted on faith if it is to be accepted at all.

The stipulation that all supernatural positions have some measure of faith in common does not, of course, entail that all religious beliefs cannot be naturalized or more perspicuously put rely solely on faith for the adoption of some religious creed. One can, of course, attempt to prove the existence of God, for example, by relying on time-honored arguments (e.g., the ontological, cosmological, teleological, etc.).[4] Other events, processes, and structures of reality believed to be of divine origin may be naturalized, at least to some extent.[5] Accepting a religious precept, however, without any further questioning or accepting some tenet such as, for example, that God created the world in six days without further investigation or reflection is to engage in supernatural thinking.[6]

Naturalization commits to removing mysterious, unknown elements from an explanation. To naturalize some idea is to explain the concept in terms that are more readily understandable. Many scholars assume that understandability, as articulated here, entails reducing some theory to a proposition that may be empirically verified or falsified, but this need not necessarily be the case. For example, there has been a good deal of interest in naturalizing ethics. To naturalize ethics entails, at least in part, interpreting how the notion of "Good" or "the Good" is to be construed. According to the ethical naturalist, the words "good" and "bad," though often used to describe actions and/or people, are unclear. The idea of what the Good is as well as the actions so described and defined by the Good are mysterious.

The ethical naturalist seeks to dispel such mystery by using different tools of investigative analysis along with dissimilar ontological suppositions than those typically employed by traditional ethicists. For ethical naturalists, the genetic and causal traits of normative thinking are more important than its imperative or intuitive aspects. Thus ethical naturalists typically place more stress on answering such questions as: "What is the origin of the Good and how did this notion come to be transmitted to humans?" Rather than on typical ethical issues such as: "What is the Good?" Or, alternatively, "What obligations do we owe to persons?"[7] Ethical naturalists either deny Hume's fork which states that an ought cannot be derived from an is (ethical imperatives cannot be derived from empirical facts) or perform a self-proclaimed end-run around such distinctions as is evident in the work of Michael Ruse and others.[8]

Answering these and other related questions regarding, what ought we to do? and, what is good? can be conducted in various ways. A non-naturalist might appeal to some higher authority such as God *simpliciter* to explain his answers to such questions. Good actions are simply those defined by God; evil actions are those that are condemned by God and *voila* a readymade answer of appropriate human conduct is provided. Those who are deemed wicked are those who transgress God's commands and various permutations on this idea are all well-known—one may commit wrong actions but have good intentions, etc. However, this general answer still leaves the naturalist perplexed as it is unclear why or how the idea of God is necessary to give rise to the concept of the Good. One could, following Socrates in *The Euthyphro*, argue along the following lines: "Is the Good simply good because God says so, or does God say that something is good because it really is good in and of itself."[9]

Non-naturalists are not without objections to these lines of inquiry, of course. One common objection raised is that of the naturalistic fallacy. The naturalistic fallacy is committed when philosophers attempt to reduce fundamental normative concepts to natural facts about humans.[10] G.E. Moore applied this label to all arguments that might try to derive ethical norms from biological facts. Moore argued for an alternative account of the Good. He argued that our sense of Good is arrived at according to some immediate, ethically primary intuition.[11]

However, again the same ontological question remains: "What capacity allows humans to possess such intuitions and why is it that some people are seemingly incapable of performing good actions?" "Why are some people evil?" Thus, the account of how some actions or people have been categorized as good needs to be justified. In attempting to answer these questions, a more naturalized account of ethics is provided by thinkers. Such accounts can and indeed have taken many different forms. One may appeal to contemporary theories of neuroscience (an abnormal brain as portrayed by a brain scan) or to biology (an abnormal DNA sequence assists in explaining the person's bad behavior, etc.).[12] The idea, again very crudely put at this point, is that the good is grounded on a naturalized faculty, that is, some biological endowment and, further, that one can empirically verify this hypothesis.

To summarize, naturalism is anathema to supernatural thinking. Supernatural thinking accepts claims on faith; no further evidence is required to support a claim. A naturalistic approach, in contrast, attempts to expose the root of some idea by grounding the concept in question on some well-reasoned articulation of facts. A naturalist tries to reveal the true ground from which some idea springs.

The naturalist adopts an *ethos* of critical appraisal; a true naturalist is committed to rebuking dogmas of all kinds whether these dogmas are grounded on faith or empirical evidence. A robust naturalism, as an activity, is one where the naturalist vigorously engages with supernatural thinking. No so-called truth is immune from possible revision. Revision occurs in the light of further rational reflection, evidence, calculation, and investigation.[13] Although naturalism does have some substantial components to it, above all, it is an attitude. Moreover, this attitude, in part, is characterized by the fervor and zealousness in which one investigates purported supernatural "truths." Thus, naturalism is not something that is arrived at but seems to be more of a way of life or what the Greeks would call an *askesis*—an exercise. The true naturalist exercises an attitude of perpetual, ongoing criticism and a disdain for all forms of idolatry whether epistemic, metaphysical, or otherwise.

In my view, Nietzsche exemplifies this ethos. Three works, in particular, demonstrate this attitude clearly. In *Twilight of the Idols,* Nietzsche argues that we must philosophize with a hammer. It is clear that Nietzsche seeks to show that beliefs need to be tapped to see if the belief in question is hollow or not. The hammer, in this case, is much like a tuning fork.[14] In the *Genealogy of Morals,* Nietzsche begins by stating that, "We are unknown to ourselves, we men of knowledge—and with good reason. We have never sought ourselves—how could it happen that we should *find* ourselves?"[15] What Nietzsche aims to do is to provide, perhaps for the first time, a genuinely naturalistic investigation into the history, origin, and subsequent development of morals and ethical practices. As he clearly states again in the preface, the goal is, "to traverse with quite novel questions . . . the so well hidden land of morality—of morality that has existed, actually been lived. . . ."[16] Finally, in the *Beyond Good and Evil*, Nietzsche concludes section one with "Suppose we want truth: Why not untruth? And uncertainty? Even ignorance?"[17] Philosophers and scientists alike forget that Truth, itself, is still a value.[18] Moreover, since it is a value we are entitled to ask why and how it has come to have the status of an invaluable value. This investigation into the very origin and value of Truth clearly demonstrates Nietzsche's commitment to a critical ethos much as I have described it above. If even Truth, truths, and truthfulness are open to investigation, then no belief is safe from Nietzsche's penetrating philosophical inquiries.

1.2 NATURALISM *VIA POSITIVA*: TWO KEY ASPECTS

The position thus far articulated is a negative thesis: I am articulating what naturalism is not but not providing any positive definition as to what naturalism is. Nevertheless, such a negative analysis is necessary given that positive articulations of naturalism are often either vacuous or annex metaphysical attachments for which no justification is forthcoming.[19] From this brief investigation, I now wish to extract two key, nontendentious aspects of naturalistic thinking. These are (1) a commitment to utilizing a reductionist, deflationist, and/or eliminativist methodology; and (2) the Causal Closure Principle (CCP). I will now spend the rest of this main section explaining each of these key components.

1.3 KEY COMPONENT 1: REDUCTIONISM

From the above discussion, it is clear that a naturalistic inquiry restricts its domain of investigation to the field of nature—though it may be difficult at this point to identify with any precision what nature denotes. However, it is unclear how naturalism accomplishes this task. One way for the naturalist to restrict the domain of investigation is by reducing some phenomenon to something else. This process, often called reductionism, takes place in a variety of ways. For example, one might think that the variety, uniqueness, complexity and fecundity of animal life clearly demonstrates that such life had a designer. However, the modern evolutionary synthesis paints a different picture. The same property of design clearly "discovered" in animal life is reduced to random gene mutation coupled with natural selection working through the sieve of environmental conditions. A supernatural explanation to account for the so-called "obvious" fact of design is no longer required: the very idea of design is reducible to simpler explanations.

In general, there are three kinds of reduction: ontological, translative and systemic. I cannot discuss each kind of reduction here so instead will focus on the two types of reduction most related to my project. These are ontological and translative reductions.

As the name implies, an ontology reduction seeks to reduce the number of entities in some field of inquiry. Entities are reduced by showing that the existence of some entity, property, capacity, etc. is explainable regarding some other objects that are already well-known. The purpose of such reductions is, invariably, to simplify. Simplification may be made for the sake of parsimony; for example, it is easier to work with a theory that has fewer entities and principles than a theory which has many. However, another reason for such simplification is philosophical: It is true to say that most individuals who naturalize some field do so not necessarily for practical reasons, but because they truly do believe that the entity to be reduced does not exist. The effects attributed to the mysterious entity may be better explained by some other thing or process.

The key for these sorts of reductionistic models to work is to ensure that the seemingly complex phenomena that are to be ontologically reduced not only are made more understandable, scientifically speaking, but do not lose essential *qualia* in the reduction process. If the phenomenon, now reduced, is, qualitatively speaking, no longer the same, then the reduction failed. A true reduction is, therefore, tough to achieve.

To concretize this point it may be useful to turn to the paper, "Raised Plasma Nerve Growth Factor Levels Associated with Early-Stage Romantic Love." This article sought to demonstrate that NGF or Nerve Growth Factor, an essential protein for the growth and maintenance of neurons, increased dramatically for individuals who experienced "falling into a state of love" during the experimental period.[20] The authors showed that NGF increased significantly for those people who self-reported falling in love. More interesting, perhaps, is that the amount of NGF decreased after approximately a year for those same participants who initially reported being in a state of love. From these findings, the authors concluded that NGF was a necessary condition for such an emotional state. It is clear that the project is ultimately driven toward finding the right chemical composition of "falling in love." If we extrapolate from this research and suggest that the feeling of falling in love could be reduced and indeed mimicked by the right chemical compound, then a successful reduction has been performed.

Naturalists may employ other techniques when it comes to restricting what truly exists in the world. This technique is that of elimination. When a phenomenon is eliminated, it is cast out from all serious discourse and subsequent debate on a given topic. "Things" once eliminated have no ontological status whatsoever. It does not exist in some vestigial form either: it is not reduced to some simpler process. Examples within the scientific literature abound and include things such as "the luminous aether" and phlogiston.[21] To be sure such things—usually abductive assumptions—may still provoke investigation, but such inquiry is relegated to the musings of the curious historians of science and not the scientist working in that field. For the scientist, such entities are no longer seriously entertained.

Why are ideas and things once eliminated no longer seriously considered? They are not taken seriously because the very scientific narrative in which they once found a place no longer exists. If we turn to a more controversial example, this can be shown. Paul and Patricia Churchland argue that the very concept of mind along with its properties, contents, and faculties should be eliminated from scientific consideration.[22] Thus beliefs, as contents of mind, do not exist because the notion of mind is simply false. Once we accept the trappings of a materialistic brain science, we must also jettison any "belief thesis" that was once part of the old narrative because it would be incoherent to hold a position where held beliefs were not causally efficacious. If one accepts that the brain is comprised of material particles (e.g., neurons) and that the firing of these neurons is responsible for thinking, beliefs lose whatever reality they once had: A belief is not being transferred from one neuron to the next after all given the contemporary neuroscience picture of mind.[23]

There are significant problems with the "no belief thesis" or as it is sometimes ironically put "the belief in the no belief thesis." The primary problem is that the old folk psychology that the Churchlands wish to replace has proven itself to be very effective over the course of thousands of years of human development. We have ample historical, interpersonal, and introspective evidence which suggests that beliefs are causally efficacious: People act on the beliefs they hold true. Moreover, intentions generally speaking serve as the vehicle for understanding and initiating said actions. In other words, they can "kick" in the sense that they can alter physical, mental, and psychological behavior and can also be kicked in that when an agent gives into a particular temptation after resolving not to, there is a feeling that a battle has been lost, and the resolution has been overpowered.[24] Also, there are some disciplines, such as cognitive behavioral therapy, for example, which have made significant advancements by taking such so-called "Folktales" seriously.[25]

It would seem imprudent to give up on such entities, such as beliefs and intentions, by eliminating them from true scientific understanding just because there is, at present, a seemingly impossible chasm to cross between what appear to be nonphysical things and the physical brain. Perhaps a rethinking of dualism and physicalism are required rather than dismissing the truths of folk psychology.

I now turn to translative reductions. These types of reductions may have different ontological commitments than the old language they try to replace, but it is not always necessary that they do. Translative reductions attempt to translate the features of some discipline to those of some other. The purpose of the translation is to show that the new language is better at handling some of the old, ossified and seemingly intractable problems with the old discipline for which the language of the discipline was in part responsible for creating. An example of a translative reduction and, incidentally, interesting technique of naturalizing can be gleaned from viewing Quine's attempt to naturalize epistemology.

For W.V.O Quine, the traditional question of epistemic justification, namely, "When is S justified in believing P?" can only be answered if we understand, first, how we come to believe what we consider being true. If the beliefs we come to have about the world are contingent on sensation then understanding how we perceive objects, that is, knowing the causal conditions necessary for perception itself, would supply an answer to the traditional question. Quine's position inverted the classical understanding of epistemology. The classical foundationalist enterprise of epistemology, which conceived epistemology as first philosophy and as prior to, and more important than science, is clearly misguided. Under Quine's view, "epistemology or something like it, simply falls into place as a chapter of psychology and hence of natural science."[26]

According to Quine, the question of justification must be replaced with the question of origination. Thus instead of asking: "When is S justified in believing P?" We should be asking: "How did the belief in P come about?"[27] "What perceptual and cognitive faculties were responsible for producing the belief?" These questions, Quine evinces, are best suited for the discipline of empirical psychology and not epistemology, at least as traditionally conceived.

Quine also altered the standard conception of epistemology in another way, too. He conceived of knowledge as a web: Every discipline from psychology to physics was interconnected via "epistemic strands." Some of these disciplines exist on the periphery of this web while others occupy a more central seat, such as mathematics and logic.[28] If Quine's web theory of knowledge is accurate, then the goal for the epistemologist is no longer one of finding indubitable truths *via* some epistemically secure method that is somehow distinct from the natural sciences, a la Descartes, but is rather one of studying the actual epistemic relationship between human beings and their environment. Since it is assumed that the sciences are the best means we have for discovering what this relationship is and its limits, the goal of epistemology is one of translating traditional epistemic questions into scientific questions. Only then, Quine believed, could we rub out the boundaries between philosophy and science to contribute to the progress of knowledge.[29]

One of the problems with this method, of course, is the assumption that the sciences are the best method for determining how in fact we acquire beliefs. More specifically, the crux of naturalized epistemology is the assumption that the justification of belief is solely determined by the origin of the belief. The problems with these assumptions, however, are first, that we seemingly go against a traditional Cartesian framework which holds that the problem of justification begins with the establishment of an indubitable foundation for knowledge *ab initio*. While one may question whether such a project could be fulfilled, nonetheless, Quine's contention does suggest that he is simply giving up on the traditional problems associated with epistemology.

The second issue with Quine's brand of naturalized epistemology can be brought into sharper focus by seeing it through the lens of Nietzsche. According to Nietzsche, all perception, whether it is that of the every day or the scientific, is shot through with evaluation. Now, on this point, Quine too, would agree. In "Two Dogmas of Empiricism" and *Word and Object*, Quine argues for a holistic position: Statements can neither be verified nor be falsified when analyzed independently from the framework in which they are embedded. For a statement to have meaning, it must be rooted within a larger framework, and it is the context along with the statement that is tested. All empirical statements are theory-laden.[30]

Nietzsche goes further than Quine in this regard. For Nietzsche, we come at a particular problem from our own distinct and unique vantage point. The same applies to empirical sciences, like psychology. These sciences, so thinks Nietzsche, are underpinned by a will to truth: a will to use what is taken as truth to wield power.[31] Empirical psychology cannot serve as a reduction even in Quine's weaker translative sense of reduction for answering the traditional questions of epistemology because such a discipline is in desperate need of a critique and subsequent correction.

Regarding Nietzsche's reductionistic tendencies, we see him employ a variety of strategies and positions in this regard. Examining what one may call, "politically imprudent actions," Nietzsche writes in *Twilight of the Idols* in "The Four Great Errors" section: "Every error of whatever kind, is a consequence of degeneration of instinct, disaggregation of will: one has thereby virtually defined the *bad*."[32] Similar reductions abound in *Twilight*. In the section "Morality as Anti-Naturalism," Nietzsche argues, "that all naturalism in morality, that is all *healthy* morality, is dominated by an instinct of life" but Anti-natural morality, Nietzsche evinces, "that is virtually every morality that has hitherto been taught, turns on the contrary, precisely against the instincts of life."[33] Clearly, the target of Nietzsche's reductionism is the Judaeo-Christian religion of all stripes. The sects of Judaism and Christianity, no matter how different on the surface, are in fact the same, according to Nietzsche's rubric, because they preach a morality that is hostile to the instincts of life.

There are obvious problems with Nietzsche's technique of reductionism as evidenced here in *Twilight*. Scholars, like Ruth Abbey, have severely criticized Nietzsche's reductionistic construal of power because the hypotheses generated from such a power narrative cannot be falsified. In his later work, Nietzsche, Abbey evinces, "now holds that if a great individual acts badly, this is a sign of declining life, making his claim about the importance of birth and lineage for greatness unfalsifiable." This issue, Abbey states, is brought into the foreground when one considers Nietzsche's example of the young man who grows prematurely pale and faded from the Four Great Errors section of *Twilight*. She writes:

> While his friends attribute his decline to illness, Nietzsche attributes his illness to decline: "*that* he became ill, *that* he failed to resist the illness, was already the consequence of an impoverished life, an hereditary exhaustion." This is a circular approach to action and identity. Bad or degenerate action is a sign of declining life; it indicates that either one's inheritance was inferior to begin with or has become impoverished, while beautiful action is a function of a good, thriving inheritance. How uninformative an approach to identity and action this is becomes apparent when Nietzsche applies it reflexively, describing the illness that forced him to resign his professorship at Basel as "that *bad* inheritance from

my father's side." If higher types falter or fail, it must be due to something faulty in their inheritance.[34]

The above is a devastating critique of the overzealous biological reductionistic tendencies of which Nietzsche was peculiarly obsessed in his final productive years. What is needed is an ontological reductionism, predicated on the general narrative of will to power, that is, in fact, informative and does not, in the final analysis, become tautologous. This concern will be one of the most difficult obstacles I face in advancing a naturalized understanding of will to power.

Thankfully, Nietzsche, at times, also offers a different kind of approach when it comes to explaining the origin and properties of phenomena. This general approach is often called deflationism. Deflationists are related cousins of reductionists but instead of focusing on the object that is targeted for reduction, deflationists concentrate on understanding the conditions which make the object possible. One way to contrast a deflationary approach to that of a reductive strategy is to examine a paradigmatic deflationist strategy. Accordingly, I examine the work of C.L. Stevenson who brilliantly deflates what he calls "the vital sense of good" or the *prima facie* "call to action" that duties and moral obligations have.

Stevenson is an advocate of what he calls a replacement strategy (though I would use the modern term, "deflation strategy") when it comes to getting at "the vital sense of good," as he calls it. Stevenson's goal is to replace questions such as "What is the good?" Or, alternatively, "What makes an action good?" and instead seeks to examine the common properties of ethical discussion itself.[35] Stevenson's reasons for taking this approach are manifold but primarily he is convinced by both Moore's naturalistic and open question arguments and yet finds that Moore's argumentation boxes the Neo-Platonist into a kind of subjectivism. For if the good is indefinable and unanalyzable and yet is grasped through some mysterious act of intuition, then it becomes impossible to compare two or more different and competing intuitions of "The Good."[36] Stevenson's solution is to show that ethical discussion is not a debate about the Good at all, but is rather a discussion about competing interests. However, just because all ethical discussion is a discussion about competing interests does not mean that the questions raised about the nature of the Good are just simply questions about what is in *my* interest. Traditional ethical issues such as "How should one act?" and "Why are hypothetical imperatives not categorical?" and so on are still meaningful questions, but these questions are neither reducible to an epistemic metric a la the utilitarianist nor an ontological understanding of the goodwill following Kant.

To show this, Stevenson attempts to get at the "vital sense of good" mentioned above. He analyzes this sense into three components: (1) Disagreement:

It must be possible to disagree sensibly about whether something is good.[37] This requirement, Stevenson evinces, rules out simple interest theories such as those put forward by Hobbes. (2) Magnetism: Judgments about goodness motivate people. This rules out Hume, according to Stevenson, for if one were to recognize that some action is good merely because the majority approve of it, then the pull of the deed itself is greatly diminished.[38] (3) Non-verifiability: Goodness can't be verified by scientific methods. This thesis is anti-reductionist and rules out questions and answers that attempt to define the good to some natural property but rules in condition one: sensible disagreement. If the good were reducible to a property or process that science could study, then it would not make sense to have the sort of ethical disagreements we currently have. Such discussions would either be incoherent, inefficacious, or worse.

Stevenson then shows that ethical discussion is mainly a type of dynamic speech or written expression. Dynamic expressions attempt to convey feelings where, in contrast, descriptive statements try to express facts with such facts, in turn, producing beliefs in people. Dynamic expressions are used differently; one uses such expressions to vent and/or to generate feelings within others.[39] Specifically, the feelings produced are those that cause one to align the listener with the position advocated by the speaker. The position is advocated because it is in the speaker's interest to do so.

The upshot of this approach is that ethics does not reduce to one's self-interest, if, that is, self-interest is defined selfishly. A wealthy speaker, for example, may advocate for a much higher taxation rate even though he may stand to lose a substantial portion of his wealth as a result of the rate coming to pass. He still has an interest in seeing this through because he may believe that such a change will greatly benefit society and he further believes that whatever benefit there is to society is greater than his personal gain: His interest in helping society is greater than his selfish self-interest. Moreover, we may still have a vigorous disagreement regarding ethical matters because there remain descriptive uses of language that are employed to support dynamic expressions. For a contemporary example which highlights this aspect of Stevenson's construal, consider the issue of weapons of mass destruction in Iraq. There has been much debate surrounding the moral correctness of the US invasion of Iraq under the Presidency of George G.W. Bush. One reason given for supporting the invasion was the belief that Saddam Hussein was producing and stockpiling weapons of mass destruction.[40] This claim was then used to buttress an interest position: No country should have such weapons, and if a country does possess these weapons then that country should be denied their use. However, notice that this belief is clearly a factual matter: in principle, it can be empirically verified or falsified (though perhaps difficult to do so in practice). Much of the support Bush had was undergirded by the belief that Hussein had these weapons. When it was brought forward that such weapons did not exist in Iraq, the initial decision to remove Saddam Hussein from power in Iraq was considered wrong by many of the same individuals who previously believed it was the right thing to do. The upshot is that ethical discussion is not pointless under Stevenson's view, indeed far from it. Although ethical utterances are dressed in dynamic language, most individuals disagree about the descriptive language that supports their ethical beliefs. These factual supports can be examined, scrutinized, and falsified and thereby alter the individual's moral stances.

Nietzsche's ethical work in my view exhibits both reductionist and deflationist tendencies. I believe that Nietzsche goes off the rails at times in his later work by clearly offering a reductionistic biological model of ethical behavior. A superior approach is available and is thoroughly Nietzschean. This method is genealogical and has more in common with contemporary deflationist theories. I reveal Nietzsche's deflationist leanings when I turn to Nietzsche's theories of truth and ethics in later sections.

1.4 KEY COMPONENT 2: THE CAUSAL CLOSURE PRINCIPLE (CCP)

A final key feature of all naturalistic philosophical positions is formally called the Causal Closure Principle (hereafter CCP). According to CCP, reality is causally closed, which is to say that all events that take place within the universe can be explained by providing a physical description of said events. Looking at consciousness, as an example, for physicalists, consciousness along with its contents, properties, and powers is dependent on a functioning brain. All of the qualities of consciousness are contingent and causally dependent on physical features; thought is entirely reducible to the brain's function.

It may not seem obvious at first glance why the mind, according to most naturalists, must be reducible to a physical entity. But the argument is that by holding two separate and distinct accounts of the same phenomenon such as thinking, feeling, etc. would entail embracing a supernatural and therefore dualist worldview. This dualist picture, however, produces an irrevocable rift in our scientific picture of how things really are because two different descriptions for the same phenomenon would both be valid. However, for the thoroughgoing naturalist, such a two-view description would entail that not all phenomena have been adequately naturalized, and this would be anathema to naturalism of all stripes. Paraphrasing Feigl, naturalism will not and cannot tolerate nomological danglers.[41] The naturalist must be committed to reducing and/or eliminating all phenomena that do not readily lend themselves to a scientific or physical account and thus CPP is often advanced as a goal for normative as well as epistemic reasons.[42]

There are many different iterations of the CCP, and it would be difficult if not impossible to examine all of them in the detail required here. I will review Lowe's, Kim's, and Papineau's respective positions. Papineau argues "that all physical events have sufficient physical causes."[43] Kim's conceptualization of CCP is very similar to Papineau's but more precise: "Any cause of a physical event is itself a physical event—that is, no nonphysical event can be a cause of a physical event."[44] Lowe argues for a somewhat different position. He states that CCP is that position where: "Every physical event contains only other physical events in its transitive causal closure."[45] I would now like to explain the support for each stance before turning albeit very briefly to my problem with CCP. I will then point toward a Nietzschean solution of CCP and develop this solution in full in chapter five.

When one thinks of a physical event occurring, it is often the case that one must think of the sufficient cause that produced it. Imagine that I am at a restaurant and leave my table to go to the washroom. On the table, I leave a half-empty can of Coke. Upon my return, the Coke has spilled all over the floor and the can crushed. Clearly, an event has taken place. It would be natural for me to think the following: "How did my drink spill?" "Who crushed my can?" It is evident from this example that I am attempting to identify a singular cause, a sufficient cause that adequately answers my questions. Moreover, the cause must suffice to produce the properties of the event in question: claiming that because a fly landed on my drink, and it was the weight of the fly that caused the can to tip over, is not a sufficient cause for the event in question. One wishes to know what event(s) triggered the Coke to fall and the can to be crushed.

Papineau's version of CCP places emphasis on what is often called the productive side of the cause equation. Causality is often about understanding the triggering aspect of cause and effect. The productive model takes into consideration the conditions that allow a particular event to happen but emphasizes the unique event which triggered these circumstances to produce the event under investigation.[46] For example, if a fire investigator were attempting to determine the cause of a destructive house fire, she would certainly look at the conditions that allowed such a fire to grow so prodigiously (e.g., flammable materials in the house, the lack of a working sprinkler system, the use of an accelerant, etc.). However, the sufficient cause might be something as simple as a lit match. The lit match, when the right conditions are present, suffices to explain the cause of the fire.

There is also a counterfactual component underpinning the model. If the match were not lit then presumably, the fire would not have occurred. This idea reaffirms the productive component of causality—to study causality is to study the discrete event that manufactures the effect under scrutiny to take place. Papineau's causal closure model suggests that to understand an event one must grasp the relevant causes, which when working in concert, and in the correct sequence, produce the event in question.

How does all this relate to mental events? Consider the following example: My right arm is raised. The raising of my arm is an unmistakable physical event and because it is a physical event it must have a physical cause, according to Papineau's model. At first glance, one might claim that I decided to raise my arm and thus the decision as a species of a more general intentional act is a sufficient cause when it comes to explaining why my right arm is now raised. Now the physicalist might retort that this decision is itself an event and therefore must have a physical cause as well. However, notice that this response would be to beg the question at hand: Mental events are produced by physical events and therefore are neither sufficient nor *causa sui*. However, even if we accepted this conclusion it would still not rule out material emergentism: It is entirely possible that mental events though initially caused by physical events, properties and structures are capable of causing events physical or otherwise and that such events are not directly reducible to mental phenomena.[47] Thus, a different version of CCP position must be put forward if physicalism is to be accepted in a non-question begging way.

This discussion leads us to Lowe's much stronger version of the position. For, according to Lowe, all events, physical, mental, or otherwise are transitively closed *vis a vis* their causal history. To show how this iteration of CCP is stronger than that of Papineau's, consider the following reply to those who obstinately hold that mental events are outside of the physical realm. Pretend that I have a paper cup full of coffee in my hand. Suppose that I am determined to squeeze the cup until it breaks but to hold onto the coffee cup, come what may. The non-physicalist would claim that it was my intention to crush the cup which then caused my hand to crush it. However, if the cup contains scalding hot coffee, and this coffee then proceeds to burn my hand, I will surely experience excruciating pain. If this intense pain then causes me to drop the cup, then my intention to crush the coffee cup has produced a non-intentional physical event: the dropping of the coffee cup. This example is intended to show that mental events can cause physical events, but that physical events can also cause mental events. Looking at the same example from a different perspective, I drop the cup because I am in pain. My pain did not come out of thin air; it was caused by a physical event: the hot coffee spilling onto my hand. Clearly, pain is a mental event that was caused by other physical events, and these physical events caused a mental event that was not intended, namely, dropping the coffee cup.

The adherent of Lowe's CCP, using the above example, will now argue something along the following lines: Since some mental descriptions and accounts are causally independent of mental events they cannot be completely determined the mental event. Thus, to give a complete causal account of such mental events is to provide at least some physical account. However, if I am to provide a physical account, then the goal must be to reduce mental events to physical accounts. Indeed, one could not provide a full account of such events like raising arms and the like, if mental events were *sui generis* because physical events can produce unintended mental states. Thus, any complete description of a physical event will be one where the mental actions of that event are wholly explained—and a full explanation of an event entails a physical description of the causes and preceding events that make up the occurrence in need of explanation. Other than accepting a deeply problematic and seemingly inherently paradoxical position such as epiphenomenalism, the physicalist evinces, one has no other option but to adopt some version of the CCP.[48]

Returning to the CCP, it has been argued in the secondary literature that the most problematic feature of the position is the issue of overdeterminism.[49] Overdetermination occurs when there are two or more independent and sufficient causes present for producing an event. If an event is overdetermined, then it is impossible to provide a full causal explanation of the event in question, and, therefore, one cannot claim that all physical events are sufficiently produced by physical causes. The classic example used to explain overdetermination is the firing squad analogy.[50]

If we assume that all members of a firing squad have a loaded rifle and each member fires his rifle at the same time killing the intended man to be shot, then we cannot trace whose bullet was responsible for killing the victim. As a result, if we then traced the full or sufficient causes that produced the physical event in question, in this case the death of the victim, we would need to trace the multitude and myriad of causes which produced the actions of each member. Doing so, however, would not produce a singular chain of causality.

The problem of overdeterminism becomes all the more acute when one examines the descriptions of physical events that seem to have mental causes as their antecedents. Let's return to the coffee cup example. Now imagine that instead of crushing the coffee cup in my hand, I decide to drink from it. Folk psychology would say that it is clear that my intention to drink from the coffee cup is a sufficient cause to explain the physical act of drinking. This event does not yet pose a problem for CPP because the true physical cause underlying my decision to now drink coffee is reducible to the firings of various neurons (e.g., a brain state) and other physiological process within my body. But if I were asked: "Why did you take a drink?" Then it becomes clear that the tracing of the chain of causality becomes harder to establish. I have a plethora of responses which seem to answer the matter sufficiently such as: "I was thirsty," "I was feeling tired" (and having some coffee would perhaps perk me up), etc. or I could answer: "I felt like it." But if we examine each of these responses it is clear that they are not causally closed. Thirst is a physiological condition and cannot be simply "willed away." Of course, we can forget about our thirst for a period by thinking of something else, but this does not will away our physiological condition, namely, that of dehydration of which thirst is a sign. The questions remain: "What caused me to take a drink?" "Was it the underlying physiological condition?" "The intention?" "Or a combination of both?" So to the response, "I was tired and needed a pick me up" would also seem to indicate that something more than a mental act is required to energize my mind. Coffee is, of course, a vehicle for caffeine. Thus, my action seems to combine both the mental intention which might be to continue to stay awake to work, etc. and a physiological condition. Here too, we have two causes that might co-arise at the same time to produce the event.

The upshot of the above discussion is that some issues which demand an answer in causal terms cannot be adequately answered by providing a physical description consisting of neurons, cells, and other essential pieces of organic matter. No, to provide the complete causal story, one needs more than just a physical description—one needs to explore as Sellars often stated, "the logical space of reasons" of which any physical theory depends for any purely physical description to convey true meaning.[51]

Thus it is clear that a physical account, while certainly part of the causal story, does not seem to be the whole causal story. The mind and more specifically a very significant capacity of the mind to form intentions, appears to be a necessary, although not sufficient condition in order to give a full, descriptive causal account of many physical events that we deem important to understand.

If the above interpretation is correct then the reduction of intentions to brain states *via* the CCP seems to imply that free will does not exist. But if this is so, then Nietzsche's ethical position, if it does, in fact, rely on something like CCP would be pointless.[52] Thankfully, Nietzsche would reject the underlying physicalism of CCP. However, it is clear that Nietzsche's theory of will to power shares many of the deterministic traits of physicalism and, as some interpreters have argued, these components render Nietzsche, a determinist of one stripe or another. For example, consider a typical section of *Will to Power*. In section 635 Nietzsche writes,

> My idea is that every specific body strives to become master over all space and to extend its force (its will to power) and to thrust back all that resists its extension. However, it continually encounters similar efforts on the part of other bodies and ends by coming to an arrangement with those of them that are sufficiently related to it: thus they then conspire together for more power.[53]

Contained within this passage is the idea of necessity: Our behavior, unbeknownst to us is an expression of an unconscious drive for power. However, if all this is true, then one of Nietzsche's principal strands of his thinking, namely, to criticize and then put forward a new ethics is in serious jeopardy. The world for Nietzsche is simply comprised of many little worlds—each and every creature perceives, acts, and calculates from its unique perspective. However, "the world remains . . . a firm, iron magnitude of force that does not grow bigger or smaller, that does not expend itself but only transforms itself."[54] Thus, one of the chief difficulties of the present book is to preserve Nietzsche's ethical project, namely to initiate a transvaluation of all values *via* the mechanism of his genealogical method, in the face of what appears to be a deterministic worldview.[55] My key to unlocking this mystery is in treating will to power as necessarily perspectival. This position will be worked out in detail in chapters three and five.

Nietzsche adopts a reductionist approach at times, but he is also clearly against the idea that causality is something that exists in itself as the "concrete of the universe" to borrow Mackie's phrase. It would be a mistake to think that a reductionist causal understanding of Nietzsche's psychology is the only available option and that Nietzsche, therefore, must be committed to some iteration of the CCP. I would argue that an alternative approach may also be identified. This method is genealogical. Briefly, the genealogical method combines a deflationist approach which examines more natural conditions that allow a particular phenomenon to exist with a logical space of reasons approach and thereby attempts to provide a fuller causal description than when either approach is adopted separately. This genealogical approach will be worked out and explained in more detail in chapter two.

The second difficulty is easier to resolve, at least in some ways than the first. The problem here lies in presenting a framework for the will to power where CCP, or some version thereof, is preserved within the framework but where the scaffolding of CCP does not rely on physicalism nor on a simplistic idea where the cause is a trigger for an effect. One possible suggestion is to adopt a different account of causality altogether. The above account is called a productive causal narrative, but there are other models of causality, too. One model that has gained noticeable attention in recent years is a powers approach. Briefly, this tactic suggests that one should not think of causality using the language and concepts of "triggers" and "conditions" only. Rather one should think of causality in terms of mutual dependent relations. Sophie Gibb provides an example that highlights this position well. She asks us to think of a vase falling on hard tile. The vase breaks. What caused the vase to break, one might ask? One explanation is to think of what caused the vase to fall; this approach would be in keeping with a productive model, and certainly, this would be in keeping with a trigger theory of causality. Another approach would claim that it was the fall that caused the vase to break. But the act of falling, by itself does not cause things to break. So what caused the vase to break?[56]

The powers approach argues that there is a gap in the explanation: just because the vase fell does not explain why it broke. A powers approach would explain the vase breaking by claiming that it was a combination of the hardness of the tile and the fragility of the vase. To provide a fuller account of this event, we need to examine the inherent properties of each object and then look at how these properties interact when they come into contact with each other. This notion of causality is necessarily perspectival and open to interpretation depending on the pragmatic framework of the investigator.

This view of causality aligns very well with Nietzsche's theory of will to power especially in relation to his bundle theory of thinghood. A key component to understanding Nietzsche's bundle position is the notion of perspective. Perspective, as I read Nietzsche, does not denote a doxastic relationship between a perceived and the mode of perception. Perspective, rather, denotes an environment of power: We do not have perspectives as we might have beliefs say, rather it is more proper to say that we are in perspectives. In my view, the powers approach to causality combined with this non-doxastic view of perspective coheres well with Nietzsche's well-known bundle position. I explain the relationship between these three in more detail in chapter five.

From the above points, a picture of naturalism begins to emerge. Naturalism is an activity: one *engages* in a naturalistic process. This process entails a simplification for the sake of clarification: It entails removing unnecessary entities, supposed laws, and postulates to render some phenomenon in clearer, more understandable terms. This desire to simplify, however, does not mean that such theories are simple: Quantum physics is a naturalized inquiry that is complex and difficult to grasp. A second related goal of this activity to simplify is either to reduce nonnatural components of the topic to be naturalized to some physical entity, quality, or process thereof, or to eliminate such components altogether. The above process of reduction is clearly ontological, but other reductions can be produced. Usually, an ontological reduction will involve translative reduction but not vice versa. The scaffolding which makes ontological reduction possible is a principle called CCP.

The process of naturalization proceeds along two lines of flight: (1) reductionism/deflationism and (2) a framework that adopts some version of the CCP. The point of this discussion is to superimpose this picture onto Nietzsche's theory of will to power such that the theory can satisfy these two conditions without absorbing the similar problematic traits often associated with these aspects. My argument, in brief, is that will to power combined with a powers approach will be able to do the work of CCP without also absorbing CCP's more tendentious aspects, namely the collapsing of free will to a deterministic causal process. However, that in addition to this advantage of using will to power instead of some variant of physicalism, that a type of ontological reductionism may be rendered that is both informative and qualia preserving.

In the following chapter, I turn to articulating other renderings of naturalism as well as documenting and critiquing other attempts made by scholars of Nietzsche to utilize these renderings to present a very different account of Nietzsche's naturalism from the one I present in this book.

NOTES

1. A recent keyword search of the term "Naturalism" in the *Philosopher's Index* reveals nearly 2000 entries.

2. See David E. Storey's *Naturalizing Heidegger: His Confrontation with Nietzsche, His Contributions to Environmental Philosophy* (SUNY Press, 2015). In the Nietzschean secondary literature, there has been robust debate regarding the nature, extent, and peculiarities of Nietzsche's naturalism. A non-exhaustive list of texts discussing these topics would include: Christoph Cox, *Nietzsche, Naturalism and Interpretation* (University of California Press, 1999). Cox's book is excellent in terms of setting up the various epistemological and ontological problems within Nietzsche's work as a whole. *Nietzsche, Naturalism and Normativity* edited by Christopher Janaway and Simon Robertson (Oxford, 2012) presents original and significant contributions on Nietzsche's ethical positions from a naturalized stance and finally there is Christian Emden's, *Nietzsche's Naturalism: Philosophy and the Life Sciences in the Nineteenth Century* (Cambridge University Press, 2014). Emden explains the intellectual milieu of the nineteenth century showing the ideational constituents that make Nietzsche's naturalism possible.

3. See, for example, John Richardson's naturalized construal of will to power in his book *Nietzsche's New Darwinism* (New York: Oxford University Press, 2004). For an excellent companion volume that treats the relationship between naturalism, Nietzsche and ethical thinking, see *Nietzsche, Naturalism and Normativity* edited by Christopher Janaway and Simon Robertson (New York: Oxford University Press, 2012).

4. There are many versions of each of these arguments. For the ontological argument see St. Anselm's Ontological Proof in chapters two and three of his Prosologion in *Anselm of Canterbury: The Major Works, Monologion, Prosologion and Why God Became Man*, edited by Brian Davies and G.R. Evans (Oxford University Press, 1998). Descartes' fifth meditation in *The Meditations*. Rene Descartes, *The Meditations and Other Metaphysical Writings* (New York: Penguin Books, 2000). For the cosmological and teleological arguments of Aquinas' *Qunique Viae* (The Five Ways), see Anthony Kenny, *Five Ways: St. Thomas Aquinas* (London: Routledge Press, 2003).

5. Michael Behe's *Darwin's Blackbox* was a rallying cry for Creationists as the book attempted to show that while natural selection worked on a macro level it did not work very well on a micro level: the sheer complexity of bio-chemistry seemed to suggest that certain structures were designed in advance; they could not have originated from sheer chance. Behe called such structures "irreducibly complex" and it is from this argument that Intelligent Design and supernaturalism by proxy, has regained some of the ground which it lost in the nineteenth century. See Michael Behe, *Darwin's Blackbox: The Biochemical Challenge to Evolution* (New York: Free Press, 1996).

6. Book of Genesis Chapter One verses 1–30.

7. See G.E. Moore, *Principia Ethica*, (Cambridge, UK: Cambridge University Press, 1903), Chapter One, The subject matter of ethics and Chapter Five, Ethics in Relation to conduct.

8. In brief, Ruse's suggestion is that the very idea of co-operation has been selected for by our very genes. In his own words he does an "end-run" around Hume's fork. See "The Biological Sciences Can Act as a Ground for Ethics" *in Contemporary Debates in the Philosophy of Biology*, Chapter Seventeen (New York: Wiley-Blackwell, 2010).

9. In section 10d of that splendid document Socrates asks perhaps the most important question in the history of Western philosophy: "Is something pious because it is beloved by the gods or is it beloved because it is worthy of piety in and of itself?" See G.M.A. *Plato: Five Dialogues: Euthyphro, Apology, Crito, Meno Phaedo* (Indianapolis, IN: Hackett Publishing Company, 1981), 6–22.

10. G.E. Moore, *Principia Ethica* (Cambridge, UK: Cambridge University Press, 1903), 17.

11. Moore, *Principia Ethica*, section 7.

12. In regard to biology, there is a gene, Monoamine Oxidase A (MAOA) dubbed the warrior gene because it has been linked to aggressive behavior in at least some studies. See "McDermott, Tingley, Cowden, Frazzetto and Johnson "Monoamine Oxidase A predicts behavioral aggression following provocation," *Proceedings of the National Academy of Sciences,* 106:7 (2008), 2118–2123.

13. This criterion, though, does not mean that theological beliefs are therefore automatically dismissed as false or are considered beliefs which cannot be naturalized. Theological beliefs may be naturalized provided that notions like God etc. can be proven to exist by relying on objective, well-reasoned premises instead of special forms of inferencing open only to the initiated.

14. Friedrich Nietzsche, *Twilight of the Idols or How to Philosophize with a Hammer*, Trans. Walter Kaufmann (New York: Penguin Books, 1990).

15. Friedrich Nietzsche, *On the Genealogy of Morals: A Polemic*, in *Basic Writings of Nietzsche* edited by Peter Gay, Trans. Walter Kaufmann, Preface section 1, 451.

16. Ibid., preface 7, 457.

17. Friedrich Nietzsche, *Beyond Good and Evil* in *Basic Writings of Nietzsche*, Part One section 1, 199.

18. When I capitalize the letter T in truth I am referring to the idea that humans can understand what the world is like in and of itself, that is, independently from some perspective.

19. For an interesting discussion on this problem, see Barry Stroud's "The Charm of Naturalism," in *Naturalism in Question*, edited by Mario De Caro and David Macarthur (Harvard University Press, 2004), 21–36.

20. Emanuele Politi et. al., "Raised plasma nerve growth factor levels associated with early-stage romantic love" *Psychoneuroendocrinology*, 31 (2006), 288–294.

21. See J.B.Conant, *The Overthrow of Phlogiston Theory: The Chemical Revolution of 1775–1789* (Cambridge, MA: Harvard University Press, 1950). See Kenneth Schafnner, *Nineteenth Century Aether Theories* (Oxford: Pergamon Press, 1972).

22. See P.M. Churchland, "Eliminative Materialism and the Propositional Attitudes," *Journal of Philosophy* 78 (1981), 67–90.
23. See P.S. Churchland, *Neurophilosophy: Toward a Unified Science of the Mind/Brain* (Cambridge, MA: MIT Press, 1986).
24. This feeling is called "agent-alienation." See my book, Brian Lightbody, *Dispersing the Clouds of Temptation* (Eugene, OR: Pickwick Press, 2015) for more information.
25. See R. Hatcher, "Insight and Self-Observation," *Journal of the American Psychoanalytic Association* 21, 337–398.
26. Quine, W.V.O. "Epistemology Naturalized," in *Ontological Relativity* (New York: Columbia University Press, 1969), 69–90, 82.
27. Hilary Kornblith takes Quine's project even further. He defines naturalized epistemology as follows: "The naturalistic approach to epistemology consists in this: question 1 [how ought we to arrive at our beliefs?] cannot be answered independently of question 2 [how do we arrive at our beliefs]. . . ." See Hilary Kornblith, *Naturalizing Epistemology*, edited by Hilary Kornblith (Cambridge, MA: MIT Press, 1994), 3.
28. See W.V.O. Quine and J.S. Ullian's *The Web of Belief*, 2nd edition (New York: McGraw Hill Publishers, 1978).
29. The term "naturalized epistemology" was first introduced by Quine in 1969, so I think it is best to begin with him. Indeed, according to Hilary Kornblith, the editor of *Naturalizing Epistemology*, Quine's text "*Epistemology Naturalized*" can be seen as the *locus classicus* of this epistemological perspective. Quine, W.V.O., "Epistemology Naturalized" in *Ontological Relativity*, 90.
30. See W.V.O. Quine, "Two Dogmas of Empiricism," in *From a Logical Point of View* (Cambridge, MA: Harvard University Press, 1953) and *Word and Object* (Cambridge, MA: MIT Press, 1960).
31. See Friedrich Nietzsche *On the Genealogy of Morals Essay One* in *Basic Writings of Nietzsche*. This entire essay is devoted to showing how the so-called "truths" of an afterlife, salvation and hell for the wicked began. See especially section 15 (484–85) where Nietzsche quotes and mocks Tertullian's veiled "truth" as a desire for revenge against the noble type.
32. Friedrich Nietzsche, *Twilight of the Idols*, Trans. Walter Kaufmann (New York: Penguin Books, 1990) Four Great Errors, section 2, 59.
33. Ibid., "Morality as Anti-Nature," section 4, 55.
34. Ruth Abbey, *Nietzsche's Middle Period* (New York: Oxford University Press, 2000), 104–105.
35. See C.L. Stevenson, "The Emotive Meaning of Ethical Terms" (1937) in *Ethics: History Theory and Contemporary Issues*, edited by Steven Cahn and Peter Markie, 6th edition (New York: Oxford University Press, 2015), 514–524.
36. Stevenson, 515.
37. Ibid., 516.
38. Ibid.
39. Ibid., 520.
40. See Robert Jervis, *Why Intelligence Fails Lessons from the Iranian Revolution and the Iraq War* (Cornell University Press, 2010).

41. H. Feigl, "The 'Mental' and the 'Physical'" in *Minnesota Studies in the Philosophy of Science*, II, 370–497. J.J.C. Smart, "Sensations and Brain Processes" in *Philosophical Review* 68, 141–156.

42. Some philosophers such as Antonio De Caro, Jaegwon Kim, and others have placed even greater weight on the *normative* rather than the descriptive direction of the Causal Closure Principle. As De Caro states: "having the social sciences and natural sciences exist side by side without the former being reducible to the latter would create an irreparable fracture in the sciences." See De Caro, "Is Freedom Really a Mystery?" In De Caro and Macarthur, *Naturalism in Question*, 188–200, 198. Jaegwon Kim whom De Carlo quotes, puts the point with a little more umph. He writes: "the failure of the causal closure domain would amount to an anachronistic retrogression to Cartesian interaction dualism." See De Caro, "Is Freedom Really a Mystery?" 198.

43. David Papineau, "Mind the Gap," *Philosophical Perspectives*, 32:12 (1998) 373–388, 375.

44. Jaegwon Kim, *Physicalism or Something Near Enough* (Princeton, NJ: Princeton University Press, 2005), 50.

45. E.J. Lowe in "Causal Closure Principles and Emergentism," *Philosophy* 75 (2000), 571–585, 581.

46. David Papineau, "Mind the Gap," *Philosophy in Perspectives*, 378.

47. For a very early article on this notion of emergence, see S. Pepper, "Emergence," *Journal of Philosophy*, 23 (1926), 241–245. For a more contemporary position, see Timothy O'Connor, "Emergent Properties," *American Philosophical Quarterly*, 31 (1994), 91–104.

48. The epiphenomenalist suggests that mental events are not the cause of physical events after all, but can only cause other mental events. There are several problematic features with this view, however. First, it seems to deny our most basic phenomenological experience which suggests that intentions can be efficacious in the physical realm. For instance, if I form an intention to shoot a basketball to win an important game and then make the shot then I am the one who decided to shoot the ball and it is I who feel jubilant and triumphant. This example, of course, does not show that my decision is made independently from more basic physical causes. Even our proximal intentions or so argues the physicalist, are reducible to more basic physical features of our brain. The point of the above example is merely to show that seemingly "pure" mental events, such as intentions, can cause physical events and that physical events (the ball going into the basket) can produce feelings (such as jubilation) which are clearly states of the mind. The epiphenomenalist, however, believes that mental events are caused by the mind alone. Thus as it now stands, the epiphenomenalist position cannot be correct, according to the lights of a naturalized approach to mind, because we cannot give a full account of all mental states by claiming that they follow from antecedent mental events.

49. See Chikwook Wan's article "Overdetermination, Counterfactuals and Mental Causation" in *Philosophical Review*, 123:2 (2014), 205–229, for an excellent overview of these problems.

50. See Jack Ritchie, *Understanding Naturalism* (Stocksfield, UK: Acumen Press, 2008), 115.

51. Wilfrid Sellars, "In characterizing an episode or a state as that of *knowing*, we are not giving an empirical description of that episode or state; we are placing it in the logical space of reasons, of justifying and being able to justify what it says." Sellars, W., *Science, Perception, and Reality* (London: Routledge & Kegan Paul), 169.

52. I examine the connection between determinism and Nietzsche's ethics in more detail in chapter four.

53. Nietzsche, *The Will to Power*, section 635.

54. Nietzsche, *The Will to Power*, section 1067.

55. Nietzsche's determinism will become all the more apparent when we turn to chapter two. In that chapter, I will examine Leiter's physiological reductionist reading of Nietzsche.

56. This example is taken from Sophie Gibb's "The Causal Closure Principle," *Philosophical Quarterly,* 65:261 (April 2015), 626–647, 632.

Chapter 2

Interpretations of Nietzsche's Naturalism in the Secondary Literature

Methodological and Substance Naturalism

In the first chapter, I examined what I took to be the essential qualities of naturalism. I argued that naturalism is a procedure: It is a process where one takes ideas about something and processes these ideas to create a naturalized understanding of the matter in question. I argued that naturalism, in all forms, has a normative *ethos* and two key aspects: an epistemology of reductionism or deflationism or in some cases eliminativism, and a metaphysical commitment to some version of the Causal Closure Principle. The plan for the rest of this book is to fit Nietzsche's notion of will to power into the framework of naturalism as outlined in the first chapter. To do this, I examine Nietzsche's philosophy, sharpened by a naturalistic understanding of will to power through the lenses of ethics, epistemology, and ontology in subsequent chapters.

There are other ways to construe naturalism, however, and some scholars have turned to these alternative interpretations both regarding explaining naturalism *qua* naturalism as well as explaining Nietzsche's naturalism in particular. My intention in this book is twofold: first, to put forward a warranted and nontrivial account of naturalism, which I think I have succeeded in doing in chapter one and, second, to demonstrate that Nietzsche's notion of will to power is a naturalistic enterprise. In this chapter, I examine alternative methods for construing naturalism, show the problems with these approaches, and then turn to examining how these models are applied to Nietzsche's philosophy in the secondary literature.

2.1 THE APPROPRIATION OF SUBSTANCE AND METHODOLOGICAL APPROACHES TO NATURALISM IN THE NIETZSCHEAN SECONDARY LITERATURE

2.1.1 Substance Naturalism

One way of defining substance naturalism or SN for short is to employ the definition proffered by Wilfrid Sellars. He states that, "Science is the measure of all things, of what is, that it is, and of what is not, that it is not."[1] Sellars obviously redeploys Protagoras' famous statement on ethical and ontological relativity by rendering naturalism in this iconic formulation.[2] At first glance it may appear that Sellars is simply parodying Protagoras; but he is not. He puts forward this formulation of naturalism in all seriousness. Moreover, why shouldn't such a rendering be taken seriously? In the popular mindset, after all, science is regarded as the unassailable metric for measuring both truth and reality.

Sellars' definition warrants further investigation, given the above considerations. The first problem with the definition, as stated, is that it is unclear just what Sellars means by "science." The definition is vague and unhelpful. Certainly, Sellars had in mind the three "traditional" hard sciences (physics, chemistry, and biology) when he made this claim, but what is it that makes each of these sciences scientific? For notice that if this question is begged—the above sciences are scientific because all sciences employ the same method—then we cannot demarcate scientific from nonscientific forms of inquiry. Thus, this first formulation needs to be more precisely stated to distinguish real sciences from non and even pseudosciences if it is to be useful.

It is important to understand in what way the term "science" is being used to study this particular problem in more detail. Is the term referential such that we are claiming that the above three sciences are the only means and measures of reality? Or, is the claim semantic in that that any current discipline capable of being a science, where science connotes a fixed meaning, can lay claim to defining the very contours and content of reality? Either side of this disjunctive leads to significant problems. Consider the first option. If physics, chemistry, and biology define what is real, then what specific principles and theories within each discipline are responsible for determining ontic reality? Should it be the case that only well-tested laws and well-accepted theories determine what exists? Can minority, fringe, or even radical positions play any role in mapping reality? Furthermore, if so, what precise role do they play?

On a related note, what becomes of mathematical entities? The three traditional sciences study things: particles/waves, molecules, and organisms. Such entities either are physical or exhibit physical behaviors. However, number, modality, etc. are not physical objects. What place then does mathematics have in Sellar's scientific worldview? This problem, often called the placement problem, is a difficult one to solve for any substantive naturalist view.

Regarding the latter option, it becomes clear that this position is also deeply troubling. If science serves to qualify a particular discipline in a robust way then surely this is because the discipline shares a common method, a scientific method with other disciplines. However, what common methodological techniques do all sciences practice and emulate? Moreover, if it is possible to articulate a nontendentious, non-vapid scientific method, is the method well-warranted? How could we tell? Could we use the method to justify the method?

Another question pertains to what some might call the "soft sciences." If we can include such disciplines, then how do we bridge the vast chasm that exists between the hard and soft sciences regarding what each respective discipline investigates? *Prima facie* the hard sciences seek to discover natural kinds of things whereas the "soft sciences," such as sociology and economics, strive to understand constructions which are not immediately given to sensory input (e.g., "society," "housing bubbles").[3] If such sciences are not included in Sellars' definition, then on what grounds are they dismissed?

Putting these questions to one side, what I take to be the most problematic feature of Sellars' metric, concerns the surrendering of an entity's very existence in the wake of new scientific research. That is, if science is the ultimate yardstick for what exists and what does not, then how do we explain when an entity ceases to exist because the scientific theory to which the entity is indexed is considered obsolete? Consider the case of Phlogiston. Phlogiston was a staple of the seventeenth century and even mid-eighteenth century chemistry. Phlogiston was thought to be the true combustible source of all flammable material.[4] What is more, there were reasons (though hardly justifiable now) to believe in the existence of this mysterious entity.[5] Nonetheless, if science is the measure of what exists then how can science produce false entities? By the very fact that Phlogiston was shown to be nonexistent (or at least not required to explain the respective chemical processes of combustion and calcification), then what was the metaphysical status of Phlogiston when it was considered a central part of science?

Contemporary definitions of substantive naturalism attempt to solve these and other related problems. Mario De Caro and David Macarthur hold a position known as "the ontological doctrine of scientific naturalism." In a nutshell, the doctrine holds that "The world consists of nothing but the entities to which successful scientific explanation commit us."[6] This definition is a much superior version of substantive naturalism than the one put forward by Sellars. First, the placement problem is a nonissue; the committed substance naturalist need not worry about the ontological status of number, modality, and mathematical objects because mathematics is simply a tool that scientists use when conducting an empirical inquiry.[7] Second, MacArthur and DeCaro appear to solve the problem regarding "unreal entities" such as Phlogiston. With the qualifier, "successful" it is clear that there is a further test a scientific explanation must pass to be under consideration for a yardstick of reality.

Still, the notion of "successful" gives one pause. If the history of science has proven anything surely it is this: It is hard to pin down what precisely endears a method to scientists let alone a theory.[8] What is a successful scientific theory? Is the answer longevity? But then again, if the longevity of a scientific theory is all that is required to satisfy the condition of a scientific theory being successful then Newton's laws of motion are far and away the clear winner. Yet, it is now well established that Newton's laws of motion do not apply to the world or the universe at large, uniformly. They certainly do not stand up at the quantum level and even if we keep our analysis at the macro level, it is claimed by some philosophers of science like Nancy Cartwright, that they apply, at best, to "rigged systems": systems with carefully defined objects and contexts.[9]

Does the term successful, then, mean congruent with contemporary scientific views held by the majority of scientists in a given field? Now certainly said theories have some degree of justification: they are, after all, supported by the majority of experts working in that particular subarea of science. However, as the history of science has shown, some views have more staying power than others, and there is no guarantee that a view believed to be true now will remain unmodified or indeed outright rejected in the future.[10]

I believe it is quite clear that Nietzsche, in no way, can be viewed as a substance naturalist in either the Sellarsian sense or improved modified sense above. Besides, Nietzsche had some degree of awareness regarding the problems already noted. Nietzsche is very critical of the so-called, "discoveries" made by scientists in his day; he is critical of both the scientists themselves and the methods they employ. We see this attitude and critique in many of his works. Moreover, he does not reserve his sometimes harsh rebuke of science and scientists to any one scientific field in particular.

As I see it, Nietzsche's criticisms regarding the substantive aspects of science can be categorized into three groups: First, he is critical of the very idea that science is the only yardstick of reality. He clearly thinks that scientists go wrong when they forget that science is actually an interpretation: a powerful and useful interpretation to be sure, but an interpretation nonetheless. The problem then has to do with the will of scientists: they are fanatical when it comes to their, "desire to halt before the factual, the *factum brutum*."[11] Nietzsche, of course, claims that the present scientific overzealousness to get at bare facts should be greatly tempered. We see this interpretation justified in many other places. For example, he writes in *Beyond Good and Evil,* ". . . physics too is only an interpretation and exegesis of the world (to suit us, if I may so!) and not a world-explanation."[12] Additionally, and most famously, "No, facts are precisely what there is not; only interpretations."[13] Scientists believe that they have discovered the true wellsprings of reality and, as such, they are not altogether different from the priests they sometimes despise. Nietzsche writes in this regard, "This pair, science and the ascetic ideal, both rest on the same foundation—I have already indicated it: on the same overestimation of truth (more exactly on the same belief that the truth is inestimable and cannot be criticized)."[14] This inestimable value of truth, though, is not, Nietzsche is quick to point out, supported for pragmatic reasons as perhaps it should be. Rather the value of truth is held simply on faith. Nietzsche worked out the problem in section 24 of *The Genealogy*. He writes: "That which constrains these men, however, this unconditional will to truth, is faith in the ascetic ideal itself, even if as an unconscious imperative—don't be deceived about that—it is the faith in the metaphysical value, the value of truth itself."[15] To be sure, this quotation should not be interpreted to mean that Nietzsche rejects the truth or the value of truth entirely. This popular "post-modernist" interpretation has all too often been attributed to Nietzsche with disastrous results.[16] At the heart of Nietzsche's criticism is that the unreflective faith in the value of truth and moreover the faith scientists have in the ascetic ideal—renouncing feeling, diligently pursuing only one method for arriving at truth (i.e. the scientific method)—is preventing new kinds of descriptions of the world. But it is these new descriptions which may be healthier than the old ones.

It is important, at this point, to understand, more fully, what Nietzsche means by truth. His criticism of truth is not unqualified: he is critical of a particular idea of truth. What Nietzsche criticizes is a view of truth that he believes to be untrue. Nietzsche argues that scientists believe that they are arriving at "Truths": absolute, unchanging facts about reality that stand true, that is, the same, regardless of who perceives them or of what happens within the world. However, Nietzsche claims, such truths are untrue: The will to power demonstrates the fluid becoming of all things. Reality does not stand still: and all things are undergoing perpetual change. Thus, scientists arrive at a falsification of reality by thinking of reality in Parmenidean Being terms: Reality is one, eternal, imperishable, and it is this thinking, Nietzsche evinces, which is unjustified. The senses, Nietzsche reminds us in *Twilight of the Idols*, ". . . lie neither in the way the Eleatics believed, nor as he believed—they do not lie at all. What we *make* of their testimony, that alone introduces lies; for example, the lie of unity, the lie of thinghood, of substance, of permanence. 'Reason' is the cause of our falsification of the testimony of the senses. Insofar as the senses show becoming, passing away, and change, they do not lie."[17]

The problem with scientists is that they are suffering from the affliction of the death of God. Scientists are so keen to replace God with something equally eternal and timeless they forget that they are placing a false idol on a pedestal, namely, the notion of timeless truths. Convictions, Nietzsche reminds us in *Human-all-too-Human* "are more dangerous enemies of truth than lies" and the assurance in pure, stable, timeless truths is one of the most dangerous "truths" there is.[18]

The second problem with science, at least according to Nietzsche, is that it rests on presuppositions which often go unacknowledged. This dilemma is similar to the first one, but here it is possible that the scientist accepts that the particular laws and specific working hypotheses she uses are interpretations, or, at best, approximations, but then makes the mistake into thinking that the sum total of said interpretations and approximations grounds scientific inquiry. This inference is an unwarranted metaphysical extrapolation and speaks to yet another problem of science: "The problem of science, Nietzsche writes, "is that it cannot be recognized on the ground of science."[19] Science cannot ground itself precisely because the scientific attitude is one that consists in ceaseless discovery, testing and hypothesizing. However, scientists, Nietzsche argues, do not wish to recognize this "truth." As Hilary Putnam puts it (drawing inspiration from Nietzsche):

> Science is wonderful at destroying metaphysical answers, but incapable of providing substitute ones. Science takes away foundations without providing a replacement. Whether we want to be there or not, science has put us in the position in the having to live without foundations. It was shocking when Nietzsche said this, but today it is commonplace; our historical position—and no end it is in sight—is that of having to do philosophy without "foundations."[20]

Even the notions of cause and effect are necessary assumptions; they too are interpretations, so holds Nietzsche. Science goes awry when it takes these notions to be absolutes. Nietzsche writes:

> Scientists should not wrongly reify cause and effect as the natural scientists do (and whoever, like them now naturalizes in his thinking), according to the prevailing mechanical doltishness which makes the cause press and push until it "effects" its end; one should use "cause" and "effect" only as pure concepts, that is to say, as conventional fictions for the purpose of designation and communication—not for explanation.[21]

With respect to scientific laws which are deemed to be eternal, complete, and self-subsisting, Nietzsche cautions scientists here, too. He writes:

> Let us beware of saying that there are laws in nature. There are only necessities: there is nobody who commands, nobody who obeys, nobody who trespasses ... There are no eternally enduring substances; matter is as much an error as the

God of the Eleatics. . . . But when will all these shadows of God cease to darken our minds? When will we complete our de-deification of nature?[22]

If methods of science are those that call for continual hypothesis creation and the repetition of experiments, then science contradicts its fundamental theorems by also seeking to ground itself on some metaphysical stratum.

Third, science requires fictions for its empirical theories to be formulated. Science works, at least, according to Nietzsche, with entities, that, strictly speaking, do not exist. Mathematical theorems, straight lines, and even cause and effect, as already shown, do not exist in the empirical world, but scientists mistakenly believe they do. Nietzsche's drive in pointing this out is not to argue against the efficacy of these ideas *vis a vis* the tremendous power of predictability science has, but to again to say that such inventions stem from a deep-seated psychological need to order the world around us. "It is the same with mathematics, Nietzsche avers, "which would certainly not have arisen if it had been known from the beginning that in Nature there are no exactly straight lines, no real circle, no absolute standard of size."[23] In *The Will to Power*, Nietzsche writes the following: "We should not interpret this *constraint* in ourselves to imagine concepts, species, forms, purposes and laws (*"a world of identical cases"*) as if we were in a position to construct a *real world*; but as a constraint to adjust a world by means of which *our existence* will be ensured: We thereby create a world which is determinable, simplified, comprehensible, etc. for us (Nietzsche's italics)."[24] However, such precise ordering produces an unintended consequence: it levels the world to a flat plane. The world becomes lifeless and bloodless, and we become lifeless and bloodless along with it. We too become mere atoms of material and take our place in the vacuum of meaning created by Laplace's demon.[25] On this general evacuation of meaning, Nietzsche writes in this regard:

> Since Copernicus, man seems to have got himself on an inclined plane—now he is slipping faster and faster away from the center into—what? into nothingness? into a *penetrating* sense of his nothingness? . . . All science, natural as well as *unnatural*—which is what I call the self-critique of knowledge—has at present the object of dissuading man from his former respect for himself, as if he had been nothing but a piece of bizarre conceit. (Nietzsche's italics)[26]

Nietzsche's naturalistic enterprise seeks to get meaning and value back in the wake of the Scientific Revolution. Thus, Nietzsche's task becomes exceedingly difficult in that he cannot discount science for mysticism, or retreat into some entombment of radical subjectivity a la existentialism. Instead, he must offer a more naturalistic description of this new, atheistic and thereby aesthetic worldview while also affirming and venerating this new existence.

Though Nietzsche is critical of what we might call the hard sciences; he does seem to be more receptive to soft sciences, like physiology. Indeed, there is a long tradition of viewing Nietzsche as a physiological essentialist—valuation is determined according to one's physiological make-up. Thus, one can predict the values of individuals by investigating their peculiar physiological constitution. If something like this view is correct—and there are many variations—then Nietzsche's polemic and critique against science, under this view is not wholesale. Rather, Nietzsche would remain firmly within the camp of substance naturalism but would not follow most naturalists in grounding the sciences on physics. Instead, Nietzsche's grounding principle, as alluded to in the preface, would be physiology.

Richard S.G. Brown in an early article entitled "Nihilism: Thus Speaks Physiology" and more recently in "Nietzsche that Profound Physiologist" convincingly shows that Nietzsche believed that one's morals along with his or her conceptions about the world, and perceptions thereof, are reducible to that individual's peculiar physiological make-up.[27] Brown argues that there are two formulations of how Nietzsche reduces moral concepts to physiological processes. He writes:

> In other words, in the first formulation, Nietzsche argues that our surface values (morality) can be read as a sign language of the underlying affects of a herd, race or individual. In the second formulation however, Nietzsche claims that it is possible to read from the physiological needs or existential parameters of a herd, race, or individual, to their respective values, that is, to be actually in a position to predict the morality or moral values that should be a reflection of the underlying physiological needs.[28]

There is a significant amount of textual evidence to support Brown's contention. Consider what Nietzsche writes in *The Genealogy*: "Indeed, every table of values, every 'thou shalt' known to history or ethnology, requires first a physiological investigation and interpretation rather than a psychological one; and every one of them needs a critique on the part of medical science."[29] Alternatively, again consider what Zarathustra says: "Truly, my brother if you only knew people's need and land and sky and neighbor you could surely divine the law of its overcomings and why it is upon this ladder that it mounts its highest hope."[30] What Brown and others in this camp argue is that one can read both a naturalized ethics *and* epistemology directly from Nietzsche's comments on physiology.

Brian Leiter, another prominent scholar, also holds what we might describe as a "physiological-type" interpretation of Nietzsche. His position is also one that cleaves to a strong physiological approach but is much more sophisticated, clearer, and, overall, philologically sounder than Brown's position. Given this endorsement, it is important to examine this stance carefully, attentively, and diligently. In brief, Leiter argues that there is a causal relationship regarding one's physiology type and one's cognitive and moral capacities. I take up Leiter's epistemic model in this section and explore the moral relationship in the section after that.

According to Leiter, Nietzsche, much like Hume before him and like Freud afterward desired to construct a type theory of human behavior. The type theory argues that human beings belong to fixed psycho-physiological types such that an understanding of these types determine and explain the cognitive faculties, actions, and behavior of individuals. "Each person has a fixed psycho-physical constitution, which defines him as a particular type of person."[31] There are two types: weak types who are impotent, reactive, prone to nursing grudges and interestingly, according to Leiter, desire to create values which serve their interests and strong types who are active, exuberant, healthy and again, according to Leiter, express values in a physical manner. In converse to the weak type, the strong construct values which come to serve their instincts.[32]

Thus, for Leiter, there are immutable type-facts about an individual: physiological and psychological traits that constitute the person and which place him in one of the categories above. These type-facts may then be used to predict, with some degree of accuracy, so thinks Nietzsche, the moral and theoretical beliefs of that one and the same person. What's more there seems to be substantial support for this view. Consider what Nietzsche says in *The Genealogy*: "Our thoughts, values, every 'yes,' 'no,' 'if' and 'but' grow from us with the same inevitability as fruits borne on the tree—all related and each with an affinity to each, and evidence of one will, one health, one earth, one sun."[33]

Now regarding a person's epistemic beliefs, such a view seems to go hand in hand with Nietzsche's well-known doctrine of perspectivism. The clearest statement of Nietzsche's perspectival view can be found in *The Genealogy*: "There is *only* a perspective seeing, *only* a perspective 'knowing;' and the *more* affects we allow to speak about one thing, the *more* eyes, different eyes, we can use to observe one thing, the more complete will our "concept" of this thing, our 'objectivity,' be."[34] There are many aspects to what some might call the perspectivist thesis in Nietzsche's *oeuvre,* and I examine these elements in more detail in chapter three, but one aspect that is immediately pertinent to the above discussion is what one might call the Epistemic Meritorious Problem (EMP). What Nietzsche identifies here, is that we come to an object with an agenda in place: we view the object from our distinctive, affective vantage point. Putting this point in Leiter's language, we view an object according to the constitution of our type-facts. As Leiter puts it, "Nietzsche effectively holds that reality exercises no epistemic constraint on our interpretations of the world (the 'facts' themselves turning out to be simply affective projections). Without any such constraint, however, it is not clear what room there could be for the idea that interpretations could have different epistemic (as opposed to, e.g., pragmatic) merits."[35] Parsing this point, we can claim that to hold a perspective, is to acknowledge, necessarily, that there is a relationship of epistemic access between a subject and an object.

However, this construal leads to problems regarding the epistemic merit of two competing perspectives that derive from different psycho-physiological types. As I see it, two questions need to be addressed: (1) How do we go about determining how direct or accurate one's access to the object is? That is, what causal relationship does the perspective establish between the subject and the object? (2) How can we definitively determine just how justified a person is in holding a belief about an object given the perspective from which he or she arrives at about his or her belief? If reality does not exercise a constraint on the beliefs we come to have, then how can one perspective be more meritorious than some other?

Leiter attempts to solve the above problem by arguing for a Purity Claim. In effect, he contends that constraint comes from within an individual. He writes in "Perspectivism in Nietzsche's Genealogy of Morals," that the Purity Claim may be defined as follows: "There exists a catalogue of identifiable factors that would distort our knowledge of the object: that is, certain interpretive interests and needs will distort the nature of objects."[36] In keeping with the Purity Claim, Leiter holds that weak individuals require some degree of falsification and filtering of perception because they do not have the constitutive faculties to see the truth of existence: that it is harsh, cruel, and chalk-full of suffering. Moreover, section 39 of *Beyond Good and Evil,* demonstrates Leiter's thesis well:

> Something might be true although at the same time harmful and dangerous in the highest degree; indeed, it could pertain to the fundamental nature of existence that a complete knowledge of it would destroy one—so that the strength of a spirit could be measured by how much "truth" it could take, more clearly, to what degree it *needed* it attenuated, veiled, sweetened, blunted, and falsified. (Nietzsche's italics)[37]

How might we establish the criterion to distinguish non-distorting needs and interests from distorting needs and interests?[38] Leiter's solution is to look to the "strong" or "choice individual." It is those individuals who are vigorous and powerful; it is those who say "yes to life," it is they who can determine the "terrible truth of reality." More precisely the strong person's affects, Leiter argues, do a better job of presenting the object as the object is, whereas the weak person's affects serve to distort the object because it is the nature of the weak to seek illusions, deceptions, and lies.[39] Strong type individuals have a more robust access to the terrible of truth of existence than the weak because unlike them they can accept life undiluted and undistorted.

There is substantial support for Leiter's viewpoint. Consider once again section 39 of *Beyond Good and Evil*: "Therefore, the strong person's motto of saying, "Yes to reality, is just as necessary for the strong as cowardice and the flight from reality—as the ideal is for the weak, who are inspired by weakness."[40] This passage and several others from Nietzsche's work supports Leiter's physiological ranking theory.[41] However, from a strictly epistemological standpoint, Leiter fails to mention the peculiar and challenging problems with this stance. For starters, we might ask: How are we to distinguish strong individuals from weak individuals? Is the adjective strong to be rendered literally or is it metaphoric? If it is employed literally, is it synonymous with those who most would classify as physiologically strong? But what do we mean by physiology? Do we mean that a person with big, bulky muscles is the Nietzschean strong type? Or is it the individual who has strong powers of recovery from injury? Alternatively, by strong is Nietzsche referring to those persons who are not biologically degenerate (whatever this may mean)?

If we turn to looking the at term from a metaphoric standpoint, then Nietzsche must mean that it is the drives within an individual which are strong. It is not the person who is strong *per se* but it is the drives themselves that seek out the hard but nonetheless real truths of reality. Which of these options is Leiter advocating?

Either option is problematic. Let us look at the last option first. If strong is meant metaphorically, then it must mean that those persons who possess these particular (strong) drives or affects in the appropriate degree and combination are capable of withstanding suffering, loss, and tragedy. These individuals are then the "chosen" individuals of whom Nietzsche speaks that can delve deeply into the very fount of human existence in all its affirmative joys and condemning tragedies. Yet if construed in this way the criterion is obviously circular: Those who possess the right affects in the proper combination are those who have the capacity to view reality undistorted and affirm the suffering and tragedy of life they encounter therein. Nonetheless, we can tell they are strong only because they can withstand the suffering and torment they then truly experience. It is clear that a metaphorical interpretation of "strong" is a circular approach we have witnessed before (in regard to Nietzsche's reductionist tendencies in *Twilight*) and does not work when it comes to justifying perspectivism.

The first option, namely, the literal interpretation is even more problematic than the metaphoric reading. I already identified the difficulty interpreting the qualifier strong in a physiological sense in that there are different meanings as to what it would mean if someone was described as strong, physiologically speaking. However, even if we bracket this question for a moment consider what a position would entail: Nietzsche's well-established argument that science only interprets reality and does so from a particular perspective is untrue. If we accept this interpretation then clearly there is only one (correct) perspective, namely, that of the biological sciences (broadly construed). All others would be merely perspectives which in this case would mean errors and falsehoods.

Nietzsche's suggestion to look to medicine, physiology, biology, and other cognate disciplines to understand how different types understand the world and how the strong types have a more accurate connection to the world is deeply incoherent for other reasons, too. Nietzsche is quite clear that the physician and scientist in his day, as already demonstrated, are infected with the priestly values of asceticism and impotence.[42] They clearly belong to the weak type who Nietzsche clearly disparages. But if all people always interpret from their physiological conditioning then the diagnoses rendered by physicians along with the biological theories constructed from the expressions of the feelings and genetic dispositions of biologists and physiologists would be merely the by-products of unhealthy, weak, heavily filtered conduits.[43] Gregory Moore highlights this tension between interpreting concepts like healthy/unhealthy, active/reactive, and life-affirming/life-denying in either metaphorical or literal terms in his book *Nietzsche, Biology, and Metaphor*. On this problem Moore writes,

> Nietzsche's Biologism is more wide-ranging more total than that of his immediate successors. Their work (Scheler, Spengler, Simmel, Lessing, Klages) also lacks the fundamental contradictoriness of Nietzsche's position—a nineteenth-century faith in the institutional authority of the biological sciences which coexists uneasily with a belief that these same disciplines are infected with false values; the characteristic hovering between literalness and metaphor, sincerity and irony.[44]

Without specifying the precise manner in which he is drawing upon the terms and concepts used in the biological and medical sciences it is difficult to comprehend how Nietzsche foresaw how health serves as the model for the strong/weak type. If the disciplines of medicine, biology, and physiology seem to be infected as well then Nietzsche's description of the strong and weak types seems at best vacuous and at worst completely and irrevocably incoherent.

I argue that there is a way to save a much weaker version of Nietzsche's strong/weak type model in the final chapter. What I argue is that one must have the strength to examine his or her feelings to determine whether such feelings come into play when assessing the epistemic merits of a particular belief. With that said, the above discussion clearly demonstrates that Nietzsche is not a substance naturalist in the "scientific" sense of the term and that if he is a substance naturalist in the strong type-fact sense argued for by Leiter, then his position cannot be redeemed. Accordingly, a more charitable and defensible interpretation must be tried.

2.1.2 Methodological Naturalism

The above section focused on some of the problems regarding a substance naturalist understanding of Nietzsche's work and more specifically a difficulty regarding how we should interpret Nietzsche's perspectivist claim under a substance reading. Leiter's purity solution, underwritten by a peculiar type-fact psycho-physiological metaphysics, was shown to be deeply problematic. I now turn to examining some of the problems with Leiter's account of Nietzsche's moral work. Leiter undergirds his account by using a different understanding of naturalism. I will examine the problems with Leiter's moral position by viewing it from his understanding of methodological naturalism and how this alternative method of understanding naturalism applies to Nietzsche's work, *The Genealogy*.

Although there are problems with the work as a whole, Brian Leiter's *Nietzsche on Morality* remains one of, if not the very best introductions to Nietzsche's position on naturalism. In this work, Leiter manages to demarcate clearly the differences between methodological and substance naturalism and argues that Nietzsche is a methodological naturalist of a very peculiar stripe. For Leiter, Nietzsche advocates a methodological naturalism that is continuous with the natural sciences—the methods, techniques, and procedures adopted by the most successful sciences are utilized by Nietzsche only toward different ends.

The principal tool Nietzsche uses to discover, what Leiter calls the psycho-physical type-fact model, is the genealogical method. Leiter makes an adamant case in *Nietzsche on Morality*, for placing genealogy in the same category as the empirical sciences, that is to say, as a naturalistic sort of investigation rather than, say, interpreting genealogy as a kind of close reading.[45] Since genealogy is subject to very different interpretations regarding its methods, goals, and value, it is necessary to explain, what I take to be the crucial aspects of this approach before proceeding to examine Leiter's take on genealogy with a more critical eye.

When I use the term "philosophical genealogy," I am referring to the method of historical and philosophical investigation developed by Friedrich Nietzsche upon his reading of Paul Ree's *Origin of Moral Sensations*. Philosophical genealogy, however, has been further refined by such continental thinkers as Michel Foucault, so this type of philosophical analysis is not peculiar to Nietzsche.[46] Philosophical genealogy is distinctive because it examines the historical origins of present-day philosophical notions, methods, values, ideas, discourses, in addition to political, legal, and social institutions. Such origins are traced and, depending on the method used, the genealogist either (1) shows how a myriad of seemingly diverse and distinct ideas and practices have their roots in one common origin or (2) shows how a regime of truth—a power/knowledge apparatus in the Foucauldian sense—is the outgrowth of some previously distinct and unconnected discourses, practices, and institutions which became woven together, interconnected and mutually supportive over a relatively short period.[47]

Although a genealogy may be performed on essentially anything, Nietzsche emphasized the importance of performing genealogies on emotions. In Essay II of the *On the Genealogy of Morals*, Nietzsche provides a paradigm model for how to go about tracing a specific feeling, in this case, guilt, to a simpler and more primordial affective state.

What Nietzsche's genealogy reveals is an entirely different story than that of the one typically given in Christian-Judeo circles. Guilt is not innate and certainly not a gift from God but a fabrication of sorts whose kernel can be found in the initial act of enclosure beginning with the very dawn of civilization itself: the in walling of humanity. Guilt is one of if not the first thread that creates the tapestry that is subjectivity.

The idea that guilt is an original formatting of sorts creating the human being from some "half-animal, half-man creature" base demonstrates that ideas, discourses, and values are born from a struggle for power. Because the first warrior-artists constructed walls and developed efficacious techniques of torture for those who attempted to flee civilization, this resulted in the blocking of natural and instinctual desires for adventure and hunting. The result was the creation of a new type of creature who expressed his or her will to power inwardly. This creature's drives turned inward carving out the faculties of subjectivity itself (e.g., introspection, conscience, guilt, strategizing and planning, internal monolog, etc.).

Nevertheless, these warriors though were soon displaced by the priestly type who took over many of the same laws as their warrior predecessors but gave new interpretations as to their origins. The priestly caste reworked and further advanced the drive toward internalization creating the soul—a substance which could be used for further self-torture.

The above is a much-simplified story of how guilt, God, and the soul came to be formed. Nietzsche fills in these details in Essay 2 of *The Genealogy*. The point in elaborating on this was to show that history, regarding civilization, begins through an act of will to power: The creation of walls is an effort to restrict the movement of others for the sake of increasing one's power. The purpose of confining early humans was to fashion them according to some ideal. Genealogy demonstrates that history is not working toward some hidden *telos* as the Whig Historian would have it, but is rather best understood as a struggle between contending forces.[48] Ideas, discourses, and practices are really the sign language of evaluation, and all evaluation presupposes evaluators. History is a struggle between groups for power.

By unmasking the origin and subsequent lines of descent of a feeling, such as guilt, the philosophical genealogist effectively demonstrates the long sign chain of interpretations that produced the current emotion.[49] A genealogist's task then, is, ultimately, to unravel the tapestry: to determine the threads used, the tools utilized, to weave the threads and the pattern, if any, the threads now make. The genealogist does not reveal an origin for an idea, practice, or feeling, but rather the conditions suitable for allowing the idea to germinate and gain hold. In addition to showing the roots and soil for the outgrowth of an idea, a genealogist also traces where the offshoots of the notion may be heading.

The above analysis as to the "true" origin of guilt to use Nietzsche's example, is referred to as the diagnostic component to the genealogical inquiry. It is for good reason: Nietzsche often called himself a physician of culture. Moreover, like any good doctor, Nietzsche develops a curative component, too. To this end, Nietzsche called genealogy the path to (*gay scienza*) or gay science.[50] Genealogy is a curative science: it exposes the flaws in the tacit beliefs we currently hold to be true.[51] By demonstrating that specific life-denying ideas or feelings long thought to be true, innate, immutable, and unchanging, are in fact mutable, contingent, and arbitrary, Nietzsche's genealogical investigations allow us to cast doubt on such modes of life and, thereby, enable us to establish new beliefs and attitudes in order to live more creatively, joyfully and indeed, experimentally than our prior beliefs allowed.

Leiter argues that genealogy shares a similar naturalistic method of investigation to the empirical sciences, but this does not mean that genealogy is substantively naturalistic. According to Leiter, genealogy, and the empirical sciences are naturalistic types of inquiry because both of these discourses share a similar method of investigation. Both the physical sciences and philosophical genealogy start from hypotheses which are empirically confirmable, and falsifiable instead of beginning from *a priori* truths.[52] More forcefully stated, it may be said that genealogy shares with the empirical sciences a *contempt* for any supernatural (and thus non-verifiable hypothesis) to explain natural phenomena, like morality. The genealogist tries to emulate the methods of the natural scientists but puts these methods to different ends. Genealogy is not substantively naturalistic or in Leiter's parlance S-Naturalistic because genealogical investigations cannot be reducible to these same hard sciences.

Leiter's position seems to steer a course between the Scylla of scientific positivism on the one hand which would reduce genealogy to a mere chapter of empirical psychology (perhaps) and the Charybdis of a purely philological approach or dare I say postmodern account of genealogy, which, as a theory, has been very often advanced in the secondary literature without much reflection.[53] Despite Leiter's clearly laudable efforts, nevertheless, the position articulated is not without problems. First, I wholeheartedly agree with Leiter's take on genealogy: genealogy is indeed a type of naturalized investigation. However, if genealogy is a type of naturalized investigation, then the search for truth itself in combination with the method one uses to discover said truths must be intrinsically valuable in themselves. However, rather curiously, Leiter explicitly argues against this position in many places. Genealogy as a naturalized type of empirical investigation into the history of morality according to Leiter, only seems to have extrinsic value insofar as it allows higher types to recognize the causal powers of, what Leiter calls, Morality in a Pejorative Sense (MPS). Only when these strong types come to recognize how they have been duped by MPS, thanks to genealogy, does it become possible for them to cast it aside making true self-flourishing possible. "The genealogy of morality, Leiter reminds us, is but *one instrument* for arriving at a particular end, namely a critique of morality" (My Italics).[54]

The problem with Leiter's above construal, however, is that Leiter fails to commit fully to genealogy's naturalized pedigree. A truly naturalized scientific methodology, after all, is not secondary to the results which you hope the method to achieve. For Leiter, genealogy, as Nietzsche's preeminent method of empirical investigation, parallels scientific thinking because it advances defensible hypotheses; tests these hypotheses by examining the relevant psychological and physical pieces of evidence which would serve to support or falsify these hypotheses and then, depending on the findings, alters or abandons said hypotheses in the face of recalcitrant evidence. However, more than this, genealogy uses the methods, theories, and procedures that comprise other empirical disciplines to create a new narrative for its object of inquiry. This sort of marshaling of evidence is anything but rare: There is an overlap between the fields of chemistry, biology, and physics such that theories in one field are only understandable and testable by using assumptions in the other. Scientists in evolutionary biology, for example, utilize theories in both biology and chemistry to make sense of the claims being made within their field.[55]

However, under Leiter's reading, physics, for instance, would only be one means for arriving at how to produce the results of physics. This rather strange proposal leads to three inconsistent results. First, looking at physics as an example, according to Leiter, CD players, atomic bombs, or launching satellites are more valuable than the method used to produce such things. However, surely this is backward: A methodological naturalist places a premium on the method one uses to discover the inner wellsprings of nature not on the springs once discovered. Leiter's true construal of naturalism would then be a product of a naturalized approach. However, this is mixed up.

Physics, rather, is the study of nature for the sake of understanding nature *qua* nature. Of course, there are instrumental interests as to why scientists study the basic building blocks of the universe, but any hard science is dedicated to getting at the truth of that which it is studying. Now if genealogy is like physics and other hard sciences because it uses a naturalized methodology then minimally this entails that it is trying to get at the truth of the matter at hand, that is, the origin and (true) value of our traditional systems of value. But if this is the case, then genealogy like other hard sciences must hold that truth, justification, and empirical warrant are intrinsically valuable for the investigation. Only an epistemological reconstruction of genealogy that places a premium on the intrinsic value of truth or perhaps better, truthfulness and justification can resolve problems pertaining to the epistemic merits of Nietzsche's genealogies.

Second, if Leiter is correct that genealogy is only one method for producing the desired results, namely, overthrowing MPS then other methods for arriving at these results are possible and perhaps even superior to genealogy. Nevertheless, if genealogy is like the hard sciences because it shares a common method, then physics, too, is valuable because it produces new technologies and therefore other theories that produce these same technologies are just as valuable or perhaps more valuable than physics as we currently understand it.

But notice that an alternative "physics" would not be different from physics but would still be physics—new theories may very well force out traditional theories of physics, but they would then be the new theories within the field of physics. If this holds for physics, then it must also hold for genealogy—no other discipline understands the means of arriving at a transvaluation of the values. It is this position, namely, the view that genealogy is the only means and method for transforming values that Leiter needs to adopt for his argument which trades on the analogical properties of genealogy and compares them favorably to other empirical sciences, to hold water. Nietzsche, in relation to genealogy, considered himself to be a physician of culture: Genealogy was the study of how we have come to accept poisoned belief systems and attempted to find the cure. Again, if genealogy is a species of method akin to the natural sciences because it uses the same methods as these sciences, then genealogy is the only means of eradicating these poisoned belief systems just as surely as the medical sciences are the only means for treating illness and disease. Other methods might be just as beneficial and salutary as medical science but these methods, once they have been understood, are then absorbed by science and become part of medical science proper.

Another problem with Leiter's construal has to do with the notion of the method itself. There are two assumptions at work: (1) All sciences share the same techniques or utilize the same methods. This claim, however, is specious. Although there have been attempts to extract a scientific method for all sciences, this attempt has turned out to be an impossible dream or deeply problematic as it revisits all the old problems of induction. While it is true that all sciences share a conviction in establishing hypotheses that are subject to empirical testing and that the results of such testing must be in principle capable of being repeated, such convictions do not make a method. Trying to go further than this as both the logical positivists and Karl Popper attempted to do in the early part of the twentieth century, led to significant problems.[56] (2) The method itself is self-justifying just because it is *the method* that the sciences use. However, as Nietzsche has already pointed out, one cannot divorce scientific practice from misinformed cultural illusions and delusions. Indeed, Nietzsche anticipated many of the standard objections as put forward by the likes of Thomas Kuhn and Paul Feyerabend when one attempts to construct a scientific method *sub species aternai*.[57]

The blind adherence to a "method" will only stultify the scientific endeavor as the history of science clearly shows. Just like Feyerabend, Nietzsche would applaud the *ethos* of smashing the idol of scientific methodology. Thus, in no way can Nietzsche be viewed as a methodological naturalist at least as Leiter interprets methodological naturalism.

Another related problem with Leiter's account, as raised by Ridley and Owen, has to do with the difficulty of epistemic authority and the intended audience of Nietzsche's *On the Genealogy of Morals*. Nietzsche's perspectival claim holds that statements are true according to some perspectives and false in others. The problem with this position is one of ascertaining which perspectives are more epistemically meritorious (or authoritative) than others. This problem was examined above. In keeping with his Purity Claim made in an earlier work, Leiter tries to work around this issue by arguing, that, since the *Genealogy* is directed to a specific audience—namely the higher types—then no justification (of Nietzsche's genealogies) is required. The book, after all, was composed for those who have the means to hear Nietzsche's message. But, as Ridley demonstrates, this answer results in a contradiction in that it shows that Nietzsche's selected audience "are not 'predisposed' to accept the authority of his standpoint after all."[58] That is, if higher types are truly different from the herd, then they would not be subject to what Leiter calls the causal powers of MPS and therefore would not require a genealogy of morality to help them throw off the yoke of morality. In sum, Ridley and Owen show that Leiter's account cannot explain how the higher types were duped by MPS in the first place. If genealogy cannot explain how an individual of one physiological type can be fooled to adopt the values of another type, then Leiter's account of genealogy does not answer the basic question of the discipline, namely, "How are new values established and how do they come to take on value?"

Leiter's construal of Nietzsche's naturalistic position may be considered to sit on the right-hand side of the naturalism continuum where Brown's approach may be interpreted as the end point of this same side. There are, however, other construals of Nietzsche's naturalism that tend toward a cultural or perhaps better put, "psychical" (and *not* psychological) methodology, broadly construed. I would argue that these approaches rest on the "left-hand side" where more importance is placed on what Sellars has called the "logical space of reasons."[59] Christopher Janaway, for example, attempts to render a different account of Nietzsche's naturalism and more perspicuously his genealogical method as a kind of naturalized inquiry than the one advocated by Leiter claiming that Nietzsche was a physician of culture and, as such, placed a great emphasis on how we, as humans become encultured. In examining how we become encultured, Nietzsche, Janaway suggests, exposes the different ways we have been fooled into believing that the source of morality is supernatural in origin. Nietzsche shows how we have been "bred." In other words, he shows how morality has been physically, psychologically, and culturally induced within us and, thusly, exposes a non-supernatural origin for beliefs we previously and mistakenly believed to be signs from God.

What is novel about Janaway's account is that culture is not flattened to some ontological reductionist scientific perspective. He argues that Nietzsche's critique of morality, as clearly put forward in *The Genealogy,* must allow the reader the opportunity to examine the fundaments of the traditional story of guilt or the origin of "Good" and "Bad" for themselves.[60] The "scientized" construal of genealogy, Janaway claims, is not only superficial (and in point of fact, vacuous as Janaway also shows) but, in many ways, wrong-headed because genealogy engages the affective drives of its readers whereas the sciences seem to expunge all emotion from its methods of inquiry.[61]

Janaway's objection to naturalism—or at least the way in which naturalism is understood by Leiter—has to do with the tendency of scientists to limit their investigations to merely physical causes. Rather, as Janaway convincingly demonstrates, psycho-physical states of individuals can neither be entirely explained by the newest discoveries in physiology or cognitive psychology (although to be sure they may be helpful in this regard) nor be explained away. For the genealogist to understand the actual engine, as it were of Christian asceticism, for example, she must examine it from the inside: from the peculiar psycho-physical state of the subject who is immersed in this belief as well as the culture which produced the belief in question.

Let us look at a concrete example. Much can be gained from studying the economic, social, and political origins of the first "Great Awakening," the early American, eighteenth-century spiritual movement. However, according to Janaway, any study that concentrated merely on these objective conditions for this cultural and religious phenomenon would remain incomplete. To truly get inside the engines of this movement, as it were, one would not only have to read the works of Johnathan Edwards, the leader of the "Great Awakening" movement but *embrace* the message of these works with both, proverbial, "body and soul." Janaway, therefore, argues that Nietzsche's true goal in *The Genealogy* is to demonstrate that equal emphasis must be placed on what we might call "subjective, lived experience" as on objective, empirical methods of inquiry. One is therefore encultured, but this does not mean that one is determined such as by Leiterean "type facts."

Although I agree with much of Janaway's analysis, and will come to investigate further features of his analysis in later chapters of the present work, I take issue with his often vague and noncommittal attitude regarding will to power. At times he seems to agree with Clark and Richardson when they claim that will to power is an embarrassment because it projects "intentionalistic, anthropomorphic language to sub-personal and organic processes."[62] At other times, he is more charitable, allowing the plausibility of Nietzsche's attempt through the will to power to highlight "an analogy or continuum between mind and organic nature positing relations that can only be described as dominance, submission, competition, and interpretation."[63] Skirting around whether the will to power can be used as a cosmological theory, Janaway supports a much weaker view: A power analysis can be profitably used, so thinks Janaway, provided that we properly constrain the scope of the analysis. To constrain the scope of analysis would entail investigating what drives human beings and how different cultures have promoted values that reflect the interests and/or instincts of those who wield power within the culture in question.[64]

I would suggest, that in arguing for the limitation of will to power to the cultural realm as Janaway does, he must uphold a robust and very traditional notion of agency. What Nietzsche exposes, so thinks Janaway, is how subjects have been duped into believing life-denying modes of existence. However, to understand how this subterfuge comes about, Janaway claims that genealogists must get inside an individual's ethical system. We must understand how the individual justifies the actual impoverished belief system he comes to hold from within the system itself. We must, minimally, enter into the individual's "logical space of reasons." Of course, Janaway will argue that far more than reasons are required; in fact, tracing the evolution of emotions is far more important to understanding what people believe and why people act on their beliefs. Be that as it may, the purpose of the genealogy, beautifully and clearly summarized by Janaway in an earlier article is to: "dissolve or explode our apparently unified present-day concepts into their more primitive psychological components. Because our moral concepts are *post facto* rationalizations of inherited feelings, to whose explanatory role we may be blind, our feelings for and against the need to be aroused and questioned, if we are to grasp the variegated psychological truth behind our concepts."[65]

However, who, exactly, is the "we" that Janaway speaks of here? Given that the "I," too, is one such "apparently unified construct" which genealogy also seeks to explode, and yet it is this same I that is expected and able to grasp the "variegated psychological truths behind our concepts," how is it that genealogy arrives at any truth? How do I know that some realization is not just another crafty rationalization? From where does intellectual reflection gain its power?

Janaway's insistence not to reduce moral beliefs to type-facts goes too far. For Janaway's position requires a relatively thick notion of I, self, person, etc. to perform a genealogical inquiry such that it is this same I who will receive the benefits of a genealogical investigation. However, this still leaves the I not just as a black box, but indeed as an epistemic ineliminable primitive and surely Nietzsche sought to go beyond this traditional conception of subjectivity. "To translate man back into nature," Nietzsche reminds us, "to become master over the many vain and overly enthusiastic interpretations and connotations that have so far been scrawled and painted over that eternal basic text of *homo natura*," is one of the primary goals of his philosophy.[66] Janaway's interpretation of genealogy as a naturalistic method is not naturalistic enough.

The difficult task then, as it appears to me when conceiving of will to power as a thick cosmological theory is not to think that Nietzsche is guilty of projecting a mind or "I" (with the usual metaphysical connotations of this term) back onto nature. Rather, the "subject" or "agent" that exists in nature, as it were, is that of desire without any metaphysical substance attached to it. However, to impute to Nietzsche, that, because such fundamental desires and drives emanate from nature and therefore Nietzsche is guilty of projecting mind onto nature, is to double the explanation: If nature has specific desires and drives then there is no need to account for these drives *via* the mind. I examine this interpretative insight in more detail when I turn to Nietzsche's theory of will to power in chapter three.

Before examining my view of will to power in considerable detail, it is important to examine one more attempt in the secondary literature to naturalize Nietzsche. Richard Schacht, in "Nietzsche's Naturalism," seeks to steer a middle way between substance naturalism on the one hand and a strict methodological conception of naturalism *a la* Leiter on the other. Thus, in many ways, Schacht's intention seems to be to show that such a continuum, as I presented it above between the end points of the logical space of reasons and hard-wired type-facts is false. He proposes that Nietzsche's naturalism is "sciental" as opposed to scientistic. He argues that Nietzsche draws on scientific inquiry along with ideas and theories taken from various disciplines within the *Wissenschaften,* as a whole, to inform his theories about human nature, normative behavior, and whatever cognitive capacities we have as humans. Schacht argues that Nietzsche's naturalism is first and foremost an attitude—it is one of recognizing that all processes, events, and occurrences within the world are to be explained by viewing the world immanently and not transcendentally. Schacht's initial reasoning here accords well with both my ethical and ontological aspects of naturalism, as articulated in chapter one (although Schacht's construal of "immanentism" is vague and incoherent as will be shown). More controversially, Schacht holds that Nietzsche does not wish to reduce such events, like the origin of morality in all its sundry forms or religious practices to a physicalist-biological model, but to understand their emergence from forms of life (*Lebensformen*).

Even if Schacht is correct in whole, it should be acknowledged that he has to walk a very thin tightrope here as it is clear that Nietzsche's task is to demonstrate that forms of life are undergirded and dependent, at least in part, on prior existing physiological conditions. This point is readily acknowledged by Schacht where he writes the following: "But he also is quite evidently convinced that human cultural phenomena, while physiologically grounded, are historically developed forms of life differing qualitatively from the biological and physiological phenomena associated with their origination and ongoing occurrence."[67] Showing both that cultural phenomena are not reducible to their physiological conditions and yet are engendered somehow from these very conditions, is a tall order, but one that is possible, at least in principle, to fill. Unfortunately, Schacht provides neither an explanation nor a justification for how Nietzsche's naturalism can reveal the physiological ingredients for the making of "moral cake" while allowing the panoply of *Lebensformen* to savor this cake from a multitude of perspectives.

The problem is that only will to power can serve as the necessary bridge between the realms of causality (the right side of the naturalism continuum) and the "logical space of reasons" (the left-side) while allowing each to be non-reducible to the other. Will to power does not reduce the latter to a mere mechanism that may be collapsed to some more primordial physiological scaffolding. On the other hand, one does not wish to collapse the realms of strict causality to cultural perspectives or mere points of view either. Unlike the other two scholars mentioned above, Schacht does not come down on either side of this dilemma because he does not recognize it as a genuine dilemma in the first place. He believes that his conception of *Wissenschaften* is both broad enough and rich enough to accommodate and inform all the different points on the continuum.

One of the problems with Schacht's approach is that it adheres to a naïve perspectival position. One sees this by examining his paradigmatic example regarding Nietzsche's censure of examining music, from only a physical vantage point. He argues that such a physical interpretation of music would fail to capture the true spirit and meaning of the music being heard: "understanding sound waves of different frequency does not equal music."[68] Schacht then goes on to write the following: "in order to understand music one must bring to bear the very different mentalities and perspectives of that which is a piece of human reality these would include the physical—scientific, physiological, neurological and psychological, others the anthropological cultural, historical biographical sociological and even the technological."[69]

However, the question remains: "How do these diverse perspectives give us a better understanding of music?" Moreover, how do all these perspectives relate to each other? If the purpose of Nietzsche's naturalism "involves employing and drawing on a multiplicity of differing perspectives and optics in the service of the interpretative attempt to broaden and deepen our comprehension of ourselves," then surely we must begin with a shared understanding of ourselves to which all such perspectives are indexed.[70] If for example, I start with the Christian ontological understanding that I am an embodied soul and that the world is a veil of tears, then I certainly can get a better understanding of what I initially take myself to be by employing different *Lebensformen*. I can view myself from the moral perspective of the Ten Commandments; I can have a better aesthetic appreciation of *my* music by understanding that many classical works were attempts to glorify God. These perspectives only come to have meaning once a firm ground, indexing such perspectives, has been previously arrived at. Schacht's point is that we can somehow get a broader and deeper understanding of ourselves by examining the myriad of perspectives on the human being without defining foremost what the human being is. But it is this very question, namely, what does it mean to be human that needs to be answered first. Are we entombed souls? Gene survival machines? Denatured and therefore existentially free beings? Risen apes or fallen angels? etc. Viewing perspectives on the human without first understanding what it is that we are viewing can only present a jumbled mess. Indeed, one would not be able to formulate a picture at all.

However, notice that to de-reify our thinghood, which is surely Nietzsche's plan, is to claim that some perspectives are untrue, and thus we foreclose certain *Lebensformen a*s a matter of course. However, how is this justifiable given Schacht's approach where all forms of *Wissenschaften* are on equal footing? For Schacht's approach to succeed, a more fundamental understanding of the world must first be advanced.

Strangely, then, naturalism for Schacht is not robust at all: it is rather a thin membrane that, presumably, applies equally to all empirical disciplines. However, if it equally applies to all disciplines then surely it applies to none of them.

I showed that there are significant difficulties in defining naturalism in the terms of methodological and substance paradigms. In addition, I think it is doubtful that Nietzsche would subscribe to either one or both of these schools of thought at least as they are popularly presented in the secondary literature. In the following chapter, I turn my attention to articulating Nietzsche's theory of will to power which I take to be the key to understanding Nietzsche's naturalistic understanding of the world. It is from this analysis that I show how the will to power may be naturalized.

NOTES

1. Wilfrid Sellars, "Empiricism and Philosophy of Mind" in *Minnesota Studies in Philosophy of Science* (Minneapolis, MN: University of Minnesota Press, 1956), 253–329, section 41.

2. "Man is the measure of all things, of what is that it is, and of what is not, that it is not."

3. See Ian Hacking, *The Social Construction of What?* (Cambridge, MA: Harvard University Press, 1997), 106–120.

4. See James Bryant Conant, *The Overthrow of Phlogiston Theory: The Chemical Revolution of 1775–1789* (Cambridge, MA: Harvard University Press, 1950).

5. Conant, *The Overthrow of Phlogiston Theory.*

6. De Caro, Mario and David MacArthur (eds.), *Naturalism in Question* (Cambridge, MA: Harvard University Press, 2004), Introduction.

7. This problem is known as the placement problem. The problem in brief is that number and mathematical truths seem especially resistant to being reduced to some aspect of science. For an interesting work that attempts to explain science without relying on number see Hartry Field: *How to Do Science Without Number: A Defence of Nominalism* (Princeton: Princeton University Press), 1980.

8. See Kuhn's discussion on Paradigm shifts in *The Structure of Scientific Revolutions* 1st edition (Chicago: University of Chicago Press, 1962).

9. See chapter one of Nancy Cartwright's *The Dappled World* (Cambridge, UK: Cambridge University Press, 1999).

10. Brian Lightbody, *The Problem of Naturalism: Analytic Perspectives, Continental Virtues* (Lanham, MD: Lexington Books, 2013).

11. Nietzsche, *The Will to power*, section 481.

12. Nietzsche, *Beyond Good and Evil*, section 14, in *Basic Writings of Nietzsche*, 211.

13. Nietzsche, *The Will to power*, section 484.

14. Nietzsche, *On the Genealogy of Morals*, Essay Three, section 25, in *Basic Writings of Nietzsche.*

15. Nietzsche, *On the Genealogy of Morals*, Essay Three, section 24, in *Basic Writings of Nietzsche.*

16. "Nietzsche has caused a lot of confusion by inferring from "truth is not a matter of correspondence to reality" to "what we call 'truths' are just useful lies." The same confusion is occasionally found in Derrida, in the inference from "there is no such reality as the metaphysicians have hoped to find" to "what we call 'real' is

really real . . . Such confusions make Nietzsche and Derrida liable to charges of self-referential inconsistency—to claiming to know what they themselves claim cannot be known." See Richard Rorty, *Contingency, Irony and Solidarity* (Cambridge, UK: Cambridge University Press, 1989), 8.

17. Friedrich Nietzsche, *Twilight of the Idols*, Reason in Philosophy, Holingdale Translation, 2.

18. Friedrich Nietzsche, *Human All Too Human,* Trans. R.J. Holingdale, Intro Richard Schact (Cambridge University Press, 1996), section 483.

19. Friedrich Nietzsche, KSA Vol. 1, 13.

20. Hilary Putnam, in *Hilary Putnam The Many Faces of Realism, The Paul Carns Lectures* "Realism and Reasonableness" (New York: Carus Publishing, 1988), 29.

21. Nietzsche, *Beyond Good and Evil*, in *Basic Writings of Nietzsche*, section 21, 219.

22. Nietzsche, *The Gay Science*, section 109.

23. Nietzsche, *Human All Too Human*, Part One, section 11.

24. Friedrich Nietzsche, *The Complete Works of Friedrich Nietzsche*, edited by Oscar Levy. *The Will to Power: An Attempted Transvaluation of All Values*. Trans. Anthony M. Ludovici. Vols I and II (New York: Russell and Russell Inc, 1964), section 521, 36–37.

25. "Pierre Laplace argued that if a demon, some super-intelligent creature with an intellect which at a certain moment would know all the forces that set nature in motion, and all positions of all items of which nature is composed, if this intellect were also vast enough to submit these data to analysis, it would embrace in a single formula the movements of the greatest bodies of the universe and those of the tiniest atom; for such an intellect nothing would be uncertain and the future just like the past would be present before its eyes." *A Philosophy Essay on Probabilities*, Trans. F.W. Trsucott (New York: Dover, 1951), 4. It is conjectured that Nietzsche had Laplace's demon in mind when writing on the Eternal Return as presented in section 341 of *The Gay Science*.

26. Nietzsche, *The Genealogy of Morals*, trans. Kaufmann and Holingdale, GM:III, section 25, 155–156.

27. Richard S.G. Brown, "Nihilism: Thus Speaks Physiology," in *Nietzsche and the Rhetoric of Nihilism: Essays on Interpretation, Language and Politics*, edited by Tom Darby, Bela Egyed, and Ben Jones (Ottawa: Carleton University Press, 1989), 133–144. See Richard S.G. Brown's "Nietzsche that Profound Physiologist" in *Nietzsche and Biology* (Aldershot: Ashgate Press, 2004).

28. Richard S.G. Brown, Nihilism: Thus Speaks Physiology, 136. Brown retains much of this view in his recent "Nietzsche that Profound Physiologist" but places a decidedly Nagelian spin on his original interpretation. To my mind, Brown represents the strongest physiological essentialist position in the secondary literature. While many other interpreters note the significance of physiological and medicinal terms in Nietzsche's thought and philosophy, they never clearly determine whether Nietzsche's discussions on physiology and health are to be taken metaphorically or if they are meant literally. For this "weaker" essentialism, see Malcom Pasley's "Nietzsche's Use of Medical Terms," in *Nietzsche: Imagery and Thought*, edited by Malcom Pasley (Berkley: California University Press: 1978), 123–158. See also Thomas Long's

"Nietzsche's Philosophy of Medicine." *Nietzsche-Studien*, Band 19 (1990), 112–128. The above two articles are paradigmatic examples of this much larger (weak essentialist) school of interpretation.

29. Nietzsche, *On the Genealogy of Morals*, in *Basic Writings of Nietzsche*, GM:I: 17, 491. Compare this with section 57 of *The Anti-Christ* where Nietzsche seems to reduce one's mental abilities and beliefs to their physiological development and body type.

30. From Friedrich Nietzsche's *Thus Spoke Zarathustra* trans. R.J. Holingdale (New York: Penguin Books, 1980), Book 1 section 9.

31. Brian Leiter, "Nietzsche's Theory of the Will," *Philosopher's Imprint* 7:7 (2007), 7.

32. Brian Leiter, *Nietzsche on Morality* (New York: Routledge, 2002), 8.

33. Nietzsche, *On the Genealogy of Morals*, Preface section 2.

34. Friedrich Nietzsche's *On/Towards the Genealogy of Morals: A Polemic* in the *Basic Writings of Friedrich Nietzsche*, edited by Peter Gay, Trans. Walter Kaufmann (New York: Random House, 2000) GM:III, 12, 555.

35. Brian Leiter, "Perspectivism in the Genealogy of Morals," in *Nietzsche's on the Genealogy of Morals*, edited by Richard Schacht (University of California Press, 1997), 347.

36. Brian Leiter, "Perspectivism in Nietzsche's Genealogy of Morals," in *Nietzsche, Genealogy, Morality*, 346.

37. Friedrich Nietzsche, *Beyond Good and Evil: A Prelude to a Philosophy of the Future*, Trans. R.J. Holingdale (London, England: Penguin Books, 2003), section 39.

38. Leiter, "Perspectivism in Nietzsche's Genealogy of Morals," 346.

39. Leiter, "Perspectivism in Nietzsche's Genealogy of Morals," 346.

40. Friedrich Nietzsche, *Beyond Good and Evil*, in *Basic Writings of Nietzsche*, section 39, 239.

41. Consider what Nietzsche writes in *Kritische Studienausgabe*: "Before we learned to understand physiological conditions physiologically, man had to deal with moralistic conditions. Consequently, the area of morality shrank extraordinarily—and is becoming small still" (9.3 [10]); see also 12.7 [6], 13.17 [3], and 13.15 [91]. Consider sections 20–23 of *The Anti-Christ* (Trans. R.J. Hollingdale, Middlesex: Penguin, 1972) where Nietzsche compares and contrasts, in considerable detail, the physiological, cultural, and social conditions required for the advent of Buddhism and those for the rise of Christianity. For more of Nietzsche's physiological and cultural conditioning explanations for specific acts of moral behavior, also see *Beyond Good and Evil* section 234, *On the Genealogy of Morals* III.17, 26, and *Twilight of the Idols*, "Expeditions," section 33.

42. See *On the Genealogy of Morals*, III: 10 "The characteristic aloof stance of philosophers, world-negating, hostile toward life, not believing in the senses, de-sensualized, a stance which has been preserved up to the most recent time and has thus won acceptance as the virtual *philosopher's pose in itself*—it is above all a consequence of the poverty of conditions under which philosophy came about and survived at all: for the longest time philosophy would *not* have been *at all possible* on earth without an ascetic covering and mantle, without an ascetic self-misunderstanding.

Graphically and clearly expressed: until the most recent time the *ascetic priest* has functioned as the repulsive and gloomy caterpillar-form in which alone philosophy was allowed to live and in which it crept around . . . " *On the Genealogy of Morals: A Polemic*, Trans. Maudemarie Clark and Alan Swensen, Intro. Maudemarie Clark (Indianapolis, IN: Hackett Publishing, 1999), 82. (Translators italics). From this passage it does not follow that Nietzsche condemns asceticism wholesale. Indeed, consider what he says in section 57 of *The Anti-Christ*: "The most intelligent men, like the strongest, find their happiness where others would find only disaster: in the labyrinth, in being hard with themselves and with others, in effort; their delight is in self-mastery; in them asceticism becomes second nature, a necessity, an instinct. They regard a difficult task as a privilege; it is to them a recreation to play with burdens that would crush all others."

43. See especially the third essay of the *Genealogy*.

44. Gregory Moore, *Nietzsche, Biology and Metaphor* (New York: Oxford, Oxford University Press), 211.

45. See Jean Granier's, *Le probleme de la Verite dans la Philosophie de Nietzsche* (Paris: Seuil, 1966) and Sarah Koffman's, *Nietzsche et la Metaphor* (Paris: Payot) 1972.

46. By the far, the clearest statement of Nietzsche's tremendous influence on Foucault can be found in Foucault's last interview entitled the "Return of Morality." Foucault says: "I can only respond by saying that I am simply Nietzschean, and I try to see, on a number of different points, and to the extent that it is possible, with the aid of Nietzsche's texts—but also with anti-Nietzschean theses (which are nevertheless Nietzschean!)—what can be done in this or that domain." See Michel Foucault, *Michel Foucault, Politics, Philosophy, Culture, Interviews and Other Writings, 1977–1984*, trans. Alan Sheridan and others (London: Routledge, 1988), 250–251.

47. See Brian Lightbody, *Philosophical Genealogy Volume One* (New York: Peter Lang Press), 2010, chapter 4.

48. See Herbert Butterfield, *The Whig Interpretation of History* (London: G. Bell and Sons, Ltd, 1963), 11.

49. Friedrich Nietzsche, *On the Genealogy of Morals: A Polemic*, in *Basic Writings of Nietzsche*, Trans. Walter Kaufmann with an introduction by Peter Gay (New York: Random House, 2000) GM III: 12, 489. A word of caution is in order in my use of the word "unmasking." It might be thought that the metaphor conveys the idea that just as when we unmask a person we reveal that person's face, in the same way we are revealing the true face or origin of a particular emotion. Certainly it is true to say that many commentators have interpreted the purpose of genealogy in precisely this way. But some scholars, such as Foucault, argue otherwise.

50. See Nietzsche's, *On the Genealogy of Morals*, in *Basic Writings of Nietzsche* preface, section 7, 457: "For cheerfulness—or in my own language gay science—is a reward: the reward of a long, brave, industrious, and subterranean seriousness, of which to be sure not everyone is capable."

51. Michel Foucault, "Nietzsche, Genealogy, History," in *Language, Counter-Memory, Practice, Selected Essays and Interviews by Michel Foucault*, edited with an introduction by Donald F. Bouchard (Cornell University Press: 1977), 156.

52. Leiter, Brian, Nietzsche on Morality (New York: Routledge, 2002), 3.

53. For two representative works in this tradition see Jean Granier's, *Le probleme de la Verite dans la Philosophie de Nietzsche* (Paris: Seuil, 1966) and Sarah Koffman's *Nietzsche et la Metaphor* (Paris: Payot, 1972).

54. Leiter, *Nietzsche on Morality*, 177. At the bottom of page 176 we find the following reminder: "In fact, as we shall see, 'need' is too strong: a genealogy is one way of getting at the critique, but it is not, strictly speaking, necessary to it."

55. The use of chemistry to explain biological processes such as the transfer of proteins between cells is readily understandable. But how chemistry relies on biological theories might seem more difficult to explain. However, there has been some interest and research to show how natural selection comes to influence chemical evolution. See Christhantha Fernando and Jonathan Rowe's paper, "Natural Selection in Chemical Evolution," in *The Journal of Theoretical Biology*, 247:1 (2007), 152–167.

56. The chief problem for the logical positivists had to do with accepting what Quine would later call the first dogma of empiricism: the idea that raw sensation is possible. Since empirical sensation is always interpreted according to some theory, then the logical positivist's program of building up science from protocol statements: bare empirical claims could not get off the ground. Popper, who of course was well aware of this phenomenon, fell victim to the other horn of this dilemma, namely, that because the theory was always impregnated with fact, one could not just test a bare theory but had to test the auxiliary hypotheses which made the theory testable. Thus one could not conclusively falsify a hypothesis because all recalcitrant experience showed was that either the hypothesis, the auxiliary hypotheses, or a combination thereof were inconsistent with the results of the experiment. See pp. 36–40 of Lightbody, *The Problem of Naturalism,* for a fuller treatment of this issue.

57. In brief, Kuhn argued that science advances as a result of paradigm shifts: theoretical models that change the very practice of normal science (experimentation, hypothesis generating, data collection, tools used for said data collection, etc.). However, paradigm shifts do not represent some Platonic model that is discovered and then put to use; rather the opposite is the case: they are discovered ". . . because the new candidate must seem to resolve some outstanding and generally recognized the problem that can be met in no other way. Second, the new paradigm must also solve more problems than its predecessor, which therefore entailed that the number of new solved problems must be greater than those solved in the old paradigm." Kuhn, *The Structure of Scientific Revolutions*, 168. A culture of disillusion with the old model must exist before a new paradigm is seriously considered. Feyerabend argues that faithfulness to facts does not advance science. In fact, if one closely examines the history of science one discovers that it is the courage to try new methods that marks scientific inquiry. For Feyerabend, there is only one method: "It is the principle: anything goes." Paul Feyerabend, *Against Mehod: Outline of an Anarchistic Theory of Knowledge*, 27–28.

58. Ridley, Aaron, "Nietzsche and the Re-evaluation of Values" in *The Proceedings of the Aristotelian Society*, 105: 171–191, 180.

59. See Wilfrid Sellars, *Empiricism and the Philosophy of Mind* (Cambridge, MA: Harvard University Press, 1997), 76.

60. See Essay one of *On the Genealogy of Morals.*

61. See Christopher Janaway's wonderful work: *Beyond Selflessness Reading Nietzsche's Genealogy* (Oxford University Press: 2007, but especially chapter 12) for more on this issue. Christoper Janaway, "Naturalism and Genealogy" in *A Companion to Nietzsche*, edited by Keith Ansell Pearson (Cornwall, UK: Blackwell Publishing 2006), 337–353.

62. Christopher Janaway, *Beyond Selflessness: Reading Nietzsche's Genealogy*, 160.

63. Janaway, *Beyond Selflessness*, 160.

64. Janaway, *Beyond Selflessness*, chapter 5.

65. Janaway, "Naturalism and Genealogy," 349.

66. Nietzsche, *Beyond Good and Evil*, section 230 in *Basic Writings of Nietzsche*.

67. Richard Schacht, "Nietzsche's Naturalism," *The Journal of Nietzsche Studies*, 43:2 (Autumn 2012), 185–212, 201.

68. Schacht, 198.

69. Ibid., 199.

70. Ibid., 202.

Chapter 3

Naturalism and Will to Power

3.1 WILL TO POWER AS COSMOLOGICAL DOCTRINE

Nietzsche's doctrine of will to power is deeply disconcerting and yet such disconcertment is very often the result of a significant misunderstanding. In this chapter, I wish to provide an outline of Nietzsche's theory of will to power along two lines: first as a theory of cosmogony which explains the inner workings of the universe as a whole and second as a theory of zoogamy which explains the development of what Nietzsche would call "life." My strategy, thus far, has been twofold: first to explain why and how the will to power is a central doctrine of Nietzsche's philosophical system and second to prove that it can be naturalized. I extend my argument here to demonstrate that Nietzsche's ontology, epistemology, and ethics can be favorably viewed as expressions of his theory of will to power. I then interpret these distinct renderings of his philosophy naturalistically.

It is hoped that Nietzsche's naturalized pedigree will also be showcased in this chapter. As was demonstrated in chapter one, naturalism, in all forms, entails a systematic reductionism, broadly construed here to include deflationism and Nietzsche's peculiar brand of naturalism—the will to power—is no exception. There will be problems with the approach I have adopted, and some of these issues will become visible as I investigate Nietzsche's ontology, epistemology, and ethics through the prism of will to power. I intend on articulating these problems as they become apparent. In chapter four, I examine three very different interpretations of will to power which may be adopted as alternative solutions to the question discussed here: "How can one distil Nietzsche's philosophy to that of a naturalized power narrative?" I argue there that each of these solutions is problematic, but for different reasons.

Will to power in Nietzsche's *Nachless* or unpublished writings is presented as a cosmological theory. Like any good cosmological theory, will to power attempts to explain the following: how things (where things are understood as middle-sized goods) come to be; the core units out of which things are constructed; how things change and why they change; and finally, what causes things to interact with other things along with the rules which restrict how this interaction takes place. After examining will to power regarding its physics, I then examine it in its organic form (as a principle regulating life itself) before turning my attention to what one might call the human or subject form of the will to power.

I begin by explaining what Nietzsche takes the will to power to be in its most fundamental state of being. Now, to be sure there is already a clear problem in presenting such an explanation because the will to power cannot be separated from Nietzsche's doctrine of perspectivism. As such to state what the will to power is, in its fundamental state of being, is to view this state from a perspective and therefore either (1) not to understand the will to power in its most fundamentally basic state of existence or, alternatively, (2) it is to entertain a contradiction: The will to power claims that all things can only be viewed from a perspective where that perspective is an evaluation. However, this fundamental truth applies equally to the will to power. Thus, one cannot provide an aperspectival interpretation of will to power without contradicting the rudimentary concept of will to power itself. This last problem is clearly and forcefully articulated by James Porter in his article, "Nietzsche's Theory of the Will to Power."[1] I address this concern more directly in section 3.2. The various epistemic and ethical problems regarding the will to power will also be treated in the above section.

In its most fundamental form, the will to power, as a whole, is a fixed quantity of energy and is the *arche* of all things. Much like the Pre-Socratics whom he deeply admired, Nietzsche, I would contend, argues that it is will to power that serves as the "material," efficient and even formal cause for the plurality of things we see in the universe.[2] "Things" are not substances in the metaphysical sense of this term following Aristotle's understanding of substance as advanced in *The Metaphysics*. Aristotle believed that he had to provide a metaphysical understanding of substance to account for how a thing might change and yet remain the same thing throughout the process of change. In a nutshell, the notion of substance/attribute constitutes Aristotle's hylomorphism. Aristotle's hylomorphism position holds that while a thing may change with respect to its accidental properties and remain the same thing, a thing cannot change as regards its essential attribute.[3] A thing is comprised of form and matter. However, things possess neither essential nor accidental attributes according to Nietzsche.

Nor can Nietzschean things be construed as abstract containers for predicates, again, following Aristotle in *The Categories*. According to Aristotle, the category, substance, is one of 10 ways (1. substance, 2. quantity, 3. quality, 4. relation, 5. place, 6. time, 7. position, 8. state, 9. action, 10. affection) in which beings may be categorized.[4] It is the category of substance alone that holds a privileged place among all other categories because it is the only category which is the subject of predicates but is not itself the predicate of any other subject.[5]

Nietzsche, in contrast, views things as nothing more and nothing less than compounded units of power. Things, to put the matter coarsely, are bundles of power. A thing is the sum of its effects and things effect and affect change through force. The theory of will to power is ultimately a material and efficient *arche* of force.

What's more, power is an energy force which seems to take on different forms or modes. The basic unit of will to power is nothing more than a quantum of power. All power quanta desire to absorb more units of power such that with the help of other such units, they become bundles of quantum units. The goal of such bundles is to overpower other units and create larger bundles of quanta power.

Desire and perspective are thus inseparable from even a single quantum; they are not attributes of quantum: One cannot talk about "desire" or "perspective" as powers which can be extracted from their underlying energetic circuitry. Quanta of power are necessarily desiring and perspectival energy formations. Nietzsche discusses this in section 634 of *The Will to Power*: "A quantum of power is designated by the effect it produces and that which it resists. The adiaphoric state which is thinkable in itself is entirely lacking. It is essentially a will to violence and to defend oneself against violence."[6]

These desiring-perspectival bundles of energy manifest themselves in wave packets. These waves take on discernible patterns of movement and seem to form assemblages with one another only to dissipate once again. Things are not stable entities: They consist of waves of forces that coalesce to form what we perceive as distinct entities only to break down and disassemble once more into smaller units of power. Nietzsche writes in this regard:

> ... the play of forces and force-waves, at the same time one and many agglomerating here and diminishing there, a sea of forces storming and raging in itself forever changing, forever rolling back over incalculable ages to recurrence, with an ebb and a flood of its forms; producing the most complicated things out of the most simplest structures; producing the most ardent, most savage things ... out of the quietest, most rigid and most frozen material ...[7]

All things for Nietzsche whether purely physical, organic, or "spiritual" are nothing more than different modes or forces of compounded energy.

Furthermore, each and every individual entity is comprised of sub-forms, and each of these sub-forms consists of its own sub-forms of energy and so on until one reaches the bare quantum nodule of power-energy.

Nietzsche was not, of course, the first thinker to reduce all things to some non-mental monism. The Pre-Socratics were the first in Western thought to ponder along these lines even before a clear demarcation was made between the conceptual distinctions of mental/physical, soul/body which contemporary philosophers utilize today. Indeed, Nietzsche drew inspiration from the nineteenth-century German materialists and, more profoundly, from their critics like Helmholtz and Boscovich. All three attempted to provide a naturalistic theory of the universe in terms that did not depend on the mind and was causally complete. The materialists sought to achieve this aim in terms of atomistic mechanics while Helmholtz and Boscovich argued for the formation of energy-force concrescences very similar to Nietzsche's base understanding of will to power.[8] However, Nietzsche found just cause to criticize both approaches. His criticism of the atomistic-materialistic framework was most severe. According to Nietzsche, the mechanistic viewpoint sneaks into its framework assumptions of traditional metaphysics such that the atom becomes much like a God particle: complete, indivisible, static, and imperishable. Nietzsche writes in this regard: "The *mechanical* world is imagined as the eye and the sense of touch alone could imagine a world (as 'moved')—in such a way as to be calculable—as to simulate causal entities 'things' (atoms) whose effect is constant (the transfer of the false concept of subject to the concept of atom)" (Nietzsche's Italics).[9] Such a starting point cannot explain physical movement, so thought Nietzsche, nor can it explain the strange phenomenon of "life" itself whose chief characteristic, Nietzsche reveals, is exploitation.

Nietzsche is critical of Boscovich and Helmholtz for different reasons. Their respective theories do not consider the inherent perspectivality of all things: things as bundles of power take up a perspective on other such things to overpower them. Perspectivism may not seem obvious in the purely physical realm, but it becomes all the more evident when one views the organic world. Organisms are organized insofar each part serves a purpose for the whole, but more importantly, organisms take up perspectives on their environment. Whether the organism is a proto-plasm to use Nietzsche's more famous example or something more advanced like a lion, there is an appreciation, as it were, of the contours and objects of the organism's environment. The organism can "assess" food sources, measure itself against rivals, and, in general, calibrate itself to its environment such that, over time, it desires to subdue the very environment itself. This aspect cannot be explained, so thinks Nietzsche, by sticking to a purely energetic model devoid of perspective. All things desire to express their power in their respective environments; it this yearning or striving which is the will component of power.

Continuing to explore Nietzsche's theory of will to power on the cosmogonic level, weaker bundles of power are absorbed by those that are stronger while both bundles whether strong or feeble, exist in a permanent state of tension and resistance to all other bundles. As Nietzsche writes in *The Will to Power*, "In its most fundamental being the will to power is ultimately ". . . a desire to overwhelm . . . until at length that which has been overwhelmed has entirely gone over into the power domain of the aggressor and has increased the same."[10] Growth for an organism or for an entire species for that matter hinges on how successful something is in using the inherent power quanta of some other thing. The successful growth of an organism turns on its ability to harness the will to power of some other entity so that this new synthesis is better able to exploit and utilize more units of power.

The synthesis produces not just a new bundle but a new perspective. Each unit of will to power, he suggests, "strives to become master over all space and to extend its force," and each encounters "similar efforts on the part of other bodies."[11] But this war of all against all comes to a truce or perhaps better put, a new front is opened such that units of power come "to an arrangement ('union') with those of them that are sufficiently related." Having thus formed a new and larger bundle, these quanta "then conspire together for power."[12] Citing this time from *The Genealogy* Nietzsche claims that "the will to life" is . . . . "bent upon power, and are subordinate to its total goal as a single means: namely, as a means of creating greater units of power."[13]

How are such units created we might ask? Nietzsche's answer: through fresh interpretations. Bundles are forced to take up different perspectives to accumulate more power. Taking up new perspectives, new interpretations, new schemes, and therefore new agendas, is the very essence of life. Looking again to *The Genealogy*, Nietzsche writes:

> All events in the organic world (*organischen Welt*) are a subduing, a *becoming master*, and all subduing and becoming master involves a fresh interpretation, an adaptation through which any previous "meaning" and "purpose" are necessarily obscured or even obliterated . . . Thus the essence of life (*Wesen des Lebens*), its *will to power*, is ignored; one overlooks the essential priority of the spontaneous, aggressive, expansive, form-giving forces (*Gestalatenden Kraft*) that give new interpretations and directions. . . .[14]

At this point, it may be advisable to examine some problems with Nietzsche's rather peculiar view of power. Examining such problems will be helpful to explicate Nietzsche's position in clearer terms. First, in regard to the question of naturalism, Nietzsche's will to power appears to rely on a robust mentalism. How so? First, bundles of power quanta clearly have desires; units of power desire to oppress others while weaker units seek to resist such oppression. Moreover, each and every unit of power desires to accumulate more power. Second, all units of power not only have desires but have goals where goal here is understood as a self-conscious desire. Instinctively a unit of power desires to express its power in a given environment. However, if a thing faces resistance on this goal, then a struggle takes place. If the fight persists, then either one of the two things or, perhaps both, will create new interpretations as to how it can best express its power. Thus, there is seemingly some recognition on the part of the stronger bundle that a new strategy must be tried. To "try a new strategy" would minimally entail that a calculation of sorts has taken place: The initial interpretation is understood not to work, and a new interpretation must be advanced for the goal of subduing to be fulfilled. However, clearly imputing such attributes to a bare unit of power entails a calculating mind.

Third, this understanding of what is needed to complete a goal presupposes that a unit of power is able to represent alternative states of affairs and further the ability to compute which states of affairs are preferable to others. Thus even a unit of power is capable of representation and making value judgments and surely this is more than enough proof to demonstrate the existence of mind.

According to some scholars, Nietzsche's will to power puts forward an anti-naturalistic view of how the world works. By conceptualizing will to power as some force that desires and interprets, Nietzsche, these scholars argue, commits the homunculus fallacy and, therefore, naturalizing the will to power becomes impossible. I examine this objection in more detail in chapter four.[15]

3.2 WILL TO POWER AS ZOOGAMY

Will to power (*Wille Zur Macht*) is the name that Nietzsche gives to explain the very essence of "life." The natural world, and the life contained therein, is often regarded as self-contained and self-sustaining. Organisms like worms, birds, and trees are all entities that take part in the various life-cycles of birth, growth, and death. What's more, such entities seem to belong to the same ecosystem in that each, in some sense, needs the other to exist. These processes are observable to the careful and patient eye of the researcher or even the avid naturalist. However, this is not Nietzsche's concern. Nietzsche is rather intrigued with the underbelly of these entities. He wishes to understand how and why such entities came to be and what the precise relationship is between these things. Unlike the biologist, however, he does not wish to study the evolutionary origin of such organisms; instead, he wishes to study and demonstrate how each form of life is merely an expression of the will to power.

To investigate forms of life with an eye to mapping the historical manifestations of will to power is to study life with the aim of discovering the creative, overflowing, form-giving qualities of life itself.[16] We might say that Nietzsche wishes to explore the "psychical" properties of life. In this regard, when Nietzsche poses investigative questions toward life itself, especially as they are raised in *The Genealogy*, such questions will appear very strange indeed. Readers who are more familiar with the standard sort of issues that biologists, anthropologists, chemists, and others pose to the question: "How did life come about?" Will think that Nietzsche has blurred Hume's fork: Nietzsche has confused questions of fact with normative questions. However, herein is the difficulty in interpreting Nietzsche: Nietzsche's questions are inherently and inextricably infused with normativity. There can be, or so Nietzsche thinks, no fundamental distinction between fact and value. Thus Nietzsche asks: "Why have certain properties become valuable?"; "What value does preservation of life have?"; "Are there higher values than mere preservation of life?"; "What forces are colluding to overthrow old values and what values will take their place?" To ask these sorts of questions is to study life with an eye to its will to power.

Nevertheless, Nietzsche's genealogical history of life and will to power is similar in some respects to contemporary evolutionary models. Nietzsche, like Darwin, defines life in rather dark, pessimistic terms. For example, "Life . . . Nietzsche famously declares in section 259 of *Beyond Good and Evil* . . . is essentially appropriation, injury, overpowering of what is alien and weaker; suppression, hardness, imposition of one's own forms, incorporation and at least, at its mildest, exploitation."[17] Exploitation is *essential* to life; there is no getting around it. It is folly, Nietzsche so thinks, to believe that exploitation within human societies will ever cease. Believing that human beings can and will learn to form relationships that will satisfy the needs of any advanced civilization without some kind of exploitation is just as foolish as believing that lions will eventually lay down beside sheep. Exploitation, which is a heavily loaded term, is necessary to all natural functioning—in interpersonal relationships with others and even in intrapersonal relationships with ourselves. I would argue that it is exploitation, in all its many hues and tones that is the very ground of Nietzschean will to power.[18]

It would also be mistaken to believe, so Nietzsche would argue, to think that those who exploit others do so because they are imperfect in character. There is no evidence for true moral evolution. Nor should we believe that "Exploitation . . . belongs to a corrupt or imperfect and primitive society: It belongs to the *essence* of what lives, as a basic organic function; it is a consequence of the will to power, which is after all the will to life" (Nietzsche's Italics).[19]

If exploitation is indeed the very essence of what lives, then what exactly is it? Certainly, we are familiar with economic forms of exploitation. Slavery, for example, is a *prima facie* means of exploitation. Wage-slavery might also be construed as another. However, Nietzsche claims that exploitation is a basic organic function and therefore must apply to all creatures in the biological realm great and small. However, to think of a wolf exploiting a sheep by simply eating it seems to go beyond the bounds of good sense. In what way would the wolf be exploiting the sheep? Certainly, he would be nourished by the sheep's flesh, but we would hardly call this exploitation. If we did call this behavior "exploitation" then we are using exploitation in a minimal sense of this word with a very broad denotation: it would apply to any relationship where one thing uses another. If this is Nietzsche's insight, then he hardly seems to be much of a philosopher at all. Certainly, he would be undeserving of the scholarly attention he has, in my opinion, justifiably received over the last two centuries.

Therefore, it behooves us to offer a stronger, more profound, albeit puzzling notion of exploitation. It might be best to compare exploitation, here understood as the heart of will to power, with the idea of evolution put forward by Nietzsche's much more famous contemporary Charles Darwin, to get a better sense of what this new interpretation of manipulation may entail.

Darwinian evolution is a complicated notion. Indeed, Darwin's understanding of evolution has itself evolved to such a degree in the contemporary literature that it is possible that he would barely be able to recognize the notion at all. Still the clearest sense of evolution is to understand that organisms are changing. What are organisms changing into? They are changing into new species. Some species change relatively quickly and some change slowly. Such is the nature of evolution. Such is the process of natural selection.[20]

What do we mean by evolution? To understand evolution, we must understand its mechanism: natural selection. Perhaps the clearest expression of natural selection remains Darwin's initial description of the term in *The Origin of Species*. I now provide the passage in full:

> If during the long course of ages and under varying conditions of life; organic beings vary at all in the several parts of their organization, and I think this cannot be disputed; if there be, owing to the high geometric powers of increase of each species, at some age, season, or year, a severe struggle for life, and this certainly cannot be disputed; then, considering the infinite complexity of the relations of organic beings to each other and to their conditions of existence, causing an infinite diversity in structure, constitution, and habits, to be advantageous to them, I think it would be a most extraordinary fact if no variation ever had occurred useful to each being's own welfare, in the same way as so many variations have occurred useful to man. But if variations useful to any organic being do occur, assuredly individuals thus characterized will have the

best chance of being preserved in the struggle for life; and from the strong principle of inheritance they will tend to produce offspring similarly characterized. This principle of preservation, I have called, for the sake of brevity, Natural Selection.[21]

Contained within this very important passage are the essential tenets of evolution as Darwin understood it. First, Darwin accepts a Malthusian economics which states that at some point in time the human population will outgrow its food supply. As Dennett explains this principle:

Suppose a world in which organisms have many offspring. Since the offspring themselves will have many offspring, the population will grow and grow (geometrically) until inevitably, sooner or later—surprisingly soon, in fact—it must grow too large for the available resources (of food, of space or whatever the organism need to survive long enough to reproduce). At that point, whenever it happens, not all organisms will have offspring. Many will die childless. Those populations that produce at less than the replacement rate are headed for extinction unless they reverse the trend.[22]

Will to power, however, is unlike natural selection in two distinct ways. First, natural selection, at least as presented above, is passive. It is the genes of species which randomly mutate; natural selection simply acts as a sieve for these genes "selecting" those that might best thrive in the current environment in which such genes are found. In contrast, the will to power is an active force; even the barest unit of power, namely the power-quantum has desires. Second, natural selection is blind in that there is no *telos* to which it is groping toward. It is not the case for the will to power: all things take up perspectives on everything else. Units of power have agendas and the foremost item in each program of anything is to exploit other things. Again, exploitation of one entity by another is not needed to explain all biological occurrences: Rabbits may flourish in a given environment because they can breed faster than their competitors, but they are not exploiting those other species which might be in competition with them for food. One may claim that they are better able to exploit their environment than another competitor, but that would be to broaden further the scope of exploitation.

In a similar manner to the metaphysical side of will to power above where compounded energy forms or bundles are forever and irrevocably in competition with other forms, Nietzsche wants to make the same claim for all organic species; they too are in competition. What do species compete over? Certainly, we are familiar with the evolutionist story—species compete against each other for scarce resources like food and land. However, this is not how Nietzsche conceives of competition. Another way of viewing competition might be taken from the world of sports. Under some sports models, the goal is to eradicate a competitor from a tournament in a winner-take-all format. Such a process ends when one team has won the championship game or series according to the prescribed rules of the contest. However, once again, Nietzsche does not envisage competition in this manner either. For Nietzsche the actual goal of this contest is to absorb other species and perhaps even more perspicuously stated, to *make* another species' energy part of one's own. A thing's goal is to force some other thing to become part of it. In essence, the will to power expresses the essential drive of all things: the sole purpose of anything is to use other entities to make itself stronger. It is this understanding of use which Nietzsche means when he refers to "exploitation."

Nietzsche captures this inherently exploitative relationship between organisms with his definition of life. Nietzsche defines "Life" as, "an enduring form of processes of the establishment of force, in which the different contenders grow unequally."[23] Force and competition have already been discussed so I will turn my attention to focusing on Nietzsche's conception of growth—surely a central concept to any coherent understanding of biology. One of the very best books in the secondary literature to discuss the relationship between the will to power and growth is Daniel Ahern's *Nietzsche as Cultural Physician*. Ahern first provides a lens for understanding *agon* (ancient Greek for "struggle") between chemical processes before turning to organic processes of growth, digestion, proliferation, and the like. According to Ahern, Nietzsche saw all natural activities to be merely the sign language of will to power. Thus if we went for a nature hike and came upon a fast flowing river working its way through a mountain pass, our first inclination might be to marvel at this beautiful, idyllic, peaceful scenery. However, according to Ahern, a battle is taking place: for "the river attempts to wash the mountain away while the mountain tries to resist this effort."[24] Even here in this peaceful like setting will to power or *agon* is at work—two "agents," the river and the mountain are locked in a battle for domination.

It is at this point that we might find Nietzsche's view of things or more accurately Ahern's interpretation of Nietzsche's view to be a wee bit embarrassing. For surely Nietzsche has projected mind-like qualities onto nature itself and thus does not seem to be a naturalist philosopher after all according to his lights. However, there is more about which Nietzsche should be embarrassed (if this were not enough already). Because, as Ahern again explains, Nietzsche holds that there has been ever increasing "spiritual" developments of will to power in the course of nature's evolution. It appears that the will to power is simply not "satisfied" with two brutes, as it were, squaring off face to face with one another because such a relationship can never get beyond the inertia of unrefined, power quanta versus power quanta.[25]

It rather seems that will to power requires (and perhaps enjoys?) two or more very different entities struggling against each other for greater units of

Naturalism and Will to Power 65

power. It is for this reason that organic life expresses a higher form of the will to power. Organic life is more dynamic than inorganic material because it alters its forms more rapidly. Thus, a Venus flytrap, to borrow Ahern's example, represents a higher form of the will to power because it must use deception to capture a fly. It alters the battlefield so that the fly is "mistaken"—it, the Venus flytrap, is not a source of food after all. It is a predator. Thus the use of deception for gaining power is one of the most important facets of Nietzsche's naturalized biology and one that, as we will see, is closely related to growth.

The above example, drawn from the organic world, also expresses another fundamental feature of Nietzsche's notion of power. Power, under Nietzsche's model, is not just about one thing competing against another for the sake of sheer domination. Nor can Nietzschean power and more precisely the desire for greater units of power, be equated with Hobbesian self-interest. Neither of these models successfully explains Nietzsche's notion of power because in its most fundamental being the will to power is ". . . a desire to overwhelm . . . until at length that which has been overwhelmed has entirely gone over into the power domain of the aggressor and has increased the same."[26] Growth for an organism or for an entire species for that matter hinges on how successful something is in using the inherent power *quanta* of some other thing. The successful growth of an organism turns on its ability to harness the will to power of some other thing so that this new synthesis is better able to exploit other things.

One of the clearest examples of this desire to exploit the latent energy forms of some other thing is the development of mitochondria: an organelle responsible, for, among other things, providing energy by generating an animal cell's ATP. According to the endosymbiotic theory, mitochondria were once single-celled organisms, not dissimilar to spirochetes that were enveloped by other prokaryotic cells.[27] The mitochondria, as enveloped cells, and over the course of millions of years, transferred all of their genes to the enveloping cell such that mitochondrial cells eventually became organelles thus leading to the development of the eukaryote cell structure. It was this eukaryote cells which broke the old and restrictive life-organizing modes of prokaryote organization, and it was this development which of course led to more complex organisms.[28] Using this example as a metaphor, Nietzsche would claim that all things seek to engulf others such that greater units of power are produced.

The desire on the part of each and everything "to overwhelm" the will of other things also holds for the interpersonal relationships we establish with other humans and perhaps, most profoundly, applies to the intrapersonal relationships we might form to ourselves. The person, as will be explained, is nothing more than a synthesis of selves.[29] There is no deep self, no primordial author of my identity. Rather the conscious self we have access to is nothing more than a commonwealth of forces. It is intensely political through and through. So too, Nietzsche surmises, it is with society. We certainly do see such battles being waged all around us. Indeed, we are all aware of political battles between "Right" and "Left" where each group simply seems to be more concerned with obliterating the other without either of them attempting to do what is best for the country which they supposedly represent. However, let there be no mistake; the root for these battles lies not in the principles themselves but the will to power. Nietzsche writes:

> . . . in nature the *rule* is not the state of distress, it is the superfluity, prodigality, even to the point of absurdity. The struggle for existence is only an *exception*, a temporary restriction of the will of life; the struggle, great and small, everywhere turns on ascendancy, on growth and extension, in accordance with the will to power, which is precisely the will of life.[30]

This passage, again, reaffirms the non-personal nature of will to power. Will to power should not be understood as one's "personal" power as it were. Nietzsche would want no truck with contemporary, new age philosophy gurus who counsel their followers to "awaken the power within." Power is far more complex than that. As Nietzsche shows in the first essay of the *Genealogy,* the will to power may turn outwardly or inwardly. If it is expressed outwardly, then the expression represents exuberance for life and the individual who expresses power in such a manner is said to be life-affirming. However, if it finds expression only in interior channels within an individual, then it will denote someone who is crooked, hateful, and full of resentment.[31]

Thus Nietzsche's "will to power" is different from the mundane understanding of power which says, that it is some "thing" that people or countries possess. In section 310 entitled "Will and Wave" of *The Gay Science,* Nietzsche once again depersonalizes the nature of power. He writes, "How greedily this wave approaches as if it were something! . . . But already another wave is approaching still more greedily and savagely than the first and its soul, too, seems to be full of secrets and the lust to dig up treasures. Thus lives waves—thus live we who will—more I shall not say."[32]

Will to power, then, denotes nothing more than the force waves of power that express *themselves* and not "us." We cannot choose our affects nor can we "choose" our emotions in the sense that we stand somehow outside of them.[33] One emotion, one thought, flows into the next from the formless ocean of life: "When we speak of values . . . Nietzsche writes . . . we do so under the inspiration and from the perspective of life: life forces us to posit values; life values through us *when* we posit values . . . " (Nietzsche's Italics).[34] And, finally, consider what Nietzsche states in *Daybreak*: "Perhaps our acts of will and our purposes are nothing but just throws—and we are only too vain and too limited to comprehend our extreme limitedness: which consists in the fact that we ourselves shake the dice-box with iron hands, that we ourselves in our most intentional actions do no more than play the game of necessity."[35] Our intentions, deliberations, and motives are nothing more than conduits through which life flows. It is folly to think that we have control over the various pieces of "furniture of the mind" such that we can arrange them as we wish. The truth is that the mind, along with our personality, character, etc. is simply an assemblage made with unknown and, perhaps, alien hands.

From this discussion, we might conclude the following: The will to power is the ultimate cosmological and biological narrative from which we, as human beings, might understand the world. Will to power explains why all things are as they are and why certain things change so much so that they cease to exist as independent entities while others seem to continue and grow by absorbing more and more power. Will to power also denotes the basic struggle of all organic and inorganic life which is to increase its share of power. Finally, it has also been shown that power is not some "thing" which one possesses. Power, rather, is more like an electrical capacity: it is something which is expressed not possessed.

3.3 WILL TO POWER AND PERSPECTIVISM

It might be prudent to discuss the other side of the will to power coin, that of perspectivism. A simplified view of perspectivism claims that facts are only true according to some perspective.[36] I refer to this position as doxastic perspectivism. My interpretation of perspectivism is non-doxastic, and I will delineate what this stance entails in subsequent chapters. Still, it is important to examine the traditional view first.

The doxastic view of perspectivism claims that no truth is true beyond the perspective in which it is indexed. There is no such thing as an aperspectival truth. Now obviously this claim combined with the thesis of perspectivism above is self-refuting, as the statement: There are no statements that are true in all perspectives is claimed to be true in all perspectives. Thus, to accept a perspectivist position leads Nietzsche, seemingly, to accept either one or both of the following claims: (1) Perspectivism is true (there is no single true account of the world; there are only some perspectives on the world). However, to assert that there is no single true account of the world is to make an assertion about the world. Putting it another way, if perspectivism is accepted as true, then it contradicts itself when applied reflexively because the central tenet of perspectivism is that we can never ascertain what the truth is independently of a perspective. Thus, there is no absolute truth. (2) Perspectivism is not true in any absolute sense, but the thesis of perspectivism is just one perspective among many. However, if we accept this proposal, then it does not follow that we should believe perspectivism. That is, the epistemic doctrine of perspectivism is no more epistemologically justified than any other epistemic theory, absolutism included. I will instead opt for a third claim: (3) Weak perspectivism, that is, the thesis of perspectivism itself, is absolutely true in all perspectives, but most other theories and assertions are only perspectively true. It is the solution Steven D. Hales and Rex Welshon adopt in their seminal work, *Nietzsche's Perspectivism.* I believe it is the only consistent doxastic perspectivist position possible.

However, it should be noted that the above discussion on perspectivism is only half the story; indeed, it is but one perspective on perspectivism. It is a purely doxastic interpretation on perspectivism. A stronger reading of perspectivism is the non-doxastic position. Under this reading, perspectivism denotes the possible forms will to power takes. Perspectives, given this reading, are strategies of domination. "Life" is but one perspective that the will to power may take. Borrowing Ciano Aydin's terminology, it is a "ground form." "Ground forms" are models of organization that have proven to be very effective in terms of gaining more power.[37] Life then, as a ground form of the will to power, is a significant development because it allows for a nuanced understanding of value. Certainly, animals can "value" various natural processes like eating, sleeping, and playing. However, the flourishing of values occurs with the development of the human being. Indeed, the notion of value can become so valuable that it may work against the very instinct of life itself. In such circumstances, people will sacrifice their lives for the sake of such values. What this shows is the crooked nature of will to power in that a form of domination can turn in on itself.

Truth is the highest value within the overall mode of life. Truth, like all perspectives, is a strategy, but truth holds a special place in this regard for it is a strategy that is necessary for all other strategies to work. Strategies for gain and empowerment must be genuine, and therefore truth remains the cross-perspectival strategy of which all other strategies must be apart. For it is because we are "chained" to the truth, as it were, that we come to accept the various truths that are told about us, and it is through these truths that we can come to know more truths about the world.

Although truth is a value, it is not a mere construction. This equation, namely that truth is merely a social construction—that society constructs truths—is sometimes made in the Nietzschean secondary literature and regrettably by Nietzsche himself in some places.[38] In Nietzsche's later work he is more consistent in upholding the value of truth. Truth is valuable precisely because its value does not change. It is the value which becomes the litmus for all other values. Nietzsche seems to acknowledge this in the very first passage of *Beyond Good Evil* by asking the following rhetorical question of truth and falsehood: "Granted we want truth: *why not rather* untruth? And uncertainty? Even ignorance?"[39] The answer, Nietzsche suggests toward the conclusion of *Beyond Good Evil*, is that we are so made, through a combination of instinct, breeding, and civilization, that we require the truth. Indeed, even Nietzsche's task of explaining how it is that we have come to desire truth proves, in a performative fashion, just how much we are beholden to the notion of truth, along with the procedures we use to arrive at truth such as investigations, analyses, and experimentation.

Truth became a perspective by which the human being could flourish. By making claims about the world, we were able to dominate it better. Such a strategy was obviously very successful allowing us, as human beings, to use our so-called "truth power" over the world and things therein. The coupling between truth and value is a rather long story. Nietzsche explores this evolution in his most analytically minded work: *On the Genealogy of Morals*. Nietzsche's method of genealogy offers the possibility of reevaluation of values by studying the emergence of values.

Thus there is a direct linkage between truth and will to power. Discovering truths about the world certainly allows us to understand it better thereby controlling it. However, Nietzsche would argue that truth (as well as deception and falsehood) are also well-known capacities that operate in the animal world.[40] Truth we might say is that perspective which enables a thing to have power over other things. However, even more, can be said. For some entity to understand another thing is to know the perspective through which such a thing operates. Moreover, to understand the point of view through which a thing operates is to realize that thing's *modus operandi* of power.

However, if all this is true then what becomes of Nietzsche's perspectivist claim? How can Nietzsche advocate a perspectivist theory of truth if truth cannot be indexed to a perspective? How can this value of truth be absolutely true such that it not only has the most perceived value of any value but indeed is the single value to which all other values are given value? Indeed, what of those quotations and passages where Nietzsche brazenly claims that the idea of Truth is a lie?[41] These are important and perplexing questions. We will turn to investigate the problem of perspectivism in greater detail in section 3.5.

3.4 WILL TO POWER AND NIETZSCHE'S ETHICS

I now wish to turn to Nietzsche's ethical position. Much has been written on what Michel Foucault might call the normative aspects of Nietzsche's ethical theory. There are many sources that outline the imperatives Nietzsche believes we should act on.[42] Likewise, there are many works which examine

Nietzsche's "character type theory" of ethical behavior.[43] Numerous works, for example, have been published on his various paradigms for virtuous behavior such as the "Overman" and "Free Spirit."[44] Moreover, once more, much has been written on the psychological make-up of different case types such as the ascetic type and so forth.[45] I do not wish to cover this much-trodden ground. Instead, I want to focus on what Michel Foucault might call the ascetic aspects of any ethical position. In *The Use of Pleasure*, Foucault argues that every ethical school of thought may be examined through two basic lenses of analysis. The normative (*nomoi*) which would include, among other things, the principles of ethical theory and the ascetic (*askesis*) aspects which concern how such principles might be put into practice.[46] Such a "how" type of analysis might be divided into two sub-categories: the practices of the self which one needs to inculcate and incorporate into his or her day-to-day living, and the ontological—what capacity, ontologically speaking, allows us to put ethical imperatives into practice? For instance, free will for many ethical systems would be the necessary ontological condition for the practice of ethical imperatives. In this section, and for the remainder of this book, I will concentrate primarily on this ontological focus.[47]

If we concentrate on this ontological question, it becomes clear that, at this stage of our inquiry, it would appear that the self, subject, individual, whatever we wish to call it, is simply the expression of the most dominant affect, or emotion at the present moment. Nietzsche seems to advocate an "expressivist" view of agency in that the agent is simply his or her actions, thoughts, and gestures with nothing left over. Action, for Nietzsche, is much like expressing juice from a citrus fruit. It is the juice being extracted that matters. The rind is discarded. In the same way, this interpretation of Nietzsche seems to suggest that we should value the action and not the actor behind the action. The intention or desire is irrelevant. All that matters is the action itself.

Nietzsche expresses this sentiment most famously in his most vital philosophical work, *On the Genealogy of Morals*. He writes,

> For, in just the same way as people separate lightning from its flash and take the latter as an *action*, as the effect of a subject which is called lightning, so popular morality separates strength from the manifestations of strength, as if behind the strong person there were an indifferent substrate, which is *free* to express strength or not. But there is no such substrate; there is no "being" behind the doing, acting, becoming. "The doer" is merely made up and added into the action—the act is everything.[48]

This passage would seem to support the extraction analogy. Still, it takes but a moment's reflection to realize that the extraction analogy blunts the thrust of Nietzsche's point. Nietzsche's hypothesis is far more radical, because, according to Nietzsche, there is nothing left over in the expression of the action. The agent is not just causally inert, but indeed non-existent. All that matters, indeed the only event which is real, is the action.

This notion of agency does indeed sound perplexing. After all, when we witness an event, we also wish to know the cause behind it. If we see it raining without a cloud in the sky, we ask: "How is this possible?" How can there be rain without a visible thing to make it rain? Surely the cause-and-effect relationship is metaphysically real. Moreover, what holds for natural phenomena must hold for psychological phenomena too, we reason. Wherever there is an action, there is an actor. An actor precedes action because the action is simply an effect of a cause much like quality is an attribute of substance. *Actio Ergo Sum*.

I will call this objection the first principle objection. Since metaphysics is often regarded as the study of first principles and it seems to be intuitively obvious, at least from the history of philosophy, that substance must come before an attribute, Nietzsche's claim that all there is, is action, seems to violate the very fundamental of metaphysical thinking itself.

Also, it would appear that Nietzsche has forgotten an age-old phenomenological insight. This insight can be clearly viewed in Plato's dialogue the *Phaedo*, written some 2400 years ago and may indeed be of even older origin. Early in the dialogue, we find Socrates trying to convince the lapsed Pythagorean, Simmias, that the soul is not purely the by-product of the body.[49] That is, the soul is both distinct from, and ontologically speaking, more real than the physical body. This view of the body-soul relationship is often called the *Soma-Sema* perspective: It is the soul which causes the body to move, and it is the soul which is immortal. The body itself is merely a tomb for the soul.[50]

One of the arguments that Plato puts forward to show that the soul is not only mere epiphenomenon in relation to the body is the argument from conflict. The soul, Plato argues, from the mouth of Socrates, is always resisting the desires of the body. However, conflict, Socrates infers, presupposes difference. Conflict, disagreement, struggle, *agon*, presupposes two or more parties in opposition to each other. Moreover, since we have all experienced this sort of turmoil regarding doing what we know is the right thing to do and merely following the passions of the body, this presumes that the soul exists independently of the body. I will call this the conflict model of the self. Nietzsche's model is false once again because it cannot account for the common phenomenon that we might call existential conflict.

I will now attempt to defend Nietzsche from the first two charges. In the final section, I demonstrate that there are some problems which remain for Nietzsche's will to power account. I will then reexamine this last objection in chapter seven.

Nietzsche's response to the first objection would be twofold. First, he claims that metaphysical thinking is grounded on grammatical syntax. That is, we are tricked by the way in which language constructs thought into believing that these thoughts and ideas represent, real, metaphysical, eternal truths. Nietzsche then offers two different accounts for this mistake: both the how and the why. The why part of this explanation is too complex and too convoluted to explain here, so I will, accordingly, concentrate on the how component. First, Nietzsche wants us to notice that our language takes a subject-predicate form. So if I were to say, "is running," this expression would not constitute a sentence because it lacks a noun; it does not have a subject. However, if I fill in this blank with Smith or Jones such that the expression now reads: "Smith is running," then this above, nonsensical expression has now been conferred meaning. It is both a sentence and a statement. It represents a complete thought and, second is making a truth claim. Metaphysics is the study of first principles or absolute truth claims. However, so Nietzsche suggests, metaphysics itself is merely a projection of grammar onto the world. We project what constitutes a meaningful sentence for us human language users onto the world where there may be no intrinsic meaning. In *Twilight of the Idols*, Nietzsche makes this connection between grammar and God more explicit. He writes: "Language belongs in its origin to the age of the most rudimentary form of psychology: We find ourselves in the midst of a rude fetishism when we call to mind the basic presuppositions of the metaphysics of language—which is to say of reason. It is *this* which sees everywhere deed and doer . . . I fear we are not getting rid of God because we have faith in grammar."[51]

Turning to the second problem that of the conflict model it is evident from the above how will to power also explains the battle, the turmoil, and the struggle we experience when we feel we are not "ourselves": Here too, Nietzsche says, power is at work. Here too, within "us," there is a struggle for power. All things, the subject, included, change because things are always in a contest or struggle for greater units of power. The subject, as a multitude of forces, is seeking more control over the several drives that constitute him or her as subject as well as attempting to overcome resistances and obstacles external to the self. To concretize this last point, we might do well to turn to a philosopher that Nietzsche greatly admired, namely, Heraclitus. Heraclitus employs the metaphor of the bow to account for how strife, within what appears to be a unified thing is not always obvious, and yet it is this same strife, this same tension, which serves as a unifying force for what were once two separate entities.

According to Heraclitus, a bow is a perfect metaphor for explaining the contest and *agon* that is taking place between all "objects" at any given moment in time. What we believe to be a unity is, instead, a carefully drawn "commonwealth" of forces that always remains in tension and strife with one another.[52] Each and every element of any "object" is both putting forth its own force while resisting the force of the other. As Guthrie, a well-respected scholar in this field makes this clearer in his commentary on the bow analogy:

> Look at a strung bow lying on the ground or leaning against a wall. No movement is visible. To the eyes, it appears a static object, completely at rest. But in fact a continuous tug-of-war is going on within it, as will become evident if the string is not strong enough or is allowed to perish. The bow will immediately take advantage, snap it and leap to straighten itself, thus showing that each had been putting forth effort all the time.[53]

Nietzsche makes a very similar point as regards the soul, self, or agent—whatever term is used by an individual to denote the executor of decisions. He argues that what we identify as a singular and stable entity is in fact, more fluid and compositional. Nietzsche writes in this regard,

> . . . for our body is only a social structure composed of many souls—to his sensations of pleasure as commander. *L'effet, c'est moi*: what happens here is what happens in every well-constructed and happy common wealth: the ruling class identifies itself with the successes of the commonwealth. In all willing, it is absolutely a question of commanding and obeying, on the basis, as I have said already, of a social structure composed of many "souls. . . ."[54]

Nietzsche adds to this point that human beings may belong to physiological "types": some people share similar drives with those of other persons. One or a group of ruling drives imposes order on all the others thus producing our "distinct" and "unique" personality. We humans, therefore, think that the "soul," the "I," the "ego," whatever one wants to call it, is in control of our actions but what Nietzsche wants us to understand is that the "ego" is just the name we give to the head drive. Since the forces that make up a "thing" are always struggling for greater power on a micro level of analysis, it is entirely possible and indeed probable, Nietzsche argues, that this head drive may change and so too our ego, personality, and consciousness along with it. Over time some drives may lose their commanding power and are reduced to obeying drives while obeying drives may become commanding drives. Thus, "obedience and commanding" are forms of struggle. It is these very forms which are responsible for producing our sense that we are a house divided: a self in conflict.

The third and related objection I shall call the akratic objection. *Akrasia* (literally, "without power" in ancient Greek) or "weakness of will" takes place when a moral agent, Smith, reasons that X is the best course of action, all things considered, and yet chooses to do Y. From this, it would seem to follow that Smith acts irrationally: His reasons lead him to believe that X is preferable over Y, and yet he chooses to ignore his reasoning.

Aristotle was the first thinker to explain this common, yet, perplexing phenomenon in terms of his theory of moral incontinence. That is, an akratic agent cannot control his or her desires: such desires are "let loose" and end up running amuck. In brief, it is Aristotle's claim that these unwanted, powerful desires get the better of the agent, as it were, and prevent him or her from making the best choice, in a moral dilemma, according to what the agent's practical rationality dictates.[55] However, if there is no actor behind the act as Nietzsche's position would suggest then once again, Nietzsche cannot account for this all too common yet profound experience.

This last objection to Nietzsche's ethical naturalism seems to be the most troublesome. As was shown, the will, according to Nietzsche, only moves forward and never backward. Much like a river, our sense of self is continually being expressed outwardly much like a river might push the flotsam that rides on its surface to the ocean. At best, our conscious awareness of our actions is merely a gauge. Our intentions, thoughts, and awareness are mere indicators of where our thoughts were and where they might be headed. Try as we might, we cannot reverse the course of these reflections. But if this is correct then there is nothing inherently ours. Our very self-constitution is constructed from actions that cannot be legislated. *Akrasia* then, given this rendering, would seem to be nothing more than a faulty gauge. *Akrasia* as a gauge, as an indicator, informs us that we had chosen the wrong action even when we knew that such a course of action was not the best choice when all things were considered. Weakness of will, and the corresponding feeling of agency alienation that usually accompanies it would not be real phenomenon according to Nietzsche. They, in fact, would be false measurements since it is not in our power to act otherwise. However, this conclusion not only runs counter to our immediate phenomenological experience but is also inconsistent with the principal features of Nietzsche's ethical philosophy. I will examine this problem in more detail in section 3.5.3 and provide at least a partial solution to this issue in chapter seven.

3.5 WILL TO POWER: PROBLEMS AND DIFFICULTIES

The preceding section demonstrated the integral role the will to power plays in Nietzsche's philosophy. Thus, a truly Nietzschean account of naturalism must consider the relation between power and the natural order. I examined this relation from three angles: metaphysical/biological, epistemic/perspectival, and ethical in sections 3.1–3.4. I now wish to focus on the potential problems that may arise by utilizing this tripartite framework for understanding will to power.

3.5.1 Ontological Problems with Will to Power

Will to power appears to be a theory of everything—it explains what the basic constituents of nature are and how, from these primal constituents, everything else is formed. However, even this rather elementary way of understanding power poses problems as to what nature itself might be independently of its parts. Kant, for example, argued for a transcendental position regarding nature. Nature is just simply the realm where all causal events are contained. Nature is already a postulate of Pure Reason in that it is assumed that all phenomena occur within the same realm. It is this realm that we call Nature.[56]

Nietzsche did not think of nature in this way. Nietzsche would call such theorizing nothing more than *a priori* or armchair hypothesizing. Of course, this does not imply that Nietzsche was a strict empiricist in the sense that he eschewed all forms of non-empirical hypothesizing. In fact, I will show that neither the *a posteriori* nor *a priori* categories are satisfactory when it comes to understanding Nietzsche's fully developed naturalist position. However, Nietzsche's basic criticism of a transcendental position is that such a position attempts to totalize something that cannot be totalized—we are providing a schema for all of nature, with us included in this schema but doing so from an aperspectival stance—a view from nowhere. Will to power is the theory which attempts to disrupt and explode the notion of narrative. Rationality, truth, and knowledge are nothing more and nothing less than attempts to totalize and absolutize something to render it more understandable. After all, man, as Nietzsche taught us at the end of *The Genealogy,* would "rather will nothingness than not will."[57]

Yet, the will to power itself is an example of the very totalizing that Nietzsche criticizes—it too seeks to render a coherent explanation for all things. Not only does it provide a framework, but it also provides succor for a brutal world in that by exclaiming that the world is brutal we are given some comfort and some means of planning against its inherent harshness. We do not suffer from false hope, and we can take action, confident that there are at least some certainties in life. Nietzsche seems to swap out one transcendental postulate for another.

However, there are more problems with Kant's model. For this container picture of nature is almost always coupled with a corresponding substance picture of things. On this reading, the universe contains distinct entities that exist independently of other things and where such things have unique qualities. Of course, this notion has been rejected in the quantum realm, but even when scientists discuss facts or principles in the biological and chemical sciences, it is clear that they are still beholden to this view. Each species has distinctive features which distinguish it from its broader genus class. Chemical compounds are comprised of elements. Each element has unique physical and chemical properties. The properties of the compound are by-products of these simpler physical units. This sort of metaphysical atomism is something which Nietzsche sought to overturn. As we have already discovered, Nietzsche attempts to overthrow this picture by presenting a relational interpretation of nature without *relata*: things are simply bundles that affect other bundles. Whether this notion is, in fact, coherent is something that will be addressed in chapters four and five.

The second aspect of this ontological understanding of will to power relates to the set of principles that regulate relations among things. A successful metaphysical theory has to explain how and why things come to be, change, and subsist. Nietzsche sought to explain these occurrences with one concept: force. Will to power is assumed to be the only real causal force in the universe. As discovered from the above section, all things in the world are held in a constant state of tension or *agon*. All things in the world compete against all other entities for more units of power. It is this competition between things that accounts for the change of some things and the subsistence of others. The causes for these changes, Nietzsche believed, could be unraveled by simply seeing the world for what it truly was: "This world: a monster of energy, without beginning, without end; a firm, iron magnitude of force that does not grow bigger or smaller, that does not expend itself but only transforms itself."[58]

However, if this is truly Nietzsche's view and some scholars suggest it is, then the problems with this interpretation of reality are manifold. My goal in this section is to state these problems as perspicuously as possible. In chapter five I will demonstrate how these problems may be solved.

Turning to the first aspect of will to power, it would seem that Nietzsche's new metaphysical account is still working with a Kantian conception of nature. Nietzsche still conceives of the world as a container. While it is true that this new world no longer contains substantive things, because Nietzsche rejects any *hypokeimenon* view of substance, his replacement for such "thing language" is no better. Things now, according to Nietzsche, are nothing more than concrescences of power. Such a so-called naturalistic translation of thinghood into force waves or packets of power, however, does not solve the problem which Nietzsche initially identified, namely, the postulation of nature as space where things exist and interact with each other. Nietzsche's problem with this view if we recall was that it was predicated as a mere postulate: an assumption. It was an abductive hypothesis which was required to substantiate a thinghood of substance in the first place. Nietzsche, it would seem, adopts this hypothesis to render his new power account of the world coherent. But, if the ground for either account of the world, namely the Kantian or Nietzschean, rest on the same assumption then it seems questionable as to why we would adopt Nietzsche's new explanation. It would appear that we have far more justification to continue using the traditional thinghood, container picture of nature.

The second objection relates to Nietzsche's construal of force. Force on its own does not seem sufficient to explain the causes and conditions for all of the events, changes, and phenomena of nature. Certainly, Nietzsche's take on the world adds a new, potentially fruitful and exciting lens of analysis. However, to see the world merely as a world comprised of relations of force seems too barren: Surely there are many more principles and many more independent causes for all the sorts of things we have in the world. Also, it is doubtful that such a description will be able to do the full work that is required of it: Nietzsche's naturalistic demands are a rather tall order. For if we recall, a reductionistic naturalist project is always a project of translation: How might we translate non-natural phenomena into purely natural terms? It has also been shown that there are different ways to fulfill this project. There can be linguistic, ontological, and theoretical translations. The chief problem with all of these methods, however, is that there is always a chance that something may get lost in the translation. As Chalmers and Jackson have shown, it is tough to translate *qualia* into scientific language without losing an essential *je ne sais quois* of the properties being translated.[59] For Nietzsche, this particular problem comes sharply into focus because even *qualia* are reducible to quantity. A bundle will be unlike from some other bundle because of the sheer number of bare units of quantum along with the mode of organization these units of power contained in the bundle take. The problem is that it seems impossible to reduce the richness and diversity of qualities to numerical quantity.

One way out of this dead-end is to adopt an eliminativist position. For if a property of something cannot be adequately reduced like a belief, for example, then we can simply eliminate it from scientific discussion. As demonstrated, there were many problems with this approach, but eliminativism always remains a live option for the thoroughgoing ontological naturalist.

The eliminativist strategy, however, is not available to Nietzsche. For Nietzsche not only desires to translate religious ideas and practices into his language of power or more accurately into a physiological-cultural interpretation of will to power, but to understand such ideas as real strategies designed to accumulate more power. He attempts to reveal the true sources of worldly and otherworldly phenomena. This approach is anathema to eliminativism.

We see Nietzsche's non-eliminativist type of reductionism exemplified in *The Genealogy*. There Nietzsche provides a psychological explanation for moral and psychical phenomena. For example, guilt according to Nietzsche is not some innate emotion peculiar to the human brain or soul. He rejects the idea that guilt is simply a biological development of our peculiar evolutionary trajectory. Nor does he accept the idea that guilt is a curse or gift (depending on how you look at it) from God. According to Nietzsche, guilt is nothing more than a contingent and historical development of a prior disposition.

Nietzsche calls this disposition the bad conscience and even this, Nietzsche claims, is historical through and through. Nietzsche, as will be discovered, does not rest his naturalism on any biological substratum: Nietzsche does not believe in using "nets" to catch his naturalist analysis. There is nothing which is not open to a genealogical interpretation.

The other problem with Nietzsche's view is the one identified by James Porter. Porter argues that Nietzschean will to power is an attempt to remove the very notion of subjectivity from nature. Nietzsche achieves this in a twofold way: First, he argues against a *hypokeimenon* or thinghood concept of substance because such a notion contains vestiges of subjecthood—things are independent objects which have definite predicates much in the same manner that subjects are taken to be individuated and independent objects that also have distinct characteristics. Instead, Nietzsche argues that a thing should be likened to the sum of its effects, but in so doing he sneaks in an assumption that is not proven, namely, that all observed effects belong to the same thing.[60] To argue that a thing is just simply the sum of its effects is still to file effects into a rigid grouping and therefore allows substance to enter through the backdoor.

However, Porter insists, there is a further difficulty: to claim that a thing or subject is nothing more than the sum of its causal effects presupposes subjectivity since we are claiming a totality for something. However, this is precisely what the will to power denies! We cannot determine the consequences of some bundle precisely because the bundle is not self-contained; it too has commanding and subjugating relations to other things and as such, we cannot determine the determinateness of the bundle. We cannot determine its totality.[61]

This same criticism can be introduced on a global level, so thinks Porter. The global picture of will to power as presented is much like a stage where the actors, "bundles of power" are constantly fighting against other bundles to gain power. However, the purpose of putting forward such a theory was precisely to deny that one can get at the truth of the world: My will projects this narrative of the will to power to make sense of the world around me. Even will to power is subject to will to power: All things, whether they are objects, statements, moral imperatives, feelings, or even theories like the will to power, are nothing more than fresh interpretations for the sake of gaining more power over something. The concept, then, is irretrievably incoherent because in articulating and explaining will to power we are attempting to totalize the world; but will to power claims that such totalization is impossible. Nietzsche, then, is committing a performative contradiction: he is evincing what cannot be evinced.[62]

With these devastating critiques, Porter then addresses the true purpose of will to power. His analysis leads to one of either two possible interpretations:

Nietzsche, Porter claims, was either aware he was contradicting himself, or he was unaware. Porter believes that it is most charitable to think that Nietzsche was aware of the above problems, and therefore he intimates that the concept should be thought of as a parable: The actual purpose of will to power is to alert us of our instinct to totalize and to inform us that totalization is impossible.[63]

This particular problem I address in the last chapter. I show that Porter sets up a false dilemma. Another and more plausible view is readymade, namely, that the will to power, as presented here, is defensible. I demonstrate and mount such a defense in the final chapter.

3.5.2 Will to Power and Knowledge

I would now like to turn to the epistemological problems regarding will to power. These epistemological aspects will relate closely to the ontological points noted above. There are at least two corresponding epistemological issues with Nietzsche's power narrative. The first has to do with the essence of knowledge. If all things are reducible in some fashion to will to power, then knowledge itself is only a means for gaining power. Knowledge, ultimately, is simply a tool that humans (and, perhaps other creatures) use to master their environment. Certainly, knowledge of the external world has proven invaluable to its mastering, but the value of knowledge does not lie merely in its instrumental value.

The other problem with this approach is that it would equally apply to Nietzsche's epistemic claim that the world is nothing more than the will to power. This claim is an attempt, on the part of Nietzsche, to control or influence thinking by proclaiming that all knowledge is already infused with power. So the claim, if true, would equally apply to itself. Nietzsche, of course, was aware of the self-referential aspect of these sort of assertions. He writes: "It has gradually become clear to me what every great philosophy has hitherto been: a confession on the part of its author and a kind of involuntary and unconscious memoir; moreover, that the moral (or immoral) intentions in every philosophy have every time constituted the real germ of life out of which the enitre plant has grown."[64]

The above problem is also closely associated with Nietzsche's perspectivist claim—that there are no truths, but only perspectives. In section 3.3 I noted how the statement might appear to be self-contradictory. However, there is a second problem in adopting such a claim: How do we determine the objective epistemic merits of two competing perspectives if the very notion of epistemic merit is itself merely relative to a perspective?

I believe that these problems can be explained. In fact, the contradictory and therefore self-refuting interpretation of perspectivism has already been answered by Hales and Welshon in their work *Nietzsche's Perspectivism*.[65] However, the second problem which concerns the objective epistemic merit of two competing perspectives is much trickier to solve. The tricky part to solving this last problem is that the solution must be non-representational. A representational, realist naturalism will always leave the question regarding the conception or perception of the object and the real object in the world, questionable. Nietzsche exposed these epistemic dangers by renouncing Kantianism. Noumenal objects or things in themselves reintroduces the skeptical challenge: "Okay, so we can know phenomena, but what of this mysterious realm of noumenal stuff?" So, Nietzsche has to present a theory that overcomes these challenges. There has to be an unmediated connection between the concepts we have of things and what these things are in themselves. If things can exist apart from the mind, then the skeptical challenge can always be raised: "How do we know that the concept we have a thing is an adequate representation of that thing?" Moreover, appealing to transcendental arguments, as Kant does, is deeply problematic.

Another solution to this perspectivist problem has been proposed by Leiter, Clark, Hinman, and others. This solution adopts an anti-realist metaphysical stance. The upshot is that all perspectives are indexed to a natural language, and therefore it is the natural language (or more accurately the language games, understood in a Wittgensteinian sense that underpins it) that provides the means and measures for evaluating the epistemic worth of a perspective.[66] The problem with this solution is twofold: It seems possible that things exist just as they are independently of a human knower. Second, such a view adopts an epistemic tribalism—whatever a community of language users deem to be true is true. However, such a position is clearly inconsistent with Nietzsche's more developed views on the origin and evolution of language. Nietzsche writes in Book Five, section 354 of *The Gay Science*, for example:

> Consciousness is really only a connecting network between man and man—only as such did it have to evolve: the solitary and predatory man would not have needed it . . . our thought itself is continually, as it were, outvoted by the character of consciousness—by the "genius of the species" which rules it—and translated back into the perspective of the herd . . . that everything which becomes conscious thereby becomes shallow, thin, relatively stupid, general, sign, characteristic of the herd, that with all becoming conscious there is united a great fundamental corruption, falsification, superficializing, and generalization.[67]

The final problem with Nietzsche's perspectivist claim has to do with error—Nietzsche needs to account for how our predictions and conceptions of the world may be false. For if it is impossible to get at the object in and of itself because we only have perspectives on it then one is entitled to ask: "How do we account for mistakes?" Surely the obvious response to this is to suggest that we do have access to immediate, recalcitrant experience and this recalcitrant experience signals that our picture of the world is incorrect. It is because of this experience that we revise our beliefs. However, if experiences are themselves indexed to perspectives, then it would appear impossible to alter our beliefs. Indeed, what possible reason could we give for changing a well-established belief if such a belief is protected from what one might call "error-experience surprise"?

3.5.3 Will to Power and Ethics

The ethical problems as only outlined in section 3.4, are also part of the general problem of taking the will to power as the ultimate explanatory narrative in which all other things must be related to have any meaning whatsoever. The most problematic point of Nietzsche's ethical position has to do with his theory of agency along with the feeling that some agents experience when they feel that they performed an action not entirely their own. The agent, if recalled, was fully expressed in his or her action with nothing left over. Indeed, the agent appears to be nothing but an unjustified assumption that traditional philosophy posits to render ethics possible: A subject must be free to be held accountable for the crimes he or she commits. This interpretation, however, is something that is only later grafted onto the notion of the subject. Before the first hint of ethical thinking in the early Plato, the subject was something already assumed to exist—as Nietzsche remarks in *The Genealogy*, the creation of subjectivity was necessary to render man calculable, predictable.[68] This epistemic practice for preferring practices over meanings is one of the essential methodological procedures of genealogical inquiry. Nietzsche makes this point quite clear in GM II 14. In speaking of these two procedures, Nietzsche remarks that, in the case of punishment, for example, the procedural is the enduring part of punishment, "the custom, the act, the 'drama,' a certain strict sequence of procedures."[69] The other aspect is the fluid element—the meaning, the purpose, and the expectation of punishment. These two aspects are distinct from each other, and we make a grave mistake if we think, as some naïve genealogists, that the *meaning* of punishment can be projected back into the *procedures* of punishment.[70] That is, the second aspect, the meaning aspect, always comes later; it has no causal efficacy on the first aspect.[71] From this, we might argue that free will is something overwritten onto the ancient procedures of punishment, but that are in no way responsible for initiating these very procedures.

However, Nietzsche's conception of morality would seem to presuppose the very notion which he rejects. Nietzsche's basic position is that there are currently or, at least historically, two types of individuals: the strong and weak. The strong were those who could endure suffering and were masters of self-overcoming. They could say "Yes and Amen" to the harshness of life. The weak, on the other hand, required subterfuge to make life tolerable. We can see this position expressed in many passages in Nietzsche's corpus but one passage in particular stands:

> Every individual may be regarded as representing the ascending or the descending line of life. . . . If he represents the ascending line, his value is, in fact, extraordinary—and for the sake of life as a whole, which takes a step farther through him, the care for his preservation and for the creation of the best conditions for him may even be extreme. . . . If he represents the descending development, decay, chronic degeneration, and sickness (sickness is, in general, already the consequence of decay, not its cause), then he has little value, and the minimum of fairness demands that he takes away as little as possible from those who have turned out well. He is merely their parasite.[72]

Despite these differences, members of either group had this in common: they both possessed a profound capacity to interpret. The weak appear to be the most curious and intriguing for Nietzsche for they provide a total reinterpretation of their seemingly meek status. They thought of themselves as conquerors because they believed that they and not their masters could endure the various tests God had put before them.[73] Likewise, the strong or nobles eventually became weak, so Nietzsche thinks because they bought into the basic tenets of Christianity. However, this raises two perplexing questions: "How does Nietzsche account for such a radical change in a group or individual's character?" "What capacity allows for an individual to alter, in sometimes rather radical fashion, his entire personality and character?" For if words have no causal efficacy—there is no downward causation—and sickness is not the cause of decay, but the reverse is true—decay is the cause of disease—then it becomes problematic to offer a drive theory of subjective constitution and behavioral analysis. There would be no point in railing against the invectives of Christian thought if thinking was simply epiphenomenalism, having no real being and therefore no real powers of efficacy as Nietzsche seems to hold in some works.[74]

The above questions, whether epistemological, metaphysical, or ethical are all equally puzzling. What's more, it was discovered that such questions become possible only if one adopts will to power as the cosmological/biological/psychological framework through which all other aspects of the universe make sense. Answering these questions entails providing a naturalized, new and very different theory of will to power than the ones that have been traditionally advanced in the secondary literature. However, before providing my answers to these queries, informed by my new position on power, it might be instructive to investigate three competing interpretations to the analysis of will to power that I have so far endorsed. These interpretations will be from the following scholars: Maudemarie Clark, John Richardson, and Linda Williams. Each has acknowledged the many ontological, epistemic, and moral problems produced by adopting a robust, ontological and, some might say, vitalistic reading of nature as I have given in section 3.1. Accordingly, they each have rendered their respective readings of will to power which serve to resolve these problems. I now turn to examining their respective ontological interpretations of will to power in the next section to show that each is inadequate, albeit in different ways.

NOTES

1. James I. Porter, "Nietzsche's Theory of the Will to Power," in *A Companion to Nietzsche*, 548–565.
2. I have inserted scare quotes surrounding the word material because Nietzsche is against a material mechanistic view of reality. Still, understanding will to power in terms of Aristotle's four causes is helpful in terms of explicating how will to power is both similar to and yet different from various Pre-Socratic theories of old.
3. Aristotle, *Metaphysics*, in *Basic Works of Aristotle*, 1032b line 14, 792.
4. Aristotle, *Categories*, in *Basic Works of Aristotle*, Chapter 5.
5. Aristotle, *Categories*, in *Basic Works of Aristotle*, Chapter 5: "Moreover primary substances are most properly called substances in virtue of the fact that they are the entities which underlie everything else and that everything else is either predicated of them or present in them." Chapter 5, lines 15–18, 10.
6. Nietzsche, "The Will to Power," in *The Complete Works of Friedrich Nietzsche*, edited by Oscar Levy, Trans. Anthony Ludovici (New York: Russell and Russell Inc, 1964), Volume 15 Books three and Four, section 1067, 431.
7. Nietzsche, *The Will to Power*, Trans. Kaufman and Holingdale, section 1067, 550.
8. An excellent overview on Nietzsche's intellectual development and subsequent critique of atomism can be found in Christian J. Emden's *Nietzsche's Naturalism: Philosophy in the Life Sciences in the 19th Century* (New York: Cambridge University Press, 2014), 105–107. For more on Roger Boscovich's theory of energy see his *A Theory of Natural Philosophy*, edited by J.M. Child (Chicago: Open Court, 1922), especially section 7, 36–38. On Helmholz, see Hermann von. Helmholz, *Hermann von Helmholtz. Epistemological Writings. The Paul Hertz/Moritz Schlick Centenary Edition of 1921*, Trans. Malcom Lowe, edited by Robert Cohen and Yehuda Elkana (Dordrecht: D. Reidel, 1977).
9. Nietzsche, *The Will to Power*, Trans. Ludovici, section 635, 119.
10. Nietzsche, *The Will to Power*, section 656, 346.
11. Nietzsche, *The Will to Power*, section 636.
12. Hales and Welshon, *Nietzsche's Perspectivism*, 71.
13. Nietzsche, *On the Genealogy of Morals*, GM II: 12, 512.
14. Nietzsche, *On the Genealogy of Morals*, Trans. Kaufmann and Holingdale, GM II: 12, 77–79.

84   *Chapter 3*

15. John Richardson in *Nietzsche's New Darwinism* argues that Nietzsche's notion of will to power, in many of his works, "leaves Nietzsche with no other alternative but to a mental vitalism, reading mind into all things." John Richardson, *Nietzsche's New Darwinism* (Oxford University Press, 2004), 64. Christopher Janaway, *Beyond Selflessness: Reading Nietzsche's Genealogy*, 160.

16. Alexander Nehamas' *Nietzsche: Life as Literature* (Cambridge, MA: Harvard University Press, 1985) has become the *locus classicus* for this position, but of course this connection was already made albeit in embryonic form by Kaufmann and Danto. For more recent representatives of this position, see Alex McIntyre's "Communion in Joy: Will to Power and Eternal Return in Grand Politics," *Nietzsche-Studien* 25 (1996), 24–41, and Bernard Reginster's *The Affirmation of Life: Nietzsche on Overcoming Nihilism* (Cambridge, MA: Harvard University Press, 2006).

17. Nietzsche, *Beyond Good and Evil*, part IX, section 259, 393.

18. This of course does not entail that Nietzschean will to power *merely* manifests itself in the form of brute cruelty toward others. The will to power manifests itself in many, many different forms. I simply wish to analyze, in further detail, an often forgotten form.

19. Nietzsche, *Beyond Good and Evil,* part IX, section 259, 393.

20. Of course Cladists would disagree with this assessment. Instead they would focus on what evolutionary adaptations were preserved in different species. That is, emphasis is placed on the shared characteristics of animals derived from a common ancestor. See R.C. Craw "Margins of cladistics: Identity, differences and place in the emergence of phylogenetic systematics." In Griffiths, P.E., *Trees of life: Essays in the Philosophy of Biology* (Dordrecht: Kluwer Academic, 1992), 65–107.

21. Charles Darwin, On the *Origin of the Species by Means of Natural Selection* (London: Murray, 1859), 127.

22. Daniel C. Dennett, *Darwin's Dangerous Idea: Evolution and the Meanings of Life* (New York: Simon and Schuster, 1995).

23. Nietzsche, *The Will to Power*, section 642, 342.

24. Daniel Ahern, *Nietzsche as Cultural Physician* (Pennsylvania: Pennsylvania State University Press, 1995), 14.

25. Ahern, 14.

26. Nietzsche, *The Will to Power*, section 656, 346.

27. Henze, Martin et al., "Evolutionary biology: essence of mitochondria," *Nature* 426 (2003), 127–8.

28. For a good introduction to the history of the study of Mitochondria, see Ernster and Schatz, "Mitochondria: A Historical Review," *The Journal of Cell Biology* 91, 227–255.

29. See Nietzsche's discussion on the soul in section 256 of *Beyond Good and Evil*.

30. Nietzsche, *The Gay Science,* section 349, Trans. Holingdale, 230.

31. See especially *On the Genealogy of Morals*, GM I: 7, 469–470.

32. Friedrich Nietzsche, *The Gay Science*, Trans. Walter Kaufmann (New York: Vintage Books, 1974), section 310, 247.

33. This does not mean that we cannot choose how we act on our emotions nor how we may understand more appropriate ways to use our affects.

34. Nietzsche, *The Twilight of the Idols*, "Morality as Anti-Nature," section 5, 55.

35. See Friedrich Nietzsche's *Daybreak: Thoughts on the Prejudices of Morality*, Trans. R.J. Holingdale, edited by M. Clark and B. Leiter (Cambridge University Press, 1997), Section 130.

36. See George Stack, "Nietzsche and Perspectival Interpretation," *Philosophy Today* 25 (1981), 221–241.

37. Ciano Aydin, "Nietzsche on Will to Power Toward an Organization-Struggle Model," *Journal of Nietzsche Studies,* 33:1 (2007), 25–48, 36–37.

38. The most famous passage where Nietzsche denies the value of truth is seen in "On Truth and Lies in a Nonmoral Sense." There Nietzsche writes that truth is: "A mobile army of metaphor, metonyms and anthropomorphisms—in short, a sum of human relations which have been enhanced, transposed, and embellished poetically and rhetorically, and which after long use seem firm, canonical, and obligatory to a people: truths are illusions about which one has forgotten that this is what they are; metaphors which are worn out and without sensuous power; coins which have lost their pictures and now matter only as metal, no longer as coins." Friedrich Nietzsche, *The Portable Nietzsche,* Trans. and edited by Walter Kaufmann (London: Penguin Classics, 1977), 46–47.

39. Nietzsche, *Beyond Good and Evil*, section 1, Trans. Holingdale.

40. A clear example of deception is the Venus flytrap noted above. But many animals engage in more conscious acts of deception. Think of the father or mother bird who pretends that his or her wing is broken. This is a strategy employed to lure a predator away from a nest. Sometimes the ruse works and sometimes the predator sees through the lie.

41. I take up this question in more detail toward the end of chapter four.

42. Classics in this area include Walter Kaufmann's *Nietzsche, Philosopher, Psychologist, Anti-Christ*, 3rd edition, 1968, see especially 211–307. For a book that examines, concretely, how Nietzsche's morality may be applied to our current disenchantment with modern society, see Bernard, Reginster, *The Affirmation of Life: Nietzsche on Overcoming Nihilism* (Cambridge, MA: Harvard University Press, 2006).

43. According to Thomas Hurka, Nietzsche advocates an ethos of perpetual self-overcoming. The goal is to take our "arrangement," to continue with the metaphor above, and continue to make it more beautiful until it is "perfected." See Thomas Hurka, *Perfectionism* (Oxford: Oxford University Press, 1996). Still other interpreters believe that our style, so to speak, is purely subjective—Nietzsche gives us license to change the assemblage of our first- and second-order qualities however we choose. We might call this interpretation the aesthetic reading of Nietzsche. For Nehamas, perspectivism ". . . seems to be precisely an effort to move away from the idea that the world (ourselves included) possess any features itself, the world has no features and these can therefore be neither correctly nor wrongly represented." See his *Nietzsche: Life as Literature* (Cambridge, MA: Harvard University Press, 1985), 45.

44. For two very different interpretations regarding the respective virtues of the *Ubermensch* see Richard White's "The Return of the Master: An Interpretation of Nietzsche, *Genealogy of Morals*," 63–76 and compare with Richard Schacht's, "Of Morals and *Menschen*," 427–449, both in *Nietzsche, Genealogy, History.*

45. For an excellent essay that articulates Nietzsche's argument against the ascetic type and hedonism as a type of action theory, see Ivan Soll, "Nietzsche on Cruelty, Asceticism and the Failure of Hedonism in *Nietzsche, Genealogy, Morality,* 168–193.

46. *The History of Sexuality Volume II: The Use of Pleasure* Trans. R. Hurley (New York: Random House, 1985), 9.

47. According to Foucault there are four different aspects to ethics. These are: (1) the ethical substance, (Aphrodisia), (2) the mode of adjustment, (3) the ascetic practices, and finally (4) the telos or goal (self-mastery) that one wants to reach by performing these ascetic practices. While the first and fourth aspects are relatively similar among ancient Greek philosophers, according to Foucault, nonetheless, the mode of adjustment, the aesthetics and practical choice as well as the ascetic practices or techne, the actual techniques used to achieve self-mastery, were quite different. See Michel Foucault's "On the Genealogy of Ethics: An Overview of a Work in Progress," in *The Foucault Reader*, edited by Paul Rabinow (New York: Pantheon Books, 1990), 353–373. Also see, Foucault's *The Use of Pleasure*, 229–246, for a fuller treatment of each of these themes.

48. Friedrich Nietzsche, *On the Genealogy of Morals: A Polemic*, Trans. Walter Kaufmann and Holingdale, GM I:13.

49. See Plato, *Phaedo* in *Great Dialogues of Plato* Trans. W.H.D. Rouse (New York: Signet Classics), 1984, 85E–86E, 584–585.

50. See Plato, *Phaedo* 66C in *Great Dialogues of Plato*, 559: Then from all this, said Socrates, genuine philosophers must come to some such opinion as follows, so as to make to one another statements such as these: "A sort of direct path so to speak, seems to take us to the conclusion that so long as we have the body with us in our enquiry, and our soul is mixed up with so great an evil, we shall never attain sufficiently what we desire, and that, we say, is the truth."

51. Nietzsche, *Twilight of the Idols*, "Reason in Philosophy" section 5, 48.

52. Those who do not understand this, Heraclitus writes {fragment 51}, "do not apprehend how being at variance it agrees with itself: there is a back-stretched connexion, as in the bow and the lyre." In Kirk, Raven and Schofield, *The Pre-Socratic Philosophers* (Cambridge University Press, 1984), 192.

53. W.K.C. Guthrie, *History of Greek Philosophy*, 1, 440.

54. Nietzsche, *Beyond Good and Evil*, section 19, Trans. Holingdale.

55. See Aristotle's *Nicomachean Ethics* VII, 1–10. See *The Nicomachean Ethics*, Trans. David Ross (Oxford: Oxford University Press).

56. See Paul Guyer's discussion in *Kant* (London, Routledge, 2006), 154–165.

57. Nietzsche, *On the Genealogy of Morals*, Essay III, section 28, in *Basic Writings of Nietzsche*, 599.

58. Nietzsche, *The Will to Power*, 1067.

59. D.J. Chalmers, *The Conscious Mind: In Search of a Fundamental Theory* (Oxford University Press, 1996). F. Jackson, *From Metaphysics to Ethics: A Defense of Conceptual Analysis* (Oxford Clarendon Press, 1998).

60. James I Porter, "Nietzsche's Theory of Will to Power," in *A Companion to Nietzsche*, 551.

61. James I Porter, "Nietzsche's Theory of Will to Power," in *A Companion to Nietzsche*, 552.

62. Porter, 552–553.
63. Porter, 554.
64. Nietzsche, *Beyond Good and Evil,* On the Prejudices of Philosophers, Trans. Holingdale, section 6.
65. Hales and Welshon, *Nietzsche's Perspectivism* (Illionis University Press, 2000). See their discussion of weak perspectivism.
66. See Lawrence Hinman's article: "Can a Form of Life Be Wrong," *Philosophy* 58:225 (July 1983), 339–355. Hinman argues that a form of life can indeed be wrong, but he must supplement his interpretation of Wittgenstein's form of life by understanding it in Gadamarian terms. Second, his interpretation of the sections in *The Philosophical Investigations* and in *On Certainty* where Wittgenstein mentions the words "form of life" is extremely charitable. Leiter also invokes Wittgenstein to buttress his position. See his essay "Perspectivism in Nietzsche's Genealogy of Morals," 349.
67. Nietzsche, *The Gay Science*, Book Five, section 354 quoted from *A Nietzsche Reader*, Selected and Translated with an introduction by R.J. Holingdale (London: Penguin Books 1977), 66–67.
68. Nietzsche, *On the Genealogy of Morals*, GM II, 9, 507.
69. Nietzsche, *On the Genealogy of Morals*, GM II, 13, 515.
70. Nietzsche, *On the Genealogy of Morals* GM II, 14.
71. Nietzsche, *On the Genealogy of Morals*, GM II, 13, 515.
72. Nietzsche, *Twilight of the Idols*, "Skirmishes of an Untimely Man," 33.
73. See Nietzsche, *On the Genealogy of Morals*, Essay one, section 14–15, 482–488.
74. See Nietzsche, *The Gay Science*, Kaufmann translation, section 127: "The feeling of will seems sufficient to him not only for the assumption of cause and effect but also for the faith that he understands their relationship. He knows nothing of the mechanism of what happened and of the hundredfold fine work that needs to be done to bring about the strike, or of the incapacity of the will in itself to do even the tiniest part of this work."

Chapter 4

Three Solutions
Clark, Richardson, Williams

In the following chapter, I examine three very different interpretations of will to power. The first account, given by Maudemarie Clark, denies the very coherency of will to power. She further argues that Nietzsche rejects will to power because he too realized it was incoherent. The principal reason for Nietzsche's rejection seems to be that will to power is an *a priori* belief and Nietzsche, according to Clark, denies *a priori* beliefs wholesale. I argue that the premises that uphold Clark's arguments are flimsy at best.

John Richardson puts forward an alternative interpretation of will to power to that of Clark. Richardson's notion of will to power is deflationary regarding both content and scope. He argues that will to power fails on a cosmological level and at best may only be used to supplement Darwinian natural selection. I demonstrate how Richardson's interpretation not only eviscerates the true insightfulness and profundity of will to power but is, in fact, inconsistent when closely examined.

Third and finally, I examine an aesthetic interpretation of will to power advanced by Linda Williams. Williams claims that will to power provokes "mirror therapy": Reflecting on the will to power helps one to overcome negative and harmful feelings and behavior. What is perplexing about Williams' work is that she claims that will to power is Nietzsche's shorthand for characterizing the nature of the world as one that is beset by individuals and groups struggling for greater power. Will to power cannot be thought of as a metaphysical or even ontological theory: it is perspectival through and through. Although coupling will to power with perspectivism, at least as Williams understands the term, may lead to incoherency, Williams, to her credit, readily understands and admits, such difficulties. Williams attempts to meet these problems by justifying will to power on a two-tiered pragmatic ground. I argue that Williams' attempt, though meritorious, leads to an internal contradiction.

4.1 CLARK ON WILL TO POWER

In her seminal book, *Nietzsche on Truth and Philosophy*, Clark puts forward several powerful arguments to show that many of the traditional renderings of will to power are incoherent and implausible. One of the most powerful arguments advanced in this regard is Clark's contention that any metaphysical interpretation of will to power contradicts Nietzsche's much-vaunted empiricism. For Clark, a metaphysical interpretation is one that is ultimately grounded in an *a priori* premise. She argues that Schacht along with many others are guilty of ontologizing will to power because their interpretations ultimately invoke *a priori* premises.[1]

The problem then, for Clark, is one of finding an acceptable interpretation of Nietzschean power that will be consistent with Nietzsche's later, more empirically minded approach to philosophical problems. Clark eventually finds an ally in Kaufmann. Kaufmann's interpretation of will to power seems the most promising because the will to power, for Kaufmann, is simply the best possible interpretation, currently available, to explain all human behavior. However, such an interpretation, as Kaufmann himself admits, leads to vacuity as "whatever is wanted is wanted for the sake of power."[2] However, if this is true, Clark argues, then second-order desires for love, riches, etc. are also at heart mere reinterpretations for the desire of power. To be more precise, there are two problems with Kaufmann's interpretation. First, power would lose its illuminating force—if everything is done for power, then nothing is. The entire point of hypothesizing will to power as the most basic driving force behind human behavior was to illuminate what appeared at first glance to be peculiar and irrational human conduct like the ascetic ideal, for example. However, if every event is done for the sake of power then every desire, no matter how nuanced, becomes flattened to mere domination. Second, if this position is correct, then it seems silly to think that any other desire would have developed independently from our desire of power. How would the desire for riches or sex evolve if every action is taken to have power over someone or something?[3]

Clark suggests that the best way to maneuver Nietzsche out of this morass is to concentrate on the writings that Nietzsche saw fit to publish while alive. In particular, she holds that Nietzscheans would do well to focus on *Beyond Good and Evil* since, "It not only contains the first articulation of the doctrine of will to power in Nietzsche's voice (an allusion to Zarathustra), but its first two parts contain four relatively detailed sections that provide a more sustained reflection on the doctrine than we find in any of Nietzsche's other books."[4] Specifically, Clark thinks that sections 9, 22, 23, and 36 are of central importance.

Clark centers most of the proceeding discussion on section 36 which presents the most extended discussion on WTP in *Beyond Good and Evil*. What Clark finds most interesting about this section is Nietzsche's very denial of the notion of will to power. I now quote the passage at length:

> Suppose nothing else were "given" as real except our world of desires and passions, and we could not get down, or up, to any other "reality" besides the reality of our drives . . . is it not permitted to make the experiment and to ask the question whether this "given" would not be sufficient for also understanding on the basis of this kind of thing the so-called mechanistic (or "material") world? . . . Suppose, finally, we succeeded in explaining our entire instinctive life as the development and ramification of one basic form of the will—namely, of the will to power, as my proposition has it; suppose all organic functions could be traced back to this will to power . . . then one would have gained the right to determine all efficient force univocally as will to power.[5]

Clark asks the reader to recognize, first, the form in which the argument is put. She claims that the argument is hypothetical in nature—"Suppose nothing is given except our desires and passions." From here, Clark explains that the argument has two premises

1. That only the world of our desires and passions is given as real, and that we cannot get up or down to any other reality than that of our drives;
2. That will is a causal power.

Therefore: Then all effective force univocally is will to power.

Clark interprets the entire passage as an elaborate *reductio ad absurdum*. Nietzsche denies that all effective force is in fact will to power. In short, the will to power is false. However, from this denial, Nietzsche, interestingly, does not believe that the idea should be thrown out into the dustbin of philosophy. Rather, Nietzsche wishes that the notion was true and philosophized as such.

Clark proceeds to outline the reasons as to why Nietzsche would think that the first premise is false. She argues that Nietzsche could not accept the first premise because it would commit him to a Cartesian position and Nietzsche, as is well known, rejects the entire notion of immediate certainties—the idea that certain beliefs are self-justifying.[6] Descartes held that the *Cogito*, short for *Cogito ergo sum*, was one such certainty. As Descartes explains, "whenever the statement, I am, I exist, is asserted or thought it is clearly and distinctly perceived to be true."[7] So too, Clark claims, Nietzsche would have to offer a similar argument with desires or drives playing the role Descartes gave to clear and distinct ideas. Clark writes: "He would have to claim, much as Schopenhauer did, that the fact that 'I will' (effectively desire) is directly present to me, it is thus 'given' or immediately certain. . . ."[8] However, since Nietzsche clearly rejects immediate certainties in the very sections leading up to section 36, then Nietzsche must deny this premise.[9]

Clark's argument for the rejection of the first premise, however, is problematic for several reasons. First, Clark conflates will with desire, but it does not seem obvious that these are the same feelings. To will something appears to presuppose agency. A dog does not will to go on a walk nor to play with a bone, but it can desire. Nor is it appropriate to call these desires needs or instincts. Playing with a favorite squeaky toy is hardly instinctual, and it is not necessary for survival, unlike food and water. However, the desire to play with *this* toy and not *that* one can present itself as an overwhelming desire in the dog as all dog owners are only too painfully aware. However, to will something does seem to be agent-directed. To state: "I will X" presupposes that I am aware of not only the object of my desire but that I am the causal agent responsible for getting what I desire. Such a thought seems to possess an agential charge. It is not always true of desire.

Thus desire or *Bergierde,* the German word that Nietzsche usually uses in the *Beyond Good and Evil,* may very well be immediate, but not necessarily certain. Clark makes yet another conflation. Certainty does not apply here because certainty is a normative, justificatory term. We state, "I know this with certainty" when we have gone through all the possible doubts and scenarios we can think of that would present epistemic defeaters for the belief in question. Desire, however, is irreducible. We need no justification to determine that we are in a state of desire. We just desire. A particular desire may require justification to be fulfilled, but that is another matter. So the first premise to my mind still holds.

Clark's second argument for rejecting the first premise conflates, once again, will with desire but in a different way. She uses section 19 of *Beyond Good and Evil* to buttress her claim: "Philosophers (like Schopenhauer) are accustomed to speak of the will as if it were the best-known thing in the world when clearly Nietzsche rejects this position."[10] To be sure, Nietzsche would agree that we know little about the will. It is often the case that I am not acutely aware of why I will what I do. Also, it is unclear how the capacity we call "willpower" works, or even exists at all. So it is true that Nietzsche, unlike Schopenhauer, thinks that the will is mysterious and is not the best-known thing in the world. However, this is because the will is infused with agential direction. There are times when we may not possess the necessary willpower, for example, to resist a piece of cake that is offered to us. On these occasions we may further feel a conflict between what we desire, namely, the piece of cake, and what we reason to be the best course of action all things considered, namely, cutting back on carbohydrates and fat. In some cases, our will wins out, and we can resist temptation, but in other circumstances, we are not so lucky—under these conditions, we feel as though a battle has been lost between our will and desire. Here is yet another reason why desire and will are not the same: It is possible for our will and desire to be aligned in one smooth action, but at other times our desires run counter to our will. Indeed, our very desires appear to have such an inexorable alien power over us at times, that when we finally yield to such desires, we experience agent alienation.[11]

Clark's argument against the second premise is powerful. In many places, Nietzsche argues that the will does not exist *simpliciter*. It is not causally efficacious. Clark quotes several passages from Nietzsche's *oeuvre* to substantiate her claim so I will not repeat all of them here but I think it is important to examine a representative passage from *Twilight:* "Today we no longer believe a word of all this. The 'inner world' is full of phantoms and will-o'-the-wisps: the will is one of them. The will no longer moves anything, hence does not explain anything either—it merely accompanies events; it can also be absent."[12] From this textual evidence Clark concludes that the ultimate causes of our actions are not the conscious thoughts and feelings with which Nietzsche claims we identify the will.[13]

The problem with this argument is twofold. First, clearly, if the will is not causally efficacious then it becomes reasonable to ask: "What, then, is the purpose of Nietzsche's moral philosophy?" Surely Nietzsche wants to show how we may go about living better lives. While it is true that Nietzsche seems to argue virulently, that not all individuals are capable of changing their behavior, clearly some are. As Nietzsche states in section 290 of *The Gay Science*: "To give style to one's character—a great and rare art! He exercises it who surveys all that his nature presents in strength and weakness and then moulds it into an artistic plan until everything appears as art and reason, and even weaknesses delight the eye."[14] These are clearly normative aims, and Nietzsche believes that by reading his books that we can become better persons even if such betterment results in further suffering and unhappiness. Nietzsche further counsels in the same section that those who fail to shape their character will never be able to give pleasure to themselves and, as a result, are "continually ready for revenge."[15] However, if Clark's interpretation of the will is correct, then Nietzsche's entire moral project is irretrievably incoherent.

Second, both Nietzsche and Clark are guilty of conflating will with feeling and affect. Will is a nineteenth-century term that does little to clarify the engine behind conscious action. It has already been shown that Clark muddles her argument by employing such language. The real non-physiological engine behind conscious action, if there is such an engine, would have to be an intention. It is our intentions that give us the impetus to make some, if not all, choices. Of course, some actions are made unconsciously, but others do seem to rest on our ability to make a conscious choice. Certainly, we do seem to be able to resist some unyielding impulses at times like eating a piece of cake that is offered to us.[16]

Now as Nietzsche rightfully mentions, we have no control over "the hundredfold processes" that are responsible for the intention that bubbles up to conscious thought: "I will not have that last piece of cake."[17] From this passage, it would appear that Nietzsche seems to hold a type identity theory of mind. Mental intentions are identical to a specific brain state. Intentions, at best, have no causal power. They are simply properties which may be reducible to a peculiar electro-magnetic-chemical state of the brain.

Certainly, present-day psychologists seem to have verified Nietzsche's nineteenth-century contention. Daniel Wegner, in his book *The Illusion of Conscious Will,* holds that mental intentions do not have any causal impact on human behavior. Intentions are not active, but reactive. They are analogous to gauges. Just as a gauge is an indication of what is happening in a drive system of a car, so too a feeling of willing which follows from some action is nothing more than an indicator; it has no causal impact because it is nothing more than a reaction of a more primordial system. Moreover, as a reaction, as a response, it cannot have any causal effect on the system which produces it.[18]

The problem with this analysis is manifold. First, let us return to the type identity theory of mind/brain interaction. One stripe of this theory holds that all mind is ontologically dependent on a human brain and that all of the furniture of the mind-like beliefs, desires, and intentions are nothing more than reflections of a human brain state. However, if this position were true, then it would be impossible for non-humans to have intentions. However, this is clearly false: It is an easy bit of business to imagine a possible world where there are intentional agents who are not humans. The above thought experiment sometimes referred to as the "Multiple Realization Argument (MRA)" would show that one cannot reduce human brain states to mental states since it is conceptually possible for non-humans to have the same mental states that we, as humans, possess.[19] Indeed it has been argued that some of the higher apes, like chimpanzees, not only possess sentience or self-awareness but may understand what it means to will some actions.[20] They can have a primitive notion of intention. Thus human neurological brain states cannot be identical to intentions.

Second, even if we remain within the purely human realm of experience, both Wegner and Nietzsche it seems, have each failed to make a critical distinction between proximal and distal intentions. It may be true that a brain state comes before the conscious awareness of a proximal intention and therefore the proximal intention is nothing more than *that* brain state. However, such a reduction would not hold for distal intentions. To see this, recall the last piece of cake scenario. Imagine Judy holds a resolution such that she will only eat one piece of cake at dessert. At anytime she is offered a second piece, she refuses it. Given this circumstance, it would seem prudent to think that it is the resolution: "I will only have one piece of cake after a meal" which is causally responsible for determining Judy's action and not Judy's brain state. Why must this be so? Because it seems very unlikely that we can identify this distal intention, namely the resolution, with a constant and persistent brain state. Further evidence for this position is all around us: We need only look to those individuals we call "strong-willed." Many people whom we might call strong willed have held the same resolutions for decades and yet the brain states of these individuals have obviously undergone tremendous changes from year to year and from decade to decade.

Thirdly, the actual problem with this line of thinking lies in cleaving to the very paradigm of thought itself. Alfred Mele's penetrating questions and criticisms of Wegner and others who claim that current neuroscience casts doubt on the efficacy of intentional actions are enormously incisive once digested. Paraphrasing Mele, we might ask: "When we argue that an intention is nothing more than a pre-conscious brain state, what actually is being ascribed here?" Mele's answer, in brief, is that the very question reveals a strange crudity in that we are still clinging to an old, antiquated notion, namely, thought itself. To believe that we humans think in thoughts is to fail to take the linguistic turn. To claim that we are thinking animals is to employ an abstraction, namely, thought. Rather, some philosophers would suggest that we are language-using animals, and therefore we must take a linguistic position to understand fully how we employ language and for what purposes. With this in mind to reduce a brain state to a thought is inaccurate from the get-go. Rather the target reduction is not a thought at all. It is, rather, a speech act.[21]

So does Nietzsche believe in the will to power and if so why? According to Clark, Nietzsche does believe in the will to power, but not for any definable reasons. Indeed, as Clark thinks she has shown if Nietzsche did, in fact, believe in the will to power for the reasons he presented in section 36 of *Beyond Good and Evil*, then he would be a terrible philosopher indeed. Instead, Nietzsche believes in the doctrine for no good reason at all other than that he would like to think that the world works this way. Clark explains that Nietzsche is simply consistent with a genuine nature of philosophy which, Nietzsche thinks, is the desire to reinterpret the workings of the world according to how it would like the world to work.

Clark interprets the famous line of *Beyond Good and Evil* section 22 which states, "Supposing that this too is only interpretation (Will to power)—and you will be eager enough to make this objection?—well, so much the better!"[22] as a confession. The very doctrine of will to power, Clark contends, "is a reading of Nietzsche's values into nature, that he, therefore, does not regard it as any truer than the idea that nature conforms to law, but that this is fine with him since he thereby remains consistent with everything he has said about knowledge and philosophy."[23] Clark further contends that " . . . his doctrine of the will to power is a construction of the world from the viewpoint of his moral values."[24]

To conclude this discussion on Clark, it seems that the entire problem with her argument is the enormous weight she gives to the assumption that if the will to power is conceived by Nietzsche to be an explanation for everything, then this entails that all meaning and values are vacuous. Such a theory that explains everything ends up explaining nothing, so Clark argues. However, I do not see how that is the case. Clark contends that if all unconscious and conscious actions and drives are mere vehicles for the attainment of power, then a true explanation for these drives and actions has not been tendered. However, if we acknowledge that power works on numerous battlefields, then it is clear that the illuminating effects of a power analysis remain.

4.2 JOHN RICHARDSON: DEFLATING THE WILL TO POWER

In an earlier work entitled *Nietzsche's System*, Richardson showed how will to power was foundational both metaphysically and epistemically for Nietzsche's philosophy.[25] Richardson still holds to this interpretation, as a philological matter of course, but now wants to provide a more defensible reconstruction of Nietzsche's position from the point of view of the empirical sciences. Such a reconstruction is necessary, according to Richardson, for two principal reasons: (1) Will to power is an embarrassing naturalistic position to hold because there is one element of this theory that is terribly non-natural, namely, its reliance on mental properties. Will to power is a species of mentalism because it ascribes full-blown mental attributes (such as agency) to nature itself.[26] (2) Will to power is not very likely to be true. Since will to power is the ultimate narrative to explain the inner workings of the universe, it is very likely to find a thing or process that cannot be explained *via* will to power and therefore such an entity or phenomenon would serve to falsify it.[27] As a consequence, Richardson goes about defending the "recessive view" of will to power which holds that will to power is not a power ontology in that it may be used to explain all things in the universe from quails to quarks, but is simply a power biology. Will to power is a narrative that, when coupled with Neo-Darwinism, can lead to new, profound, and testable hypotheses.[28]

Richardson concentrates his analysis on those things which are responsible for valuation. In keeping with Richardson's anti-mentalism approach, he, therefore, focuses on analyzing physical drives. Richardson wants to show how we can go about naturalizing will to power by demonstrating how the drives within our body are directed toward some end. Furthermore, Richardson seeks to put forward a coherent position that is non-cognitive since Nietzsche's thoroughgoing naturalist position rejects cognitive, epistemic positions on many occasions.[29] So a drive-end must reveal how everything in the drive is a culmination of this end while also showing that the seeds of the end were not already contained in the drive.[30] It is a rather difficult challenge, but Richardson thinks that Darwin may be of assistance to Nietzsche with this task. For Darwin, too, deflates the importance of the human being by showing that the human species is not some natural kind of thing but a process, a form that has a long history and one which might eventually have an end.

However, before Richardson can preside as minister over this marriage, he must make the groom (Darwin) more appealing to the bride (Nietzsche). Richardson's first task in this regard is to show that Nietzsche's reading of Darwin is terribly off base. First and foremost, Nietzsche misreads survival. Survival is not that which is "selected for." It is rather the reproduction of offspring that is selected for. Reproductive fitness is the contemporary term now employed by most Neo-Darwinists when discussing selective processes. This term applies not just to the reproduction of offspring regarding the sheer number of offspring produced by a species, but also to viability, longevity, etc.

However, by far the biggest problem with Nietzsche's reading of Darwinism concerns his reading into Darwin or perhaps more accurately Darwin's spin doctors, the notion of an end or *telos*. Under Nietzsche's reading of Darwin, natural selection has been working toward the end we currently observe, namely, the flourishing of a liberal, democratic civilization. Intention, progress, freedom, sexual desire, self-preservation, etc. are concepts that are already infused in the very notion of evolution or so Nietzsche's reading of Darwin assumes. Nietzsche writes on this point: "There is no such thing as the 'instinct of self-preservation' the search for that which is pleasurable. The avoidance of that which is unpleasurable, explains everything necessary about the drive. . . . There is no instinct to preserve oneself through the species. That's all mythology. . . . Sexual lust has nothing to do with the procreation of the species!"[31] This explanation is, of course, a grave misinterpretation of Darwin. However, it is from this misconstrual that leads Nietzsche to postulate his end for the human being which is equally infused with agency. It also leads Nietzsche to postulate a consciously rich biological theory which serves to explain how this goal may be understood and brought about, that is will to power. Richardson writes in this regard: "Here too Nietzsche appears to anthropomorphize life, by attributing a certain intentional and representational content to it, and using this content to explain what organisms do. Indeed, he readily attributes 'perspectives' to all of these drives. So despite his attacks on our mental model, it is hard not to suspect that he falls back on it in thinking of wills and drives."[32]

Richardson's critical conclusion, as seen above, may not seem obvious at first glance, but it becomes clearer as we cash it in. For some process to work toward some end or be goal directed in any fashion, there must be something within the process that intuitively directs the process to the end. Richardson calls this intuitive directness "pre-giveness." This notion of "pre-givenness" however, is equated by Richardson as a mental disposition that can "see" its way to some destination. The drive already has, no matter how obscure it might be, a representation of the desired result. Drives with ends must already possess a representation of what the drive is intended to direct. However, such a position, Richardson avers, allows the end to explain the causal behavior of the drive. All this is too easy.

After a rather belabored analysis of functionality, Richardson develops his own "towardness" of will to power that seeks to work its way out of the drive-end quagmire discovered above. He writes, "Will to power is a disposition to cause a certain result, that is power" and further that past—actions of some organism (such as an amoeba eating and growing)—caused (produced) this disposition.[33]

However, how can dispositions be produced without a pre-given end? Richardson answers this question by examining Nietzsche's notion of breeding. Despite being a central concept for Nietzsche, breeding, Richardson declares, has been widely misunderstood and insufficiently scrutinized in the secondary literature. Nietzsche employs the idea in several distinct ways. Nietzsche recognizes that breeding, either by humans or by some other force, redirects a developmental process already at work in nature toward new ends. Perhaps the best example of this is something Nietzsche calls the "bad conscience." The bad conscience was produced as a result of those great warrior-artists who created the first walled towns. When these early rulers then decreed laws with punishments for those who broke them, the bad conscience was born. The drive for mastery, freedom, cruelty Nietzsche claims, turned inward against these early proto-human creatures because they would now be punished if they acted on these drives. However, the drives do not disappear; they simply found new channels of expression. "That will to self-tormenting," Nietzsche avows, "that repressed cruelty of the animal-man made inward and scared back into himself, the creature imprisoned in the "state" so as to be tamed, who invented the bad conscience in order to hurt himself after the more natural vent for his desire to hurt had been blocked."[34] The bad conscience is the name given for the fear and anxiety that would be produced in these creatures if they disobeyed the laws of the state.[35] The point in mentioning this example, however, is to show that such warrior-artists did not act so as to create the bad conscience, a distant forbearer of guilt. Their desires were healthy, at least according to Nietzsche. They simply wanted to assert their power.[36] New and powerful feelings and thoughts can come into existence without intention. Drives are bred without a clear direction. Under Richardson's interpretation, drives remain the basic engine of lineage for Nietzsche, but these drives can be exapted for different purposes. Thus drives can retain an end, but this end need not be conscious; nor is the end non-revisable.

What then is the relation between the will to power and selection? According to Richardson there are two possibilities:

1. He (Nietzsche) offers will to power as a life-will that is, explanatorily, fully basic and prior in particular to natural selection;
2. He offers will to power as a product of natural selection and uses selection to explain (why or how there are) these wills.[37]

Likewise, there are two ways we can apply these insights to Nietzsche. First, as competing hypotheses about his one real position or second, as coexisting aspects or moments of his position, as layers or levels within it.[38]

Richardson argues against the first view by averring that such a position would entail a form of mentalism. Will to power cannot run counter to natural selection for two reasons. First, if we are to reconstruct will to power as a naturalistic doctrine, then it would be ludicrous to throw out the most warranted and fruitful biological theory we have, namely, natural selection, which explains the inner wellsprings of nature quite well. Natural selection both explains why organisms change but is also consilient with genetics; the "how" of fitness, whether direct or indirect is entirely explainable in terms of gene mutation and replication. Second, if we are to keep a naturalistic position, then we must start with the most basic level of understanding, namely, the physical and work our way to explain the mental. Nietzsche, however, starts with the mental and then proceeds to extrapolate and project mental attributes onto nature when none need be present.

Richardson, therefore, argues for the second view and proceeds to develop two possible alternatives. Selection is, in a particular way, for power; but in what way? Richardson outlines two possibilities: "(1) a function or goal shared by some or many selected drives or (2) a higher-level structural end of selection itself, which somehow squeezes in alongside or under Darwinian survival."[39] The problem with the second, of course, is that it would appear that we are back to a metaphysical understanding of will to power. Will to power would be a *telos*, an end of natural selection and *voila* a new mentalism is born. Accordingly, Richardson will argue for the first position.

How does Richardson understand this reinterpretation of Nietzschean selection? Richardson writes, "In better moments he treats drives as designed by selection. They are so designed simply *qua* drives, in that organisms are crucially rendered fit by being equipped with plastic dispositions (drives) physical set ups with causal tendencies that are plastic toward certain ends."[40] Plasticity is an important aspect of natural selection theory. Since genes and, indeed, entire biological structures can be co-opted or exapted by natural selection, Richardson argues that drives too, if they are to be explained *via* natural selection models, must also be capable of this exaptation. Perhaps the best analog to this process of drive plasticity is the phenomenon of convergent evolution. Convergent evolution is a process where organisms develop the same biological characteristics even though their ancestors are only distantly related. An obvious example of such a process is the evolution of the eye. Birds are not directly linked to mammals in regard to their phylogeny, but they too have developed a keen sense of sight independently of mammals.[41]

Richardson sums up this view by noting: "The drives that have best served reproductive success and that dominate drive economy of most organisms are drives whose goals involve some control, either over other organisms, or over other drives in the same organism. It's not really the pleasure of the outcome, but the power or control it takes, that shows us what selection actually favors in drives."[42]

One of the problems with Richardson's views is his overly bombastic and mistaken criticism of what he calls "mentalism." Richardson is of the opinion that any drive which takes a goal for itself represents the goal before itself in some manner, and therefore that drive must, minimally, possess some sort of primitive consciousness. Richardson instead holds that will to power is selected for as a drive much as a gene might also be selected for because of its phenotypical trait. The problem with this view is that genes do not become conscious. However, in this case, the drive, namely, will to power, does, in fact, become aware of its end. The drive, it would seem, then, becomes conscious of what it is driving toward. Striving for power for the sake of power is a drive that many humans fall victim to. So either there is something terribly wrong with the analogy or we must accept some form of mentalism. Even this conclusion, however, is a false disjunctive because there is a third alternative: Nietzsche is claiming that once we become self-conscious of this, the power drive, it is no longer possible to view other drives like sex, fame, wealth, etc. without also imputing an end desire to them as well. That is, without imputing some type of "pre-givenness." It is this view which I develop. I demonstrate in chapter seven that once the capacity of character reflection comes onto the natural scene as it were it becomes impossible to reduce it to any simpler function.

The second problem with Richardson's approach is that he adopts a passive reading of selection. Selection acts as a sieve: Genes and their expressions are the true engines of change in the world. All selection does is to promote those genes which may proliferate in an environment. However, selection may also work in a top-down fashion. As Neil Campbell has noted, environmental pressures can cause certain genes to turn on and off. The base pairs of DNA are then adapted within the organism according to the ecological niche. The environment can direct the process of gene replication in a "top-down" fashion. It is, for this reason, biologists are becoming increasingly interested in the phenomenon of "co-emergent evolution."[43] This fact, may, upon first reading, appear to be consistent with Richardson's aversion to relying on "the mental" to explain natural events and animal behavior. Animals, Richardson might declare, are not determined by ends where there is a clear representation of the end in mind (although this point is very clearly debatable), but by instinct. Thus, even if co-emergent evolution is true this simply shows once again that we need not require the representation of an end to make sense of the so-called "goal" of a drive. Drives may alter and indeed become transformed as a result of where they are expressed: Some environments will cause some drives to be expressed but not others. Here too, the mental is not needed. Far from undermining Richardson's thesis, co-emergent evolution acts a further buttress of support.

The above point, if it is accepted—and pressed further—serves as a hidden acid corroding Richardson's position from the inside. For one thing, the position is no longer as self-contained as perhaps Richardson would like it to be. Richardson wants to preserve the uni-directionality of will to power. However, if we accept a multidirectional account of natural selection then will to power loses much of its force. Whither will to power? Natural selection along with physical geography serve to both describe and explain the emergence, growth, and flourishing of organic species and inorganic matter alike. However, even physical geography, so argues the emergent evolutionist, can change depending on the dynamics of an ecosystem.

For an example of how the organisms of an ecosystem can change the very physical geography of the environment they inhabit, consider the phenomenon called "trophic cascade effects." Trophic cascade effects occur when a predatory apex group is reintroduced into an environmental niche producing a significant change in the ecosystem by altering the behavior of other creatures that share the same ecosystem, who then modify the behavior of others and so on.[44] The effect of such a reintroduction is immediate and felt by all organisms within the ecosystem. One provocative and intriguing case of such a reintroduction was the repopulation of wolves in Yellowstone National Park begun in 1995. Since 1925 wolves were simply non-existent in Yellowstone: They were actively hunted, both in and around the park for decades.

The argument for their total extirpation rested on the ground that wolves were dangerous predators that would harm park visitors and nearby livestock on farms bordering the park. The initial purpose of reintroducing wolves was to check the white-tail deer and elk populations of the park. In the absence of wolves, the deer and elk population had vastly increased and, despite efforts to curb their populations, nothing seemed to work. Reintroducing wolves would help to curtail the growth of these populations in a completely natural way. However, another issue at play was the significant loss of many of the indigenous grasslands of the park. The deer and elk populations had grazed so much of the vegetation that vast areas of the park, but especially its valleys, were now barren of vegetation.

However, once the wolves were reintroduced, though few, they immediately changed the behavior of the deer and elk. Both groups of herbivores began to feed in safer areas of the park that offered better protection for their young fawns and calves. Moreover, as this occurred, the vegetation and in general reforestation of the park began to take place. The "greening" of the park led to the proliferation of many smaller indigenous inhabitants, such as songbirds, rabbits, and beavers, species that were thought to be nearly extinct in the park.

So far so good we might claim: The ecologists who reintroduced wolves to Yellowstone anticipated these developments. However, there were some developments that no one expected: The wolves changed the very nature of Yellowstone's river banks. The extirpation of wolves from Yellowstone in 1925 meant that the park's rivers increased in hydraulic capacity—because elk and deer, no longer had a natural predator, they freely ate all of the riparian vegetation along the borders of the rivers of Yellowstone.[45] However, riparian vegetation acts as a natural buffer against soil erosion and helps to maintain rigid river channels. With the loss of this particular kind of vegetation, rivers became increasingly wider and deeper. When the wolves were reintroduced, they changed the behavior of elk immediately such that the elk no longer ate along river banks. Within six years, the rivers of Yellowstone became more inelastic and returned to their traditional narrower channels because much of the riparian vegetation, but especially cottonwood had regrown: all on account of the reintroduction of a few dozen wolves.

What this example underscores is, that, while natural selection may be part of the causal story concerning explaining the evolution of species and alteration of an ecosystem it cannot be the entire causal story. Physical geography also plays a role in explaining the results of reintroducing wolves into Yellowstone Park. However, even physical geography cannot explain the impetus to remove nor reintroduce the wolves. Only a narrative which explains the psychological and all too human reasons as to why wolves were first evaluated as a problem and then reevaluated as a solution, can tie together all these accounts. Human beings can no longer be separated from these ecological studies because it is we humans who have had a significant causal impact on every ecological niche. Only by translating man into nature and nature back into man do we have any hope of understanding the world; this is the key to naturalizing will to power.

4.3 LINDA WILLIAMS: WILL TO POWER AS MIRROR

The third reading of the will to power is one given by Williams. In her book, *Nietzsche's Mirror: World as Will to Power* she argues that will to power's true importance stems from the incisive and insightful powers it gives to the one reflecting upon it. Will to power, Williams avows, is "Nietzsche's lens through which he interprets the world—his shorthand way of suggesting that experience be viewed as differing struggles for superiority between humans."[46] Such interpersonal struggles are best interpreted as struggles between different representative forces: for example, slaves versus masters. Following Deleuze, Williams makes a distinction between two different kinds of will to power. The first she calls positive, active, and forward-looking while the second she classifies as reactive and negative.[47] This interpretation is largely founded on the distinction Nietzsche makes in the first essay of *On the Genealogy of Morals*. There, Nietzsche compares the values of the master type and the slave type by using the analogy of birds of prey and sheep. Birds of prey act out of instinct—they pursue their natural drives—these drives are considered good in themselves. There is no separation between desire and "the Good"—what is desired is that which is Good and that which is Good is that which is desired.[48] More to the point we might say that the hawk's latent instincts are beyond good and evil. The purpose of Nietzsche's genealogical investigation is to jettison any lingering normative questions that might remain once he offers his redescription as to the actual origin of morality. The lambs, on the other hand, do not have values of their own. Their values stem from an interpretation of hawk values. What is "good" for the lambs is not to be eaten by hawks and what is bad for lambs is when they are not protected and are easily eaten. The lambs reinterpret what is "bad" for the hawks as "evil."

In a similar manner, the analogy suggests that moral values, or what Brian Leiter calls MPS (Morality in a Pejorative Sense) are nothing more than negative, reactive reinterpretations of active, noble values. For example, the commandment, "Thou Shalt not Steal" is a reaction to a prior act, namely, that of stealing. As a commandment, it is a condemnation of the act stealing which is instinctual and, therefore, the act cannot ground itself—it is parasitic on more primordial evaluations.

To be sure there is much to be said for this interpretation, but there are obviously many problems with this account. I do not wish to expose the naiveté and simplicity of Nietzsche's analogical reasoning, provided here in the first essay of *The Genealogy* because the account is itself a genealogical first rendering, as it were, and is therefore not his final analysis on the subject. In any case, the upshot of Williams' approach is that one may use the idea of the will to power and more specifically the knowledge of eternal recurrence, as a mirror to understand the self: that is, either as a positive and life-affirming individual or as someone negative and reactive. This interpretation of will to power Williams calls the "mirror thesis" and I will use this terminology as a shorthand for discussing her overall position on the will to power.

The mirror thesis puts forward two ideas: First, by that by simply reflecting on the will to power, one can get a better understanding of oneself. More specifically, Williams counsels that one can use will to power as a lens through which to view what one is feeling. One reflects on either the truth status of will to power or eternal recurrence to produce, what, for Williams will be, a curative effect. To think about the truth status of will to power entails, minimally, that will to power is true. This reflection entails two stages according to Williams: First, one must come to understand the hard "truth": that all truths are simply expressions of valuation and therefore of power. Facts are value-laden; it is, therefore, impossible and indeed incoherent to describe the world or even oneself objectively where objective here is understood as taking an aperspectival stance as regards reality.[49]

Second, this reflection and acceptance of what is, presumably, a hard, primordial truth then awakens many and hitherto dormant feelings in the individual regarding how one feels about the value-ladenness of truth as such. Such an idea may be either freeing or enslaving, depending on one's psychic constitution. Reflecting on how one feels about the will to power reflects one's true character, according to Williams.[50]

Reflecting on eternal recurrence, however, is perhaps a more powerful and potent excavator for such feelings. Williams believes that eternal recurrence is perhaps the best means of unearthing both positive and negative aspects of will to power. Eternal recurrence is best expressed in section 341 of *The Gay Science* where Nietzsche writes:

> How, if some day or night a demon were to sneak after you into your loneliest loneliness and say to you, "This life as you now live it and have lived it, you will have to live once more and innumerable times more; and there will be nothing new in it, but every pain and every joy and every thought and sigh and everything immeasurably small or great in your life must return to you—all in the same succession and sequence—even this spider and this moonlight between the trees, and even this moment and I myself. The eternal hourglass of existence

is turned over and over, and you with it, a dust grain of dust." *Would you not throw yourself down and gnash your teeth and curse the demon who spoke thus? Or did you once experience a tremendous moment when you would have answered him, "You are a god, and never have I heard anything more godly."* (Emphasis mine)[51]

According to Williams, entertaining the mere idea of eternal return causes one to release powerful feelings which give rise to further reflection. If one gnashes his teeth at the very thought of the idea that one's life has been lived countless times in the past exactly as it is now and will be relived countless times in the future without such much as one iota of difference—then one's will to power is expressed negatively. One is much like the slave types described above. If on the other hand, one cherishes the idea then one is clearly expressing the positive valence of will to power.

Contained within this concept of the mirror thesis are two ideas: a descriptive claim and a normative claim. First, using either the first or second method presupposes the truth of will to power. Eternal return is a test to determine what I shall call one's "will to power expression valence" (i.e., whether positive or negative) but for the test to be meaningful one must believe that the type of will to power expressed is truly a mirror for what one is feeling. Thus at least two of Nietzsche's most controversial ideas must be held true by the individual who takes the mirror test seriously: will to power and eternal return. Williams, in a rather protracted study of eternal recurrence recognizes the logic of the above sentence but goes to great lengths to deny the Truth of will to power. According to Williams, will to power is ultimately justified in aesthetic terms. This ground for the will to power poses significant problems as will be shown below.

There is a second clandestine normative claim advanced by Williams in advocating one to undertake this "test": Once one's will to power is expressed one should act on this information. One should strive to express her or his power in more positive ways. I now wish to examine each claim in more detail below.

Turning to the descriptive claim, it is incumbent on Williams to explain both how the process of mirror therapy works and how efficacious it is. To summarize, if the individual feels disempowered, fearful, anxious, etc. upon thinking about the will to power, then these feelings reflect the nature of the person's sense of self. One can then use this reflection to realize that such views of oneself are not life-enhancing, but clearly life-denying and then use this further realization to change one's behavior. Therefore, the true purpose and value of will to power, at least according to Williams', is at best pragmatic: The will to power is a self-therapeutic technique each of us may put to use to manage the self better. The ultimate foundation for the efficacy and adoption of will to power, according to Williams, is aesthetic: One may use will to power as a way of refashioning the self to live, presumably, a more positive, life-affirming existence.[52] Williams is not unique in this regard—there have been many defenders of the aesthetic will to power position.[53] What is exceptional to Williams' thesis, however, is her understanding of the multifaceted epistemic and metaphysical problems associated with developing this idea. I will not explore all of the issues concerning Williams' construal for there are many. Instead, I will focus on the causal, metaphysical, and epistemic problems with her account.

4.3.1 Causal Problems with Williams' Account

The main casual problem with Williams' therapeutic techniques has to do with the twofold stage of the mirror theory itself. The first stage requires that the reader believe in the "hard truth" of will to power. The belief in this truth causes a process of what one might call belief falsification to occur: The individual is confronted with the disturbing and unnerving idea that all of her beliefs whether conscious, tacit or otherwise, are inflections of power. The individual is then forced to entertain the notion, perhaps for the first time, that all of her beliefs are unjustified. Will to power provokes one to engage in such reflection and thereby causes one to reevaluate one's most deeply held, cherished beliefs.

After this initial stage of belief falsification, there is the second stage of reflection which I call the "mirror therapy stage." During this juncture, readers use Nietzsche's ideas as self-reflecting mirrors: By thinking about how we feel about the will to power, we get a better sense of who we are as persons, that is, whether we are reactive and negative or positive and active. Such an acute perception of ourselves, facilitated by will to power, may force us to change our behavior for the better.

The overall problem with this technique, however, has to with the relationship between the two stage processes of the mirror theory itself: the belief falsification stage and the reflective stage. If we now turn to the belief falsification stage of will to power, it is implied that Nietzsche's accounts of truth, his genealogy of ethics, his critique of metaphysics, etc. are capable of undermining well-justified, deeply embedded beliefs held by the reader. For example, most educated persons might believe various scientific "truths": natural selection, quantum theory, etc. Such theories are taken to be True: The statements which make up the model correspond to how the world works, independently of some perspective. Presumably, then, any claim which is inconsistent with these theories is false. Reflecting on these truths, however, through the lens of will to power, Williams avers, can be quite revealing and disturbing for the will to power causes one to reevaluate the objective (here understood as aperspectival) pedigree of the sciences. The sciences are not absolutely True. Williams clarifies and defends this position when she writes the following: "Nietzsche's stance as I read him is not to eliminate the scientific perspective but rather, to remind it that it is perspectival we should recognize that such truths are mistaken insofar as they put forward an aperspectival view."[54] There are several ways to interpret the above statement, but all of the main contenders are deeply problematic. First, I would like to examine robust and weaker interpretations of the claim. The problem with a full-bodied interpretation of the above quotation by Williams is that to receive science in this way is to deny the scientific perspective entirely. The consequences of denying the scientific perspective are disastrous for William's interpretation of will to power. Will to power is either inconsistent with the scientific perspective or is justifiable provided that we hold a metaphysical position of will to power. To see this, consider the first disjunct: Science is only one such perspective on reality; other equally legitimate views of reality are possible. This interpretation is clearly false even from the scientific standpoint. For to hold a scientific perspective is simply to hold the view that science is the only justified view to have on some topics; other views on the same subject matter are simply mistaken. Although to be sure there are tensions within each respective scientific field and not all scientists within the same area of study agree, questions about laws of nature in the three traditional fields of scientific inquiry: Physics, chemistry, and biology, are investigated within each respective science. From the scientific perspective, these are the only justified views within these fields and indeed the only legitimate views on these topics outside of them. Under one reading, reminding scientists that their perspectives are not aperspectival they are, too, just perspectives, is tantamount to saying that other perspectives on the same issues scientists traditionally investigate are equally valid. This claim is both false and one that Nietzsche rejects in many places.[55]

Under another reading, one may hold that scientific perspectives are not aperspectival because all views are shot through with power. All positions are products of will to power. This interpretation leads to two, distinct sub-interpretations. The first is a robust claim: The will to power is the only perspective through which to view the world, and this point of view says that all perspectives are willful interpretations of reality. This thesis is a metaphysical view and is one that as I will show below, Williams must ultimately adopt to render her position consistent. Unfortunately, however, Williams rejects this metaphysical construal of will to power.

I now turn to the alternative interpretation. To interpret will to power, under this framework, to understand it as that theory which simply reminds us that all investigation is agenda driven, is to embrace a much-weakened iteration of will to power. However, if the will to power simply means that any investigation is interest driven, then there is no justification for Williams' rather radical interpretation. Will to power would be a rather banal claim—for what investigation whose goal is to arrive at truth not agenda driven?

4.3.2 Williams' Position on Self as Viewed through the Mirror

The second problem with Williams' approach has to do with her notion of self. The purpose of the mirror theory is to use will to power as a therapeutic device: One subjects oneself to the test of will to power or eternal return to see how one feels about these ideas. One then scrutinizes such feelings to determine whether one is life-affirming or life-denying. Williams neither reveals nor investigates the constitutional qualities of self that make such reflection possible. Perhaps equally troubling, Williams does not disclose the inner wellsprings of action that allow the self to modify its behavior. In point of fact, the self that Williams articulates and defends is anathema to the expressivist idea of self that Nietzsche argues for in many passages within his *oeuvre*.

Williams implicitly holds that we can stand back, detached from our vested interests and perspectives to see ourselves or at least our emotions for what they truly are. The issue with this position, though, and incidentally what is conspicuously absent throughout Williams' book, is a discussion regarding how Nietzsche believes that the self, too, is simply a constitution of warring drives. The self, too, is subject to will to power. According to Nietzsche, the self is much like a political state with different warring factions. These factions serve effectively as the self—the self who changes moods, the self who suddenly strives for things, the self who is taken to have a specific personality, etc. is at least, according to some passages, within Nietzsche's texts, nothing more than a manifestation of more primordial drives. This position was well-noted in chapter three. However, the notion of a conscious, reflective, self-detached subjectivity existing independently of the body or indeed existing independently of oneself (such that one can view the self's true interests and agendas from some non-perspectival standpoint and so forth) is a nonsensical absurdity according to Nietzsche. If all this is correct and we assume that Williams holds the standard position on the Nietzschean self as advanced here, then what is one seeing when one uses the will to power as a mirror as she suggests?

The standard interpretation of Nietzsche's drive theory of subjectivity holds that whatever "us" there is, is nothing more than a construction of competing drives. The self is nothing more than epiphenomenon: it has no causal powers of its own. Drives, according to Nietzsche, are responsible for directing both our behavior and our perception. However, if this is the case then two troubling questions arise for Williams' position: First, what truths are revealed by reflecting on the will to power? According to the dominant reading of Nietzsche's drive theory, a la Leiter, the drives are responsible for interpreting reality where interpretation here means that reality is construed as existing independently of the self. Far from viewing one's self in a more truthful light, the picture of oneself reflected back when one employs will to power, in the vein that Williams suggests, is more likely to be the image of one in a funhouse mirror: some features would be hideously distorted. Surely any truth revealed is simply that of the drive responsible for presenting the image.

Second, even if we accept that we can view the truth by utilizing eternal return, such truth would be irrelevant for we could do nothing to change ourselves. The self, Nietzsche writes on many occasions is an effect of physiology; it is produced entirely by processes that we have no control over. It is therefore causally inert. Assuming a Leiterean or Brownian reading of Nietzsche's view of self as discussed in chapter two, even if one could see one's emotions more clearly by utilizing Williams' mirror therapy cure, there is absolutely nothing one could do to change oneself. Without a further articulation of the "subjecthood" of subjectivity itself, Williams' account cannot explain how mirror therapy works. It would appear that either Williams upholds a traditional account of subjectivity where the subject is not determined by its physical constitution and therefore where the will is free at least to some extent from motive (whether the motive is psychologically or physiologically grounded) or she must choose a fatalist view of self a la Leiter.[56] If the former, then she clearly rejects Nietzsche's notion of self, but in so doing rejects will to power because not all things can be explained *via* power: the self would exist outside the narrative of power. On the other hand, if Williams chooses the latter approach then mirror therapy is possible, but only in the form of diagnosis—no cure could be causally efficacious.

4.3.3 Williams and Epistemology: Decoupling Truth from Belief

The final problem with Williams' interpretation has to do with her views on truth and will to power. Truth, according to Williams, is nothing more than a secretion of will to power. This position is, of course, not new: Many scholars have argued that Nietzsche does not believe that objective truth exists and further that truth may be deflated.[57] That is, a proposition such as "This is true" is retranslated to mean: "This is necessary for my survival, etc." In general, the difference between these earlier, pragmatic, will to power approaches and Williams' is that Williams is more aware of the many problems that emerge when it comes to articulating and defending such a view. Williams makes clear that she fully understands the logical implications of this position. She notes the two imminent dangers: (1) If the will to power is true then it becomes a metaphysical theory—there is absolute Truth after all. However, this is a conclusion that Williams clearly rejects. (2) If all truth is merely an expression of the will to power then the statement, "The will to power is true" is just simply another manifestation of power. However, this view would entail that will to power is no more true than any other position; it is simply an expression of one's will to power. It is a mere evaluation, an opinion. Nevertheless, if the will to power is itself just another evaluation then why use it as a test as Williams proposes?

It might be wise to consider this last problem in further detail because it may not be immediately obvious how the above conclusion, namely, the very test Williams proposes is pointless. To see why it is useful to compare Williams' discussion of eternal recurrence to the problem regarding will to power identified above. In chapter three of her work, Williams provides an analysis of the long-posed question relating to the truth of eternal recurrence. In the secondary literature, scholars have been divided as to whether eternal return is put forward by Nietzsche as a true, cosmological theory about the universe or whether it is simply a normative test that one may use to enhance one's life by forcing one to think about the weight that all choices have.[58] The presumption being that all choices will recur an infinite number of times presses upon us to fully understand the significance we give to even the most trivial choice. As Williams notes, citing Magnus, this either/or interpretation between cosmological or normative interpretations is not a true exclusive disjunctive at all for the normative is clearly parasitic on the cosmological. Williams paraphrases Magnus here stating: that for one to use eternal recurrence one must also accept the idea as true. If the idea were not true then the individual would either (A) not subject herself to the test because there would be no point or (B) not take the results of the testing very seriously because it would only be one possible test to choose from among many others to which one may subject themselves.[59] Thus, to use eternal recurrence as a test of one's life is to believe in the truth of the cosmological position.

Building as she does on Magnus' above argument, Williams does a wonderful job of collapsing the "either/or" interpretation of eternal recurrence. However, she does not seem to realize that her interpretation of will to power causes the same difficulty she exposes so well—for the will to power is a mirror test too, but because it is a test, it must be believed to be true by the tester. If it were not, if it were simply considered one perspective among many others—possibly an infinite number of other such perspectives—then it too would not be taken seriously, and thus it is doubtful that the test would be initiated by the tester.

Williams' solution to this problem, though not explicitly stated as such, is to offer an aesthetic justification for the test. The test, she writes, allows us to "engender a more passionate and aesthetic view of the world. It is the subject of infinite interpretations eternally revisited."[60] This response, however, seems to contradict her initial interpretation, namely, that will to power reveals uncomfortable and, presumably, real truths (since if such feelings were not true they would not be uncomfortable truths) about ourselves which we must recognize. Now, Williams cleaves to an aesthetic appreciation of the myriad of perspectives one may take on the self by using mirror therapy. Yet here again the same problem regarding eternal return is revived: If either the self or world is the subject of infinite interpretations then surely such a test would not compel us to move forward with the aim of changing our behavior, assuming, that is, that we are free to do so, but instead would cause us to freeze in our very tracks; there would be no point perceiving ourselves from these perspectives if they too did not track our true selves. The will to power would not be a test at all but really a matter of taste and once more it would lose its importance because it, like eternal return, desperately needs to be believed true in order for the test-taker to take it seriously.

There is yet another issue with Williams' suggestion, and it has to do with the relationship between the will to power and the so-called "truths" it reveals about our true self. Even if we accept her suggestion, namely, that seeing the world through the lens of power produces new aesthetic avenues for self-exploration, Williams neither explains how this is epistemically possible nor desirable. Assuming that we decouple Nietzsche's notion of self from his theory of will to power (a cause of concern, as we saw, in the last section), we might reasonably ask two related questions regarding how will to power achieves such results. First, how does using will to power, as a test, cause negative, deeply held narratives to collapse? Second, once such self-stultifying beliefs are demolished, how does will to power, underwritten as it is by an artistic interpretation as a form of therapy, open up new possibilities of existence?

The answer, according to Williams, is that beliefs are causally efficacious. Since the mirror therapy process is underwritten by the beliefs a subject has about herself, Williams must assume that beliefs are effective vehicles of agential change. Beliefs, all by themselves, she explains, are responsible for altering values. She writes in this regard: "Beliefs empower people. According to Nietzsche, people believe certain ideas because they help people live and get around in the world, but he wonders why these helpful ideas must be called True (Williams' capitals)."[61] Williams then further argues for two positions: (1) The notion of "Truth" is not necessary because we can use different couplings other than belief and truth such as belief and necessity, for example, which perform the same function as truth and belief.[62] (2) To regard beliefs as True entails that I place the actual importance of my beliefs outside of myself. Beliefs are only important to me provided that they satisfy an external condition, namely, that of Truth. This view, however, is dangerous according to Williams' reading of Nietzsche because Truth is an external condition imposed on a belief and thereby it is the outer condition outside of the individual that empowers the belief, not the individual. Williams writes in this regard: "Again by pretending that the Truth of beliefs originates from the world external to humans, the beliefs' alignments with these objective facts confer power to them and by extension to the humans who hold them."[63]

I think it is fair to say that there are a plethora of problems with these statements. I now examine each statement in turn. First, we might delve further into the question: What makes a belief necessary for me? Let's say a professor believes, wrongly, that the colleagues within his department are plotting against him because he has some rather robust and compelling evidence that suggests they do not like him. From this evidence, he believes that their ultimate goal is to get him fired. Let us further suppose that the colleague is right in thinking that his fellow workmates do not like him, but that there is no evidence, whatsoever, that they wish to see him fired, or that his work is held in contempt. Nevertheless, the professor believes, for whatever reason, that his colleagues are planning to get his tenure terminated.

The professor uses his beliefs, unjustified as they are, in a rather Nietzschean fashion, to increase his scholarly activity: The belief that his firing is imminent motivates him to publish even more articles and more books of high scholarly worth. Providing a Nietzschean analysis, he attempts to exact his own form of revenge by making his colleagues jealous of his scholarly accomplishments. However, notice that the impetus for his achievements is derivative from the mistaken view he has about his colleagues' views of himself. It is this belief that motivates him to succeed further in his career in the hopes that he will be able to pursue another, better and more prestigious position. The belief is not true but necessary because, without the conviction, the scholar would be less motivated to publish and therefore would not be as competitive on the job market as other scholars.

The question I propose is the following: Is believing that a belief is necessary because it helps one to achieve goals that matter to one enough to motivate someone toward achieving those very goals? Consider the scholar in the above example. If the scholar were to employ Williams' suggestion in divorcing belief and truth and substituting "necessary for me" in the place of truth it is doubtful that he would be as motivated to publish. He may believe that his colleagues, holding him in contempt, wishing to get him fired and so forth is necessary for him to publish. However, I argue that belief must rest on the further belief that his colleagues actually do hold him in contempt and that his colleagues really are trying to get him fired. Assuming that conscious belief is an engine for action, as Williams assumes here, I would argue that consciously believing that something is merely necessary to motivate one is not enough: Only a belief *regarded* as true would provide one with the impetus to act on the conviction.

It is for this reason that truthfulness cannot be replaced by any other substitute: it is a stopgap measure; it prevents further inquiry and investigation regarding the truth of some matter. Believing in the "Truth" of some belief is necessary for action assuming beliefs themselves are causally efficacious as Williams clearly assumes. However, notice that one does not believe something to be true merely because it is necessary (at least not consciously): because if one did then truth would lose its power. The truth of the belief would be reducible to what is necessary for me. Acting on a proposition believed to be true or believed likely to be true provides the causal impetus and normative justification behind action.

This point may be further illustrated by turning to Williams' own example, namely, her struggle to overcome her negative feelings regarding her body-image. I argue that her very analysis reveals the impotence of any belief-narrative divorced from truth. Regarding how she feels about her body-image, Williams writes: "When I step out of the shower, there I am in full view of my mirror. Most of the time I am not too keen on what I see. I start thinking I should exercise more, eat better, get in better shape. I could say that my mirror tells me this, but of course it does not—it just reflects the image of my body. I am the one who is nauseated by what I see."[64]

Williams believes she has an ugly body. She believes that she is not attractive, and it is this belief, assumed to be true by her; that produces a real affective response—she feels nauseous upon seeing her body when coming out of the shower. Williams continues:

> But my nausea is based on my standard of values. My body is unacceptable if based on the Madison Avenue media and fashion values of creaseless, waif-thin, but preferably big-breasted female bodies. If I adopt a new value standard one that values wrinkles, pregnancy stretch marks and cellulite, I'm beautiful! But the mirror tells me neither that I am ugly nor that I am beautiful. I place those values on myself according to what standard for beauty I have chosen either by adoption or creation, for myself.[65]

In a rather powerful way, the mirror clearly does tell her what is beautiful! Before Williams either consciously chooses to think of her body according to a different standard of values, she experiences nausea. This gut reaction is both a strongly felt emotion (I am disgusted with myself) and a judgment (I am ugly), and it is clear evidence that our perceptions of ourselves are not freely chosen: Before there is the choice there is feeling. It is this inseparable connection between belief and feeling that Nietzsche identifies quite clearly throughout all his work: thought cannot be detached from its organic substrate. Thought cannot be detached from the conditions of breeding and physiology that make it possible. More precisely, Nietzsche declares: "Feelings and not thoughts are inherited."[66] Both feelings and beliefs must be confronted for self-experimentation to occur. What's more such feelings must be recognized as truth-candidates—statements that can be further investigated, found to be warranted or conversely, improbable.

Williams goes on to explain that she has been suffering from feelings of self-loathing regarding her view of her body-image for the past 20 years. Assuming this is true, and there is no reason to doubt the veracity of this statement the question then becomes: "Why is it so difficult to throw off this clearly debilitating idea?" The answer, in my view, is that such an assessment has not been falsified. Entertaining different value standards from other cultures does very little regarding casting off debilitating views. The way to throw off a view is to investigate it and to demonstrate that such a view is false or at the very least unjustified; it is this goal of debunking debilitating perspectives that Nietzsche identifies as the very purpose of genealogy.

The purpose of genealogy, as briefly entertained in chapter two, is to offer a new description for feelings and thoughts by demonstrating that the old description and explanation of such feelings and/or beliefs was not terribly well-justified. Thus, I would argue, by denying the truth of truthfulness we deny the intrinsic value truth has from the human perspective. No other coupling substitute will have the same value as truth and therefore no other notion can perform the same work as truth.

This discussion leads to several interesting questions regarding the status of truth and indeed the power and concept of truthfulness itself in Nietzsche's work. If one were to ask Pontius Pilate's question of Nietzsche, "What is truth?" there are several ways he might respond. Postmodern readings of Nietzsche often conflate Nietzsche's sometimes vicious attacks against Truth with attacks on truthfulness and even truths. However, I would argue that there are at least three ways Nietzsche conceives of truth. The first is what we might call a nominalized theory of truth—we extrapolate from the idea that there are truths to Truth much in the same way that Plato is guilty of nominalizing goods into the Good.[67] This way of thinking about truth, claims that propositions do in fact reflect reality as reality truly is. As I will show in chapter six, this is a position that Nietzsche firmly rejects in many places. Second, there are truths, pluralized where Nietzsche suggests that there are facts but that facts must be indexed to some perspective or narrative. Turning to the *The Genealogy* we see Nietzsche admitting of this pluralized notion of truth when he discusses how the genealogist should investigate humankind's moral swamp ground. He implies in essay one, section one that genealogists should keep their "hearts as well as their sufferings in bounds and (to) have trained themselves to sacrifice all desirability to truth, *every* truth, even plain, harsh, ugly, repellant, unchristian, immoral truth.—For such truths do exist" (Nietzsche's Italics).[68] Again in the earlier work *Human-All-Too Human*, Nietzsche suggests that there are some givens, some truths that sciences have captured. He writes, "All we require, and what can be given us only now that the individual sciences have attained their present level, is a chemistry of the moral, religious, and aesthetic conceptions and sensations, likewise of all the agitations we experience within ourselves in cultural and social intercourse . . ."[69] Here Nietzsche is at his most positivistic and implies that science, but especially chemistry can reveal the true wellsprings of our physiological conditions and thus the ground for many of our philosophical disciplines. But notice that even in *The Genealogy*, Nietzsche reaffirm, his positivistic stance in Note 2 of the first essay. He writes, "Indeed, every table of values, every "thou shalt" known to history or ethnology, requires first a *physiological* investigation and interpretation rather than a psychological one; and every one of them needs a critique on the part of medical science (Nietzsche's Italics).[70] And, finally, in the KSA, we have the following passage: "When I think of my philosophical genealogy, I feel myself connected with the mechanistic movement (reduction of all moral and aesthetic questions to physiological ones, of all physiological ones to chemical ones, of all chemical ones to mechanical ones."[71] Moreover, as we will come to discover, Nietzsche unearths and strategically employs well-known facts to prove his three hypotheses of *The Genealogy*. Nietzsche clearly demonstrates that the genealogical method of investigating moral phenomena is epistemically superior to that of the English utilitarians such as Spencer for two main reasons: (1) Because genealogy can make better sense of the statements recognized as facts by both groups (the genealogist and utilitarians). (2) Because genealogy can unearth deeply embedded, unconscious facts about humans whereas utilitarians must stay on the level of conscious sensation (i.e., Pain and pleasure). Thus, the utilitarians of the nineteenth century could only offer, at best, a limited and superficial reading of human psychology. Nietzsche accepts that there are facts but that facts are not discovered through disinterestedness—indeed one must be polemical to discover such facts in the first place.

However, of more importance is Nietzsche's later shift from truth to truthfulness. The relation between truth and truthfulness is the third way in which Nietzsche probes the nature and value of truth. This divergence from thinking about the truth on its own terms, independently from a will, from an actor engaged in seeking the truth, and thinking about truth as intrinsically linked to a will to be truthful, represents an important watershed in Nietzsche's thinking. For he now recognizes, in *The Genealogy* especially and elsewhere, like Book Five of *The Gay Science*, that an investigation into the nature of truth is necessarily coupled with a will *willing* to launch the inquiry. Thus, any answer given to the question "What is truth?" Is never complete because there is always something outside of the examination, namely, the will engaged in the inquiry. This insight means that standard objections to deflationist accounts of truth will not apply in Nietzsche's case but indeed provoke a new thinking regarding the relationship between justification and truthfulness.

This shift in emphasis from truth to truthfulness first appears in *Beyond Good and Evil*. In the very first aphorism, Nietzsche asks: "What in us really wants truth?"[72] This question is in keeping with Nietzsche's new accent on the actor who desires to reveal the truth, along with the attitude required to reach the truth. For the attitude, Nietzsche avers, cannot be so easily separated from what we suppose the truth to be. If we view the truth to be what actually exists outside of our perception of things, then it stands to reason that we must be objective, unprejudiced to arrive at this truth. However, it is not just this method but the willingness to adopt the method which Nietzsche now questions in his mature work. In GM III: 27, Nietzsche affirms that once the fundamental question of truthfulness is raised, namely, "What is the meaning of all will to truth?" then and only then will morality perish for truthfulness leads to the realization that, above all, humans desire the security of meaning, of narrative.[73] We would rather will nothingness than not will because even here we are secure in the belief that we are the ones doing the willing. Although we are no longer certain of God, we are confident of our own agency. Truth, Nietzsche concludes in section 375 of *The Will to Power* "is really only a word for the will to power."[74] Truth proves to be a disguise for completely other feelings and drives.[75]

It is this desire for truthfulness that Nietzsche traces from the practices of priestly asceticism to the scientific attitude of the eighteenth and early nineteenth century to nihilism at the end of the nineteenth century in Essay III of *The Genealogy* which comes to occupy his mature thought. As Nietzsche demonstrates historically and concretely, the search for Truth is intimately tied to truthfulness.[76] Although truthfulness begins as a Christian virtue, it is like unripened fruit: Truthfulness becomes important for the scientist as the scientist seeks to discover that which is objectively true and therefore concocts a method that devalues perspective, feeling, and instinct. But even here truthfulness is still "sour": The scientist is still working with the assumption that his method can arrive at an objective Truth and that there is an objective Truth to be found. The attitude and compunction to be truthful continues to ripen with atheists and nihilists who begin to turn the desire to be truthful back onto itself. Only then, Nietzsche evinces does truthfulness reveal the real value of Truth: security. Being in possession of Truth is being in possession of something that does not change, that which remains eternal.

Truth, as a goal of truthfulness, is the third sense of truth which Nietzsche examines so earnestly in his mature writings. Truth here is not defined as a mirror on what actually exists (first sense) or even a fact embossed within a belief system (second sense) but is far more personal: Truth here is defined as the result of one's honest inquiry. This dyad of truth/truthfulness is as

I demonstrated above, results in a new dyad of stopgap/normative measurement and means. Moreover, in his mature writings, Nietzsche explains why. For to arrive at the truth, through a method thought to be truthful, is ultimately to coronate some belief. It is to recognize that some statement is the final destination point of some road that is already deemed to be the right path because of some deep-seated desire: security. Moreover, just like any king or queen so coronated, the secretions of this truth's power make themselves known. This relation between truth, truthfulness, and power will be spelled out more explicitly in chapter six.

What is of interest here, in connection with Williams' work, is the braking power, the stopgap power of truth. Why do we cease an investigation? There are several reasons, and Nietzsche embraces all of them depending on the kind of truth one discovers. Some "truths" are accepted because particular individuals or groups lack the cognitive power to criticize them. Warriors, Nietzsche tells us, were confused by their priestly competitors and eventually accepted, adopted, and most importantly *felt* the truths the priests taught. They went against their very instinctual nature as warriors *qua* warriors and became dupes in the language of Leiter to MPS. On other occasions, Nietzsche suggests that some lack the will to investigate further. Some people may have the intellectual capacity to question a so-called "truth" but fail to do so because they need tartuffery and illusion. Such individuals accept readymade truths because they cannot accept the tragic sense of life where suffering is just a matter of dumb luck: it befalls the good and wicked alike.[77] Still, other truths are deeply embedded within the very psyche of humans. Whether this is because of our natural biological endowments, our breeding or society or more likely a combination of all three, such beliefs as cause and effect, the law of identity, basic inference forms of logic, etc. are deemed true because we cannot think our way around them. In essence, they serve, as Wittgenstein might say, as "forms of life": they are the very background conditions that make any thinking possible.[78]

What's more, there is some support for Nietzsche's contention. In their recent paper, "Epistemology for Beginners: Two- to Five-Year-Old Children's Representation of Falsity," Olivier Mascaro and Olivier Morin study the ontogeny of a naïve understanding of truth in humans.[79] Their paper is fascinating for several reasons, but most striking is their claim (given a rather optimistic reading of epistemology) that toddlers as young as two can, at times, recognize false from true assertions. Mascaro and Morin's Optimist Epistemology Hypothesis holds that young children have the conceptual understanding to treat, correctly, assertions that make false representations of states of affairs as false. Where toddlers are unable to identify false representations correctly as false, Mascaro and Morin argue that this is because they reconstruct the testimony of some speakers, but especially primary caregivers, "in a way that makes them true."[80] This research suggests that we are hardwired to think about truth and yet to understand even at the age of two that truth and more especially falsehood have values and therefore benefits and consequences—it is not a good idea to call out a primary caregiver as a liar! It is this seemingly biological/social need to be truthful coupled with the need to discover truthfulness in others—even if it means we must reconstruct falsehoods in others to make them truthful—which explains both how and why we cannot give up on truth. Yes, truth no longer plays the same epistemic role it once did, but Truth still plays a vital normative role especially in regard to how we relate to ourselves. This research, only in its infancy, confirms why Williams cannot decouple belief from truth; for without truth, action would never take place and willing would never occur. We would (A) either be forever stuck in a Socratic *aporia* because an investigation without truth would be interminable or (B) we would act from some irrational impulse that we could never reason through and ever truly justify.

In this chapter, I examined three very different interpretations of will to power. The first interpretation denies will to power outright. I hope to have demonstrated that denying will to power, as Clark does, effectively serves to neuter Nietzsche's philosophy and render many parts simply incoherent. Moreover, the will to power can be defended such that it allows for new methods of interrogation and illumination to come to the surface again contra to Clark. Turning to Richardson, his account of will to power effectively serves to render it subservient to natural selection. However, two problems emerge: first it proved impossible to demarcate a clear role to will to power once it has now been reduced to a further corollary of natural selection. Why not work with the present model of natural selection to account for the twin developments of will and freedom within the human being? Second, there are cases restricted to the biological realm where one must reckon with agency.

The problems with Williams' approach are manifold, as demonstrated, but the chief problem is her denial of truth. A proper naturalization of will to power must preserve the value of truth. This intrinsic value of truth is preserved only when one recognizes that one cannot replace the coupling of belief with truth for any other substitute. The problem, as presented here for my purposes, is one of preserving this value of truth while also supporting the perspectival and, therefore, inherently infinite evaluation that is celebrated in Nietzsche's theory of will to power. I work out these problems in chapter six.

With all that said, I have encountered a rather difficult problem regarding the alethic relation between the will to power and truth. If the will to power is true, then it is a species of metaphysics because it becomes the one principle and indeed narrative for explaining all that transpires within the universe. If it is not true, then why believe the will to power? While it is possible to believe in the will to power using different couplings other than truth, such as necessity for example, it was shown that such couplings could not do the work of truth. Truth is a unique value that is conferred onto statements and therefore adds a special normative property onto an assertion. It is this peculiar property of truth that Williams could not explain: An aesthetic approach to "belief acceptance" may have a higher power valence than a competing assertion regarded as true by some subject, but it cannot replace the *gravitas* the subject gives to the declaration accepted as true. Truth is a very special value which is only granted to some statements and not others; this value does come to impact how we view the statement if a subject accords the statement this exalted status.

I resolve this last problem in chapter six by adopting a deflationist view of truth in the first sense. I argue following Rorty and others that it is really justification that bears the epistemic load and not truth. However, I also demonstrate that Nietzsche would not go along with Rorty's "little" justificatory program and argue that Nietzsche is actually a virtue foundherentist in terms of how he justifies his claims. Finally, I examine how truthfulness comes to play an integral role in Nietzsche's naturalized epistemology.

NOTES

1. See Maudemarie Clark, *Nietzsche on Truth and Philosophy* (Cambridge University Press, 1990), 1–5.
2. Walter Kaufmann, *Nietzsche, Philosopher, Psychologist, Antichrist* (Princeton University Press, 1968), 511.
3. Clark, 210.
4. Ibid., 212.
5. Nietzsche, Friedrich, *Beyond Good and Evil*, section 36, in *Basic Writings of Nietzsche*, Trans. Walter Kaufmann, 237–238.
6. Clark, 33.
7. Rene Descartes, *Meditations on First Philosophy*. Meditation Two in *Rene Descartes, Meditations and Other Metaphysical Writings,* Trans. Desmond Clarke (New York: Penguin Books, 2000), 24.
8. Clark, 214.
9. See especially section 34 of *Beyond Good and Evil.*
10. Nietzsche, *Beyond Good and Evil*, in *Basic Writings of Nietzsche*, section 19.
11. As the name implies, agent alienation occurs when we feel detached from an action taken. See Brian Lightbody, *Dispersing the Clouds of Temptation*: *Turning Away from Weakness of Will and Turning Towards the Sun* (Eugene, OR: Pickwick Press), 2015.
12. Nietzsche, *Twilight of the Idols* II, section 5.
13. Clark, *Nietzsche on Truth and Philosophy*, 215.
14. Nietzsche, *The Gay Science*, section 290, Trans. Holingdale, quoted in *A Nietzsche Reader*, 237.

15. Nietzsche, *The Gay Science*, Trans. Kaufmann, section 290, 233.

16. This is a contention put forward by Richard Holton. See his book, *Willing, Wanting, Waiting* (New York: Oxford University Press), 2009.

17. See Nietzsche, *The Gay Science*, Trans. Kaufmann, section 127.

18. See Daniel Wegner, *The Illusion of Conscious Will* (Cambridge, MA: MIT Press, 2002).

19. There are many different versions of this argument but Hilary Putnam's and Jerry Fodor's seem to be the clearest and most devastating to all brain-type identity theories of mind. See Hilary Putnam's "The Nature of Mental States" in *Mind, Language and Reality: Philosophical Papers, Vol. 2* (Cambridge University Press, 1975). See Jerry Fodor's "Special Sciences or the Disunity of Science as a Working Hypothesis" in *Synthese*, 28 (1974), 97–115.

20. See Daniel J. Povinelli's controversial book: *Folk Physics for Apes: The Chimpanzee's Theory of How the World Works* (Oxford University Press, 2003).

21. See Alfred Mele's, *Effective Intentions, The Power of Conscious Will* (Oxford University Press, 2009), Chapter Two Conscious Intentions and Decisions.

22. Nietzsche, *Beyond, Good and Evil*, in *Basic Writings of Nietzsche*, section 22, 220–221.

23. Clark, *Nietzsche on Truth and Philosophy*, 223.

24. Clark, *Nietzsche on Truth and Philosophy*, 227.

25. John Richardson, *Nietzsche's System* (Oxford University Press, 1996).

26. John Richardson, *Nietzsche's New Darwinism*, 46–52.

27. Richardson, *Nietzsche's New Darwinism*, 50

28. Richardson, *Nietzsche's New Darwinism*, 52.

29. Richardson, *Nietzsche's New Darwinism*, 51. See Nietzsche's *The Gay Science*, section 127 and *Twilight of the Idols,* chapter 6, section 3.

30. Richardson, *Nietzsche's New Darwinism*, 35–45,

31. KSA IX, 234.

32. Richardson, *Nietzsche's New Darwinism,* 23.

33. Richardson, *Nietzsche's New Darwinism,* 27.

34. Nietzsche, *On the Genealogy of Morals*, GM II: 22, 528.

35. See Book II section 14 of Nietzsche's *On the Genealogy of Morals*.

36. Nietzsche, *On the Genealogy of Morals*, GM II, section 17, 522–523.

37. Richardson, *Nietzsche's New Darwinism*, 46.

38. Richardson, *Nietzsche's New Darwinism*, 46.

39. Richardson, *Nietzsche's New Darwinism*, 53.

40. Richardson, *Nietzsche's New Darwinism*, 53.

41. Nobel S. Proctor, *Manual of Ornithology: Avian Structure and Function* (New Haven: Yale University Press, 1993).

42. Richardson, *Nietzsche's New Darwinism*, 55.

43. See Neil Campbell, *Biology* (Menlo Park California, Benjamin and Cummings 1991). Also see George F. R. Ellis, "On the Nature of Emergent Reality," in *The Re-emergence of Emergence: The Emergentist Hypothesis from Science to Religion,* edited by Philip Clayton and Paul Davies (Oxford University Press, 2006), 79–109.

44. Robert Beschta and William Ripple, "Trophic Cascade Effects in Yellowstone: The First 15 Years after Wolf Reintroduction," *Biological Conservation* 145:1 (January 2012), 205–213.

45. See Robert Beschta and William Ripple, "The Role of Large Predators in Maintaining Riparian Plat Communities and River Morphology," *Geomorphology* 157–158 (July 2012), 88–99. Also see, Marshall, Hobbs, and Cooper, "Stream Hydrology Limits Recovery of Riparian Ecosystems after Wolf Introduction," *Proceedings of the Royal Society B-Biological Sciences* 280 (April 2013), 1756.

46. Williams, Linda, *Nietzsche's Mirror, The World as Will to Power* (Lexington MD: Rowman and Littlefield, 2000), 129.

47. Williams, *Nietzsche's Mirror*, 38. See Gilles Deleuze, *Nietzsche and Philosophy*, Trans. Hugh Tomlinson (New York: Columbia University Press, 1983).

48. See Nietzsche's fable of the lambs and hawks in *On the Genealogy of Morals*, Essay I, section 13, 480–482.

49. Williams, *Nietzsche's Mirror*, 103.

50. Williams, *Nietzsche's Mirror*, 115.

51. Nietzsche, *The Gay Science*, section 341.

52. Williams, *Nietzsche's Mirror*, 125–126.

53. For a paradigmatic aesthetic interpretation of the will-to power, see Arthur Danto's *Nietzsche as Philosopher* (New York: Columbia University Press, 1969). Also see Alexander Nehamas' "Nietzsche: Life as Literature" (Cambridge, MA: Harvard University Press, 1988). Nehamas makes an interesting connection between aestheticism and perspectivism. He writes, "Nietzsche's aestheticism is also connected with perspectivism in another way. The philology of the world, which I mentioned above, not only provides him with a literary model for many of his views but also motivates him to create what we may call a literary product. Nietzsche's positive thinking consists . . . in the presentation, or exemplification, of a specific character, recognizably literary, who makes of these philosophical ideas as way of life that is uniquely his. The fact that this character is unique, that it is not described in a traditional sense, and that it is produced in a way that prevents it from ever being a model for direct imitation allows Nietzsche, as we shall see, to persist in his perspectivism without being obliged to construct positions which are merely negative," 3–4.

54. Williams, *Nietzsche's Mirror*, 130.

55. See Nietzsche, *Twilight of the Idols* III "Reason in Philosophy" section 3 "Today we possess science precisely to the extent to which we have decided to accept the testimony of the senses . . . The rest is miscarriage in which reality is not encountered at all."

56. See Paul Katsafanas, discussion on deliberation in section 2.1 of his book, *Agency and the Foundations of Ethics, Nietzschean Constitutivism* (New York: Oxford University Press, 2013).

57. See chapter five of Arthur Danto's *Nietzsche as Philosopher* (New York: Columbia University Press, 1969) and Christoph Cox's *Nietzsche, Naturalism and Interpretation* (University of California Press, 1999).

58. See Bernd Magnus' *Nietzsche's Existential Imperative* (Bloomington: Indiana University Press, 1978) for the *locus classicus* discussion on these different interpretations.
59. Williams, *Nietzsche's Mirror*, 114–115.
60. Williams, *Nietzsche's Mirror*, 123.
61. Williams, *Nietzsche's Mirror*, 103.
62. Williams, *Nietzsche's Mirror*, 103.
63. Williams, *Nietzsche's Mirror*, 103.
64. Williams, *Nietzsche's Mirror*, 118.
65. Williams, *Nietzsche's Mirror*, 118.
66. Nietzsche, *Daybreak*, section 30.
67. I am inspired to describe Truth in this manner by Richard Rorty. Rorty often called Truth a nominalized and grotesque interpretation of truths. I will come to show that Nietzscheans like Cox are correct in thinking that Nietzsche is a deflationist with respect to the idea of Truth and that, as for Rorty so it is for Nietzsche—justification does the heavy lifting in Nietzsche's theory of knowledge. What I reject is Rorty's little theory of justification. I will examine Rorty's theory of deflationism in more detail in chapter six.
68. Friedrich Nietzsche, *On the Genealogy of Morals*, Trans. Walter Kaufmann and R.J. Holingdale, edited with Commentary by Walter Kaufmann GM I:1, 25.
69. Nietzsche, *Human-All-Too-Human*, 1.
70. Nietzsche, *On the Genealogy of Morals*, Trans. Walter Kaufmann and R.J. Holingdale, GMI: 17, Note 55. Compare this with section 57 of *The Anti-Christ* where Nietzsche seems to reduce one's mental abilities and beliefs to one's physiological development and body type.
71. Nietzsche, *Kritische Studeinausgaube (KSA)* Vol. 11. Section 26, 432, quoted from Christoph Cox's *NietzscheNaturalism and Interpretation*, 216.
72. Nietzsche, *Beyond Good and Evil*, section 1.
73. Nietzsche, *On the Genealogy of Morals*, III: 27.
74. Nietzsche, *The Will to Power*, 375.
75. Also see Section 344 *of The Gay Science* and section 1011 of *The Will to Power.*
76. See section 357 of *The Gay Science* and *On the Genealogy of Morals* III: 24.
77. The mark of one's capacity for truthfulness has in Nietzsche's view a physiological condition. As Nietzsche writes in *Nietzsche Contra Wagner*: "Only great pain, that long, slow pain in which we are burned with green wood, as it were—pain which takes its time—only this forces us philosophers to descend into our ultimate depths and to put away all trust all good-naturedness, all that would veil, all mildness, all that is medium-things in which formerly we may have found our humanity. Out of such long and dangerous exercises of self-mastery one emerges as a different person, with a few more question marks—above all with the will to question more persistently, more deeply, severely, harshly, evilly and quietly than has ever been questioned on this earth before." *Nietzsche, Contra Wagner* in *the Portable Nietzsche, The Portable Nietzsche*, Trans. and edited by Walter Kaufmann (London: Penguin Classics, 1977).
78. "It is no doubt true that you could not calculate with certain forms of paper and ink, if that is, they were subject to queer changes—but still the fact that they changed

could in turn only be got from memory or from other means of calculation. And how are these tested in their turn? What has to be accepted, the given, is—one could say—forms of life." Ludwig, Wittegenstein, *Philosophical Investigations,* Trans. G.E.M. Anscombe, edited by Anscombe and Rhees (Oxford: Blackwell, 1959), 226.

79. Mascaro, Olivier and Morin, Olivier, "Epistemology for Beginners: Two-to Five-Year-Old Children's Representation of Falsity," in *PLOS ONE* 10:10 (October 2015), 1–20.

80. Mascaro and Morin, "Epistemology for Beginners," 4.

Chapter 5

Naturalism and the Human Being
Nietzsche's Naturalized Ontology

Things, according to Nietzsche, are not static objects. Things, rather, are relational entities—they are held together by multiple sets of relations. These sets, in turn, are held together by further relations and so on until we arrive at the bare quantum of will to power. Without over committing, ontologically speaking, it would be accurate to claim that things are, at a minimum, bundles of relations. What precisely are these relations? Well, as suggested, at a minimum, these relations are ones of power. All relations are power relations.

However, what does it mean to state that all relations are power relations? Obviously, I need to say something more about the relation, as it were, between relations. I also need to say more about "middle-sized goods" and, finally, how these things may be viewed as relational entities. It is necessary to explain all three aspects of these relations because power, otherwise, would have very little explanatory cachet. It is certainly true that undertaking a power analysis can illuminate facets of an event or action which might otherwise go unnoticed. However, can more be said? The purpose of this section is to show how we may extend the power narrative as advanced in chapter three, to illuminate more facets of human behavior, organic action, and chemical interaction.

A power narrative can help to shed new light on a well-known phenomenon. Clark, in *Nietzsche on Truth and Philosophy,* contends that an analysis of rape, through the perspective of power, is revealing. It reveals a very different cause of rape than the "sexual desire" approach. The "desire approach" postulates that the rapist rapes because he desires to fulfill some sexual need. A power narrative reveals something different altogether. The actual motivation of the rapist is not a sexual need at all. The rapist does not have an unquenchable sexual urge which must be fulfilled at all costs. To make this claim is to see such an event as a mere predator-prey dyad relationship. It represents an attempt to naturalize the event, but not in a particularly good or useful way. To naturalize an event in this way is to offer an explanation that reaches ground zero: Rape is an event in which the rapist engages, to satisfy some sexual urge and sexual urges are basic to the human animal. However, once this ultimate ground is reached, it becomes difficult to change the cause of the action.[1]

The alternative power approach reveals a much more complex set of relations. It examines the event as a reflection of how men view women and speaks to the psychological make-up of the rapist. Such an analysis, as proven in the secondary literature on the subject, has provided new and insightful directions for further research leading, hopefully, to rape prevention.[2]

However, one can also go too far with this power approach as Clark duly notes. For if the analysis of power is taken too far then it can have the exact opposite effect: instead of illuminating the possible reasons for an event, it instead acts as an impediment to further understanding. If everything is power, then all events and things are reduced to power relations, and this entails a peculiar vacuity.

Accordingly, this section will seek to accomplish three things. First, I want to provide a comprehensive and consistent ontological position on the ontology of a thing. Second, I will then explain how things relate to other things or perhaps more clearly put I will explain what I take to be the engine of change among things in the inorganic and organic world. Thus, just as Darwin will claim that natural selection and scarcity are the engines that alter species, I will explain why things become different from what they were, from a power analysis. Third and finally, I will show that a power analysis is not vacuous as Clark and others imply, but is deeply meaningful.

To accomplish these related tasks, I will first work on the ontological status of an individual thing. Next, I will explain how individual things relate to other things. Finally, I will explain how all things fit together, as it were, in the world. In other words, I will show how we may think of the world as nothing more and nothing less than an intimate tapestry of power relations.

Steven D. Hales and Rex Welshon in their seminal work *Nietzsche's Perspectivism,* go a long way to resolving the first of these problems. Unfortunately, however, they do not seem to grasp the correct solution that their investigation affords. In general, they argue that Nietzsche adopts a bundle theory of thinghood. However, there are at least three different stripes of bundle ontology in Nietzsche's *oeuvre:* the aggregationist or conjunctivist view, the constellationist view, and the organizationist view. The problem, as they understand it, is to analyze which of these positions is the most coherent and, second, which is the most truthful to Nietzsche's philosophy. My interest is to provide a coherent power position first and foremost. Whether my approach coheres with *all* of the things Nietzsche has to say about bundle organization, is of secondary importance.

The aggregate position suggests that bundles are much like heaps. Such heaps, however, are not of smaller, individual things, like sticks, for example, rather such bundles are bundles of properties. So, for instance, a coffee mug is a bundle of attributes—cylindricalness, voluminous, color, hardness, etc. Such properties are lumped together in a common region of space and appear together with some temporal regularity and consistency at least insofar as they are perceived by some consciousness. Our consciousness, according to the aggregationist perspective, does not create the bundle, however. It plays no role with respect to the thing's constitution. What precise properties the mug might have independently of a mind is unknown. The object is a mere aggregate of properties that are sensed by some mind.

Welshon and Hales show that Nietzsche makes a strong case for this conjunctivist view in many different places in his work. For example, Nietzsche writes:

> The world apart from our condition of living in it, the world that we have not reduced to our being, our logic and psychological prejudices, does not exist as a world-in-itself; it is essentially a world of relationships; under certain conditions it has a differing aspect from every point; its being is essentially different from every point, every point resists it and the sum of these is in every case quite incongruent.[3]

Such a view of thinghood, though, raises the following question: "What would the world look like independently of human observation?" At times Nietzsche seems to suggest that the world exists independently of people, and it is characterized simply by a chaotic and disorderly flux of events. Nietzsche writes in this regard: "Not to know but to schematize—to impose upon chaos as much regularity and form as our practical needs require. In the formation of reason, logic, the categories, it was need that was authoritative; the need to, not to know, but to subsume, to schematize, for the purpose of intelligibility and calculation."[4] However, it is also apparent, from Nietzsche's later writings, that he sees significant problems with such a view. First, Nietzsche queries, "How do we know that the world, in itself, is characterized in such a way?"[5] Second, if it is assumed that objects are much more than their sensible qualities because we are assuming that the object will have the qualities that I attribute to it independently of my observation, then it becomes perfectly reasonable to ask the following questions. "What is the ontological nature of those things (namely us) perceiving these qualia?"; "What qualities do I add to the thing I am observing?"[6]; and "How are we able to constrain the boundaries of these properties of a thing to a common spatiotemporal location?" Finally, "If the world truly is a mere plenum of becoming then why do we seem to perceive relative property stability among objects?"

To his credit, Nietzsche gives an answer to these tough questions. In his early work, he suggests that it is we, as human beings, who impose logic onto the world to schematize it. Logic makes the world not only simpler but, more importantly, calculable. The law of identity, for example, stipulates that A is A: a lion is a lion, or a rabbit is a rabbit. We must believe that such things remain the same from moment to moment to ascribe properties to them. Moreover, we ascribe properties to such things to (or "intending to") control our environment. As Nietzsche writes: "He for example, who did not know how to discover the 'identical' sufficiently often in regard to food or to animals hostile to him, he who was thus too slow to subsume, too cautious in subsuming, had a smaller probability of survival than he who in every case of similarity at once conjectured identity."[7] Some animals, Nietzsche contends, survived because they made an identity claim, which was, in a strict sense, mistaken. Identity is nothing more than an illusion, but it is a necessary illusion because it allows species to survive and thrive.

However, there are obvious problems with this solution. First, Nietzsche clearly wants to argue that human beings, and other animals that had a seemingly innate ability to "subsume" other things, survived while those who saw things as they truly were, such that there were no things, no substances, but flux and change only, perished. However, if projecting the concept of identity onto the world helped us to survive in a hostile environment then surely it has some measure of warrant. It does appear to be an accurate depiction of the world as the world is in itself. On another reading then, one might claim that it was we who saw the world as it truly was. Consider the following example: No two rabbits are identical, but all rabbits provide nourishment. Animals that were able to make the distinction between accidental properties of something (some rabbits are brown, and some are white) and the essence of something (rabbits are a source of food) thrived. Thus, from the same evidence that Nietzsche evinces for the position that logic sprang from illogic, one could claim that human beings and other animals, were simply using a more powerful understanding to look past mere superficial appearances and to see the thing for what it truly was.

Nietzsche provides a unique account of organic taxonomy here, but it does lead to a second problem. Nietzsche divides organisms into two basic groups: those who can see the world for what it is and those who order the world for the sake of subsumption and mastery. Let us call the first group the "true viewers" and the second group the "subsumers." Now, how exactly is such mastery achieved? What does this process of subsumption entail? It would seem that the subsumers would need some special status in the world precisely because it is the essence of the subsumer class to subsume. However, if this is the case, then it does not seem possible that the subsumer class of things is a mere aggregate of properties because this group possesses an identifiable essence. They have a unique power which allows them to subsume. What, then, allows such creatures to have this power? The obvious answer is that there must be some underlying ontological structure either of their bodies, minds, brains or of a combination thereof, which is responsible for correctly understanding the properties that belong to certain things. However, if this is true then the conjunctivist is incorrect: Subsuming animals can identify the actual order of the universe, and we would, therefore, need a very different ontological position with a view to present an accurate understanding of this group. Indeed, one might even claim, given Nietzsche's naturalistic leanings, that it would be of the utmost philosophical importance to be able to explain how and why such a group of animals can impose not just any schema onto the world to master it, but the correct schema.

This inference is not lost on Nietzsche. As Nietzsche suggests elsewhere, the actual goal of philosophy, if this picture of the world is, in fact, correct, would be to understand the entity or entities which are capable of sifting order from this supposedly pure chaotic flux of raw becoming. "The question is whether there could not be many other ways of creating, adapting, falsifying is not itself the best—guaranteed reality; in short, whether that which posits things is not the sole reality."[8]

However, something is wrong here, too, as Nietzsche eventually comes to realize for this view of subjectivity is not compatible with his fully naturalized construal of will to power and perspectivism. The clearest passage in Nietzsche's *oeuvre* where it becomes abundantly clear that Nietzsche has no empirical evidence to support such a "subsumer hypothesis" subtended as it might be on a conjunctivist position, is found in *Beyond Good and Evil* section 15. Nietzsche writes:

> What? And others even say that the external world is the work of our organs? But then our body, as part of this external world would be the work of our organs! But then our organs themselves would be—the work of our organs! It seems to me that this is a complete reduction ad absurdum, assuming that the concept of a *causa sui* is something fundamentally absurd. Consequently, the external world is not the work of our organs![9]

Following Clark, we can understand this passage as an elaborate *reductio*:

1. Assume that the essence of our organs is such that they organize the world for us.
2. The world along with the things in the world have no independent structure; no essences. (the conjunctivist position).
3. The organs are things in the world.
4. But if the organs are things in the world then they too have no essence (2, 4)

Therefore our organs cannot be responsible for organizing the world for us.

Clark nicely summarizes the upshot of the argument: "It follows that empirical accounts cannot provide a basis for equating reality with the chaos of sensations since they must presuppose that sense organs and bodies are real."[10] In other words, the sense organs must be taken as real entities with essential structures if the conjunctivist position is to go through. However, it is the very crux of the conjunctivist position to deny this possibility. The only other possibility is to hold that the sense organs themselves are merely mereological schematizations of sense data. However, if this is the case, then we are left with an infinite regress as we require some other organ to schematize these organs and so on.

It should now be obvious from this discussion that a different theory on bundle ontology must be tried. The second approach to bundle organization is what Hales and Welshon, following the work of Nehamas, call "the constellationist position." The constellationist position holds that things are formed by some other thing taking a perspective on some object. So, for example, the constellation Ursa Major (the Great Bear) consists of several smaller asterisms including the Little Dipper (or Plough). Now one may always ask: "What is the ontological status of the Great Bear?" or "What is the ontological status of the Little Dipper?" The constellationist position asserts that the Little Dipper *only* exists because human beings can *only* see certain stars with the naked eye. Humans have then traced these stars to form some design. In analogous fashion, the constellationist theory of bundle organization holds that entities only exist because some thing has taken a perspective on them.

There are several important points to this position that need to be considered carefully. First, we may notice that constellations have some objective properties. Human beings are not responsible for creating stars. However, we are responsible for placing these stars within an imagistic framework for easy reference. Second, such asterisms are causally efficacious. Star systems are still used for marine navigation. We can discover in which direction we might be headed if sailing a ship, by noting that Polaris or the North Star can be found by finding the handle of the Little Dipper.

Now at first glance, this position might seem to be very similar to the aggregationist position discussed above. However, upon further reflection it becomes evident that it is not because, for the conjunctivist, properties are detached from things—all that the thing is, is simply a bundle of *qualia*. However, from the constellationist point of view, parts of a thing exist independently of the constellated thing in question. The stars which form the Little and Big Dippers have existed for billions of years. Such stars existed long before human beings indeed even before the earth was formed, but it is we, as human beings, who then reconfigure the light from these stars into discernible and rather homely patterns. Thus, it would seem that the constellationist view holds a two-tiered view of reality. There is a lower tier of reality which consists of real, ontologically subsistent objects. Such objects exist independently of human observation. However, there is then a second order of reality where some other entity constructs narratives out of these objects. These constructions occur for the sake of power. For example, asterisms have been useful in a myriad of ways: They are obviously useful for navigation, but they have also played significant cultural roles as they were the muse for the creation of myths and stories about the origin of the heavens and human beings. Also, they were then used as proof that such stories were true and thus came to play a role in the consecration of the political and social powers of shamans and, later, temple priests.[11]

Second-order objects, like the asterism, Orion's Belt, are manufactured from perspectives of power. There is some support in Nietzsche's *oeuvre* for this position. Nietzsche, at times, suggests that things are constructed according to biological, pragmatic, and cultural needs. As Nietzsche writes in this regard: "It is essential to determine what concepts and formulas must be: means for comprehensibility and calculability. Practical application is the goal, that man be able to help himself to nature . . . Science: the conquest of nature for the ends of man."[12] The same point is put a different way in *The Will to Power:* "Truth is therefore not something true, that might be found or discovered—but something that must be created."[13]

This position is more consistent than the aggregationist/subsumer position examined above. All vestiges of essentialism have now been expunged; so it would seem. All things, including human beings, are mere constructions of other things. Once again, constructions are manufactured for the attainment of power.

While this view constitutes an improvement because it appears to be more coherent, internally speaking than the aggregationist view, it has its set of complications. The first of these has to do with the hitch of internal organization. It appears *prima facie* that some bundles are organized by some interior principle. In other words, it would be very problematic to use this position to explain how and why some things have a long-standing and consistent organization. Indeed, the only way to explain the long-standing organization of some things would be to ascribe some essentialist ground to the construction. As is evident this theory of bundle organization must still rely on the ontological primacy of thinghood. The designs we create from stars as humans are clearly ontologically contingent on the stars themselves. Thus, second-order organization, namely the design of the asterism, in this case, is clearly parasitic on real, substantial things. As such, we, therefore, do not have a bundle theory at all. We are rather defending a property-physicalist position. Former physical things, like stars, are the *really*, real stuff that make up the universe.

Bundles of these things are properties that belong to a group of things, but not to each thing itself.

To complement this "two-substance view of thinghood," we also have a "two property view." Some of the qualities of these concrete things are inherent to the thing in question such that they exist whether someone observes them or not. However, other properties are manufactured according to cultural needs that are shot through with power. Accordingly, these manufactured qualities would seem to be parasitic on the primary, self-sustaining properties of the thing in question. However, if this is true, then, once again, Nietzsche does not subscribe to a bundle ontology after all.

The question at hand is: "Can we go deeper?" "Can we use a bundle position to show that even stable objects, like igneous rocks, for example, are nothing more and nothing less than bundles of qualia?" The final view of bundle power quanta organization attempts to do just that. This position is what Hales and Welshon call an organizationist or internalist view. This view holds that there is some fundamental structure or principle which holds bundles together. Many passages in Nietzsche's *oeuvre* serve to support this rendering of bundle organization. Most of Nietzsche's proofs for this position come in examples drawn from the biological world. For example, Nietzsche believes that our very physical bodies are nothing more than bundles organized by chains of nutrition. All organs and major somatic systems of the body, such as the immune, lymphatic, etc. are connected via a complicated network of nutrient linkages. Human bodies are not bundled from another bundle's practical need as the constellationist believes. Nor is the human body a mere aggregate of properties that somehow coalesces to form a consistent and self-sustaining entity. The human body has its unique mode of organization. What's more, this mode of organization is formatted along the lines of power. Hales and Welshon in their seminal work, *Nietzsche's Perspectivism,* make this point crystal clear:

> Each unit of will to power, he suggests, "strives to become master over all space and to extend its force," and each encounters "similar efforts on the part of other bodies." (WP 636) This *Bellum omnium contra omnes* (the war of all against all) ends in a truce, in which the units of power come "to an arrangement ('union') with those of them that are sufficiently related." Having thus formed a new and larger bundle, these quanta "then conspire together for power."[14]

All things are composed of bundles of quanta power. Bundles exist because there is some internal mode of relation that ties properties and presumably sub-bundles and sub-sub-bundles, together. The body is an excellent example of how such a view may be rendered coherent. Single-celled organisms evolve into multicelled organisms. Multicelled organisms evolve into multi-organ organisms, and so on. Every biological unit from the nutrients within a cell, to the individual cell, to cell tissue, to organs, and the body as a whole do battle until a truce of some sort is achieved. *Agon* or struggle is possible because all biological units share the same perspective or battleground. In this case, it is nutrition. Nutrition is the mode of power which allows objects to gain more power.[15]

One of the problems with this account is that it seems to avow a rather robust essentialist position. Though the organizationist eschews the notion of substance or essence, nevertheless, defining principles of the organization, come to adopt the same role. However, surely Nietzsche would reject any view which comes to take any thing or principle to be absolute and eternal. However, this is what we seem to have in the organizationist position.

Another impasse has been reached, or so it appears. Clearly, organizationism has several advantages over constellationism. The organizationist can deny the substance/attribute view of metaphysics while also being able to explain relative permanence. Objects are relatively stable, at least regarding their properties, because they are organized by some inherent principle of organization. The constellationist, as argued, has difficulty explaining such relative permanence. It seems impossible to deny that atoms, quarks, and animal cells are relatively stable entities which have existed, at least in the case of quarks and atoms, for billions of years exactly as they are now and will remain just as they are long after human beings become extinct.

Constellationism, however, does have several distinct advantages over organizationism. For the constellationist holds that things are constructions of power made by some other thing. This view advances two important points: (1) It helps to explain how new objects can come into the world. Objects are fundamentally creations and only exist because some other thing finds these creations useful for the attainment of power. (2) It denies any inherent *telos* to a thing. A thing only comes to have the properties it has because of the perspective some other entity has on it.

Given that both positions have advantageous properties that the other lacks, is it possible to combine both without contradiction and without losing these properties? I would argue yes. Take the following example of acid rain. Sulfur dioxide is the primary component in the formation of acid rain. The chemical reaction in which sulfur dioxide bonds with hydrogen molecules with the help of the catalyst nitrous oxide has been well-collaborated. The chemical understanding of this process along with the corrosive properties of water which result from this reaction are well-known. However, acid rain is not just a chemical reaction relegated to the tomes of meteorologists and chemists. Acid rain is a serious environmental problem that came to spawn a political and social movement.[16] Acid rain is a relation: of course, it denotes the way in which sulfur dioxide bonds with hydrogen molecules, but it also denotes and connotes much more than that. Acid rain is an environmental occurrence that clearly showcased the fragility of the globe. Such a phenomenon is international in that some countries experience the devastating effects of acid rain even though they do little to produce much of it.[17] Acid rain is or should be a concern for all human beings because it can eradicate entire species of flora and fauna. However, because it is such a significant issue, it can be constellated, co-opted. It can become a mere tool used by a political party, for example, to gain power.

To be clear, I am not suggesting that acid rain is simply a social constructionist kind of thing merely because it is not a natural sort of thing. To attribute this view to my interpretation would be a gross misunderstanding and oversimplification of the point I wish to make. Indeed, it would be a false dilemma. The point is to put into question what natural kinds of things are. Many philosophers argue that a natural kind of being is one where the properties that belong to that entity exist independently of human interest and action.[18] That is to say; they are mind-independent: whether humans exist or not the properties of natural kinds of things remain what they are. The example of acid rain raises the issue of whether it makes sense to speak about natural things independently of human categories and, most importantly, human actions. As I try to show, all attempts at understanding, according to Nietzsche, are valuations of power. Thus, to use the categories of "natural" or "social constructionist" kinds of things when discussing entities is to place a valuation on the world. For Nietzsche, the task of the genealogist is to understand why the value has been placed. He, therefore, does not directly answer such questions as: "What makes a natural kind of thing natural?" However, instead, he compels us to think about the evaluative conditions that make such questions possible. For example, if Nietzsche were investigating acid rain in the twenty-first century he might ask the following questions: "Who benefits from creating this sort of division between the natural and social worlds?" "Why would someone insist on treating acid rain as a natural kind of thing?" "What epistemic and ontological conditions allowed such a division to be created?" Acid rain is not a natural type of thing; indeed, no thing, strictly speaking, given will to power is a natural or social form of anything because all things are simply relations. The example of acid rain demonstrates how science can be co-opted: when one thinks of acid rain one does not think of sulfur dioxide but rather the environmental impact of said rain. Acid rain denotes and connotes more than just rain that is corrosive; it is a complex, real phenomenon created by human beings and thereby gives rise to a myriad of different meanings according to the agendas and values of those who think about it. One cannot divorce the forces that make the investigation of acid rain possible as a phenomenon from the conditions that give rise to it.[19]

Based on this example, we can see what a merger between the constellationist and organizationist positions might look like. On the one hand, the organizationist can hold that some things exist *inter alia* of human perception. There are relatively stable yet relational units of power that make up all things in the universe. These units are bundled according to some internal principle. In the above example, the sulfur dioxide which causes acid rain is double-bonded to oxygen. This chemical bond, when bonded to hydrogen molecules becomes a corrosive water-based liquid. As rain is something that is required for all human life, we have a natural vested interest in any unusual chemical reaction that might put such a valuable resource in danger. Therefore, it is only appropriate that, when such a threat arises, human beings will take notice. However, it is in the taking notice where constellationism comes into play. For, as Nietzsche so eloquently put it, "contemplation without interest is a nonsensical absurdity."[20] An object garners and warrants contemplation only insofar it is capable of affecting the enhancement or detriment of power for some entity. Once the basic power organization of something is realized, however, the object then is transformed into a "danger" or a weapon depending on the perspective taken. The object is repackaged, reevaluated by being related to the agenda of the interested party.

Still, this hybrid organizationist-constellationist position is not without flaws of its own. The chief flaw of this attitude is that it gives little room for power to operate as an explanatory concept. One might claim that while a power analysis illuminates certain features of acid rain as a social and political phenomenon, it has no bearing on the chemical process itself. Even more problematic is that our best naturalistic explanation for this process seems to be at odds with the will to power. Will to power projects a vitalistic life force onto things that appears, at first blush, unnecessary. Most things can be fully understood without having to turn to this power narrative. So what is the point of will to power? Why postulate it?

I respond to these objections by noting two things: First the task of Nietzsche's naturalism is not to get at what a thing is. This traditional goal of epistemology, which was to understand what something truly is, is now deemed incoherent since all things are merely relations. Things, as I have shown, are nothing more than bundles that have an internal organizing principle but may always be constellated or absorbed into some other bundle. If this is correct, then it is possible to have a proper understanding as to how a bundle is organized from an internal perspective. Thus it is not always necessary to understand things from the viewpoint of power when one examines the internal constitution of a thing, but this does not mean that such a perspective is not always possible. Since all things are related to all other things, one can never truly understand a thing unless one understands all of the myriad ways in which such a thing relates to everything. Acid rain, for example, would not exist as a chemical reaction, if the earth did not have the planetary orbit it has. Indeed, one might wonder whether an atmosphere capable of producing life would exist at all if this orbit had been slightly different from what it is. Acid rain exists, in part, because of the earth's spatial relation to the sun. Everything is, in some sense, organized according to some higher principle. Borrowing the notion of a ground form from chapter two, we might say that there will always be progressively broader and broader ground forms. Some of these forms exist on the organizationist side of the will to power continuum while others exist more on the constellated side.

On the other hand, it may be possible to change the very chemical constitution of acid rain itself. It might be possible, though perhaps unlikely, to manufacture goods without producing any pollution at all. This example shows that to speak of natural kinds of things is inaccurate. We can change a chemical compound by understanding the forces that make up the compound in question. When we do so we are surely exerting our force, our power on such a thing. Why would we do such a thing? Simple: for the attainment of power.

As far my second response is concerned, I argue that such a "vitalistic" conception of power need not be postulated as the driving force for *all things*. Vitalism is not the essence of the world it is only the essence or engine of will to power from the human perspective. Will to power is what drives all human behavior, but insofar as it is the driving force behind an entity, and all entities are related at least in some fashion to all others, it is true to say that will to power is, therefore, a relationship that truly exists in the world. I am therefore not "projecting" will to power onto the world as some interpret Nietzsche doing to render the concept coherent. Nor is will to power simply another narrative that allows me to see the world from a new perspective as Williams argues. Rather we relate to the world from and through the channel of will to power. However, perspective here is simply a relation. Thus one cannot make a firm ontological distinction between human beings and the world because the world, from my standpoint, my perspective, is nothing more than the set for all relations within the world. Indeed, even this way of relating to the world is still just another relation within the world. Moreover, one cannot relate to the world from a non-relation, relation. When we relate to something, anything, even inorganic matter, Nietzsche evinces, we do so with an agenda in mind, interest. Will to power is "real" and not just a projected notion of mind "writ large" because it is a real relationship which exists in the world. It is the relationship that we form to other things, and this relation is always one of interpretation: "We may not ask who then interprets? For the interpretation itself is a form of the will to power . . . as an affect. The world it is well to recall here, is will to power."[21]

Thus, my view of will to power may be best thought of as a non-physical emergentism. Emergentism is usually taken to mean that certain properties of physical things cannot be reduced to the sum of the material thing's parts. They come to exist because of the way in which the thing's parts are organized. This position would be a general definition for physical emergentism. So what then is non-physical emergentism? A non-physical emergentism would suggest that power is an emergent property of force. Force is a relation between things. Just like the relation between oxygen molecules and sulfur in the sulfur dioxide in acid rain. However, since all things may be further reduced to smaller and smaller bundles until we arrive at the simple quantum of will to power, it would not be correct to call Nietzsche's position a physical emergentism. Rather the correct view is that power emerges as a unique relation from the relations of force which exist in the universe. Power is simply that relation which relates to itself as a force. Power, then, is the narrative to be employed to understand both the conscious and unconscious motivations of an individual or group. However, it is the narrative, force, in all its myriad manifestations, for example, physical, gravity, weak and strong forces within the atom, electromagnetism, that should be employed when dealing with the non-conscious.

A non-physical emergentism allows one to hold to the common aspects identified in chapter one as belonging to all naturalistic theories: naturalism is reductive. Naturalism is a critical ethos, an immanent critique of the assumptions, narratives, and discourses we learned to accept as unvarnished truth. Naturalism remains committed to understanding the internal causes responsible for producing the various things and events as found in the world. All processes, as well as all things themselves, are reduced to *quanta of* power. However, this reduction avoids some of the problematic features associated with reductive physicalism. The problems for the reductive physicalist were twofold: (1) There is a problem of reducing sensory or internal *qualia* to physical objects such that the target of the reduction becomes flattened. We saw this in chapter one where the feeling of "romantic love" was reduced to Nerve Growth Factor. (2) Physical reductionism taken in conjunction with the causal closure thesis negates free will. If all actions are the result of prior physical causes then free will, as a capacity becomes causally inert. My position avoids these two problems because the reduction, in this case, is non-physical and because it is non-physical, dynamism is built into the very explanation of all phenomena. Even physical entities are comprised of smaller bundles of power quanta. These, in turn, exist in a state of tension and flux with all other bundles within the bundled-thing. This explanation may make more sense if we turn to a concrete example.

Take Nietzsche's genealogy of guilty. Nietzsche does not simply reduce guilt to the bad conscience. The phenomenon of guilt is both affectively and cognitively different from negative feelings of "bad conscience" first experienced by humans who were enclosed by their captors whom Nietzsche calls "the blond Germanic beasts."[22] What Nietzsche shows is the genealogical development of bad conscience from the confluence of different powers. These powers included the inherent biological drives contained within the human being, the social constraints that contributed to the breeding of specific drives within the majority of individuals, and the advent and growth of Christianity (which further energized, crystallized, and transformed the feeling itself). My account provides room for the logical space of reasons because reasons are themselves perspectives of power in that they are attempts to totalize some entity or some relationship. They are, in effect, attempts to gain knowledge about some entity.

I now wish to take this opportunity to explain what if any adherence Nietzsche would have to CCP. In chapter one, I examined some of the problems with CCP from a causal productive paradigm and suggested that a new "powers" approach would be more in keeping with Nietzsche's position. The above reconstruction of Nietzsche's bundle view of ontology is mutually reinforcing with a powers approach. A powers approach, as expressed by John Heil, holds that entities, on an ontological level of understanding, exist in a "causing" relationship. Heil's best example of this relationship is the playing card analogy. If one were to take two playing cards and prop them up forming a triangle house, what, he says, is the cause of the structure? According to Heil, one would need to note several causal relationships: The cards are in a causal relation of mutual, structural support, the table acts as a foundation for the cards giving both cards stability, and gravity would be another cause forcing the cards to slope downward.[23] Though, a person was the initial productive cause for propping the cards up, once this original causal relation is removed other relations must hold to explain the reasons for the card-house.

This approach is in keeping with Nietzsche's bundle theory above. Believing that there is, in reality, a definitive, productive cause or causes for some event is to engage in illusion. It is akin to assigning an actor behind some action. It is, at best, an effort to simplify to make the world explainable, knowable, and therefore predictable. "We have absolutely no experience of a cause. . . . In fact, we invent causes after the schema of effect: the latter is known to us."[24] According to Nietzsche relations of force exist between things and even within things, but causality in the productive, triggering sense is something that is assigned based on pragmatic needs. Consider Gibb's zero-oxygen chamber example in this regard. Pretend there is a scientist in a zero-oxygen chamber striking a match on the strip of a matchbox. Because there is no oxygen in the room, the match will not light. However, if someone were to open the chamber, letting oxygen in just as the match was being struck, we might exclaim that the cause for the match lighting is the oxygen being let into the room and not the striking.[25] This example shows that assigning causality to reality is a mistake.[26]

However, despite Nietzsche's vitriolic attacks against causality, it does not follow that he would argue against a powers approach. In fact, in many places, Nietzsche seems to endorse the position I articulated above. Consider section 112 of *The Gay Science*: "Scrupulous scientific observation uncovers a manifold one-after-another where the naïve man and inquirer of older cultures saw two separate things."[27] Moreover, again consider what Nietzsche writes in *The Will to Power*: "One would like to know how things in themselves are obtained; but behold there are no things in themselves! . . . Something unconditioned cannot be known; otherwise it would not be unconditioned!"[28] Nietzsche is not a "fictionalist" when it comes to the "causing" powers of things. It is consistent to claim that Nietzsche would uphold a version of CCP in that the world is causally closed or better put "forcefully closed" and that all events and interactions can be understood if one were able to understand the relations of force *and* power holding between all things.

I now wish to respond to one of the most incisive criticisms in the secondary literature concerning will to power. If we recall, Porter argued that will to power was inconsistent on two levels: first, regarding how it treated things and second, on a global scale in explaining the agonic relationship between things at large. Porter argues that the problem is one of totalization: On a local level, will to power views things as simply the sum of their effects. They are totalized. However, this cannot be correct because a thing cannot be adequately understood on its terms but only in relation to other things. We could never discover the sum of an item's effects. On the global scale, will to power attempts to totalize all relationships by claiming that they can be understood by using a common narrative namely the perpetual strife existing between all things and the overcoming of said strife when one thing absorbs some other thing hoping to become stronger as a result. However, Porter argues that will to power denies the very ability to understand the world from some absolute aperspectival standpoint. In claiming that will to power be a final totalization of the world, this theory, Porter contends, does what it deems to be impossible: it understands the world from a position that is external to it.

How do I respond to this objection? I think a sufficient response must be threefold. First, Nietzsche cannot completely divest his thinking from a subject/predicate comprehension of the world. Since Nietzsche must express his positions in language and language or at least Western languages, as Nietzsche demonstrates, are underwritten on a metaphysics of subject/predicate format, even grammatical syntax resists what Nietzsche is desperately trying to communicate. Nietzsche is, it is fair to say, trying to communicate the incommunicable but that does not mean that such an idea is incoherent.

Responding to Porter's claim on the local level, he is right: One cannot hold that a thing is just merely a sum of its effects for to make this assertion we detach this thing from the preexisting interrelationship it has to other things and the intrarelationships it establishes to itself. However, it is clear that when Nietzsche speaks about a thing in this way he is totalizing a thing according to a prearranged constellation: He detaches a thing from the intimately woven fabric of will to power to answer the question: "What is a thing?" Moreover, to respond to this question or indeed any matter is to render the question intelligible. Thus, Porter's analysis mistakes an instance of a clear performance of will to power, on the part of Nietzsche, with a descriptive claim. Anytime we think of a thing we do so with an agenda in mind. It is impossible, so Nietzsche thinks, to exercise power by thinking of all the relations and *relata* in the world. Will to power selectively cognizes a particular thing with a specific purpose in mind. To discuss what the thing is, is an attempt on the part of some will to explain the intelligible character of that thing and thus requires that an evaluator selectively cognizes a thing according to a predetermined, though, thoroughly constelled perspective.[29]

Turning now to Porter's global criticism, I object to Porter's description of will to power as just another attempt to totalize the world. Certainly, if this were the case, then Porter would be right in criticizing Nietzsche. However, a more apt analysis would be that of realizing that Nietzsche's statement, "the world is will to power and nothing else besides!" is not a totalization of the world but is an announcement: it screams what the secret characteristic of the world is. Will to power as a secret discovery about the world does not come from an attempt to stand outside the world and to totalize it: to provide some inductive generalization that could be used to describe, with some accuracy, what all relationships and *relata* within the world have in common. Rather it is to penetrate into the very wellsprings of the world to discover its heart.

What's more, Nietzsche endorses this position in section 36 of *Beyond Good and Evil*. He states there that, "The world seen from within, the world described and defined according to its 'intelligible character'—it would be 'will to power' and nothing else."[30] The key part of this quotation lies in comprehending the notion of "intelligible character." We, as humans, cannot help but totalize: We cannot resist to creating stories to explain how things are, how they were and how they will be. This predisposition, nay this prejudice, is a necessary aptitude and instinct of being human. Will to power is the name Nietzsche gives to describe this narrational capacity that marks us as human beings *qua* human beings. However, we do not need to apply this attitude to will to power reflexively thereby showing that the claim is either tautologous or self-referentially inconsistent. Rather it is best to think of will to power, as Nietzsche indicates in the above passage, as a necessary infusion at all attempts of thinking, investigation, discovery, reflection, intention, imagination, and valuation and any other mode a mind may take. Such patterns of thinking are invariably shot through with willing; they are permeated with clear attempts to render something intelligible, such that one can better control it. To realize this truth or better capacity and limitation from within the human perspective is to strip away all the glosses and permutations of thought to reveal its hidden desires. It is not to group all thoughts into a category to discover what they have in common. It is one of understanding that some perspectives, are cross-perspectively true: The perspective of will to power is one that applies to every corner of inquiry, every relationship we enter into, every fact that we come to know about the world. Explaining the idea of cross-perspectival truth for Nietzsche, Hales and Welshon illuminate this notion in the following passage:

> That we are unable to conceive of the laws of logic not holding shows nothing except that we are forced to adopt a certain perspective in order to think at all. Hence, there are according to Nietzsche as interpreted here, universal or absolute truths for humans, only far fewer than philosophers have traditionally thought. Note that in characterizing absolute human truths it is not claimed that they are true outside of perspectives or true extra-perspectivally. Rather, the claim is that there are truths that are truths within all human perspectives, that is that there are cross-perspectival truths.[31]

In thinking of will to power as another cross-perspectival truth that holds true in all perspectives is not to contradict oneself as Porter claims. Though, as we will come to see in chapter six, it is preferable to call what Hales and Welshon describe as a "necessary truth" as a capacity and limitation. Will to power is the only necessary relationship that is infused within all relations. It is this so-called "truth" or primal channel in which all thought flows, does not come from an aperspectival stance but rather comes from understanding that it is a basic feature of thinking itself.

In conclusion, Nietzsche rejects a triggering view of causality but would seem to adopt at least implicitly, a powers approach as described above. Nietzsche is a naturalist because he accepts CCP in that the world is causally or forcefully closed and that all events are explainable in terms of what nature has afforded. However, there is a place for the mind: One can and must switch from examining the causing powers of bare force which are responsible for producing some phenomenon and the causing powers of power—where human interest and agenda take center stage. With that said, the above division is itself only a schema of totalization: It is impossible, conceptually, to truly separate force understood as "natural causing powers" from human valuation.

With the metaphysical problems relating to will to power now solved, I will now turn to discuss the epistemic issues about the will to power identified in chapter three.

NOTES

1. See Clark, *Nietzsche on Truth and Philosophy*, 210: "The enlightening character of contemporary accounts of rape in terms of power, for example, seems dependent on the implied contrast between the desire for power and the desire for sex."
2. See, for example, Roy Baumeister, Kathleen Catanese, and Harry Wallace, "Conquest by Force: A Narcissistic Reactance Theory of Rape and Sexual Coercion," *Review of General Psychology* 6:1 (March 2002), 92–135.
3. Quoted from Steven D. Hales and Rex Welshon, *Nietzsche's Perspectivism* (Carbondale, University of Illinois Press, 2000), 70. (Quoting Nietzsche's Nachlass translated as *The Will to Power*, section 586.)
4. Nietzsche, *The Will to Power*, WP 515. Also see KSA XIII 333–334.
5. See Friedrich Nietzsche, *Human, All too Human*, section 9: "We view all these through the human head and cannot cut this head off; though the question remains, what of the world would still be there if it had been cut off."
6. See section 57 of *The Gay Science*, "That mountain there! That cloud there! What is "real" in that? Subtract the phantasm and every human contribution from it, my sober friends! If you can! If you can forget your descent, your past, your training—all of your humanity and animality," 121.
7. Nietzsche, *A Nietzsche Reader*, Trans. Holingdale, *The Gay Science*, section 111, 60. See also *Daybreak*, section 117: "A thirst, the habits of our senses have woven us into lies and deception of sensation: these are the basis of all our judgments and 'knowledge'—there is absolutely no escape, no backway or bypath into the real world! We sit within our net, we spiders, and whatever we catch in it, we can catch nothing at all except that which allows itself to be caught in precisely our net."
8. Nietzsche, KSA XII 396.
9. Nietzsche, *Beyond Good and Evil*, section 15.
10. Maudmarie Clark, *Nietzsche on Truth and Philosophy*, 123.
11. See Jeroen W. Boekhoven, *Genealogies of Shamanism: Struggles for Power, Charisma and Authority*, Barkhuis, 2011. Also see chapter one of Henri Ellenberger's, *The Discovery of the Unconscious* (New York: Basic Books), 1970.
12. Nietzsche, KSA 61 XI 91.
13. Nietzsche, *The Will to Power*, section 552.
14. Hales and Welshon, *Nietzsche's Perspectivism*, 71.
15. For a detailed argument supporting this view, see my book, *Philosophical Genealogy, Vol. 2* (New York: Peter Lang Publishers, 2011), chapter 7.
16. See the article, "Acid Rain" (Salem Press Encyclopedia, January 2014).
17. Ibid.
18. See the article "Natural Kinds" in *Stanford Encyclopedia of Philosophy* by Alexander Bird, http://plato.stanford.edu/entries/natural-kinds/.
19. This may seem that I adopt a conventionalist position. I will demonstrate how a power approach will help to renaturalize acid rain.
20. Nietzsche, *On the Genealogy of Morals*, Preface, 2.
21. Nietzsche, *Beyond Good and Evil*, 36, also see KSA XI 611.
22. Nietzsche, *On the Genealogy of Morals*, GM I: 11, 478.

23. John Heil, *The Universe as We Find It* (New York: Oxford University Press, 2012), 119. I realize that Heil is a particularist but this does not mean that his notion of power causality cannot be exapted for my purposes.

24. Nietzsche, *The Will to Power*, section 551. Also see KSA XIII 98.

25. Gibb, "The Causal Closure Principle," 631.

26. See also section 112 of *The Gay Science*, Trans. Holingdale: "Cause and effect: such a duality probably never occurs—in reality there stands before us a continuum of which we isolate a couple of pieces. . . ."

27. Nietzsche, *The Gay Science*, section 112.

28. Nietzsche, *The Will to Power*, section 555. See also KSA XII 154.

29. I discuss the concept of selective cognition in more detail in chapter seven.

30. Nietzsche, *Beyond Good and Evil*, section 36, Trans. Holingdale.

31. Nor does this imply that we as human beings have some species perspective vantage point on the world distinct from all other species. Again, we must always keep in mind that all species just like all other things are always undergoing changes. Hales and Welshon, *Nietzsche's Perspectivism*, 33–34.

Chapter 6

The Human Being and Naturalism
Nietzsche's Naturalized Epistemology

Many scholars in the secondary literature have argued that Nietzsche is clearly a non-foundationalist regarding his epistemic justificatory commitments.[1] However, some go much further, and draw, in my view, an unjustified inference. These same scholars argue that Nietzsche is not only a non-foundationalist but a non-cognitivist. They interpret Nietzsche's remarks on truth and reasoning to mean that he also believes it to be impossible for human beings to have any epistemic purchase on the world. Human beings are only afforded perspectives: We have no direct access to the world and, therefore, there is no *interpretandum* which is not already an *interpretans*. All we have are mere perspectives, so these interpreters hold.[2]

Nietzsche himself seems to endorse the "meager perspective view" on occasion. Indeed even in speaking of will to power, Nietzsche admits that it too may just be an interpretation: "Supposing that this also is only interpretation–and you will be eager enough to make this objection?—well, so much the better."[3] Compare further what Nietzsche writes on epistemic judgment from *Beyond Good and Evil*: "My judgment is my judgment: no one else is easily entitled to it—that is what such a philosopher of the future may say of himself."[4] However, this epistemic position has the following consequence: Since language is itself merely a schema of interpretation which is infused with power, then it too cannot be a means to discover the true identities or essences concerning things. Thus interpretations can only be validated by their life-giving qualities because facts are normatively laden. Yet, if facts are normatively laden, then there can be no objective ground from which to measure the accuracy of two very different sets of facts about the same thing. Indeed, even Nietzsche's premium normative valuation, which is that of adopting a healthy *ethos*, is itself just that, a valuation. Such a valuation is not value neutral and therefore would seemingly only carry weight for those who were already so inclined to accept the assessment as true. Such an interpretation leads to an impassable quagmire in that Nietzsche cannot provide non-normative support for his unique and, what he believes is the correct view, namely, bestowing the highest possible value to life itself. His philosophy would seem to be nothing more than a mere matter of taste or an "enthronement of taste" as Habermas so eloquently put it.[5]

Two related issues need to be addressed: Nietzsche's epistemology and his ethics. In this chapter, I will concentrate on the epistemic side of the equation and in the next I will focus on the ethical. I will begin by examining Nietzsche's view of justification. I argue that Nietzsche is a non-foundationalist on the question of justification, but that he is also a non-coherentist too. Thankfully neither of these positions exhaust all justificatory theories. I will show that Nietzsche is best understood as a foundherentist and more precisely as a virtue foundherentist. This unique outlook will be explained below. The second aspect of the epistemic questions concerns Nietzsche's views on truth. This issue, is, as anyone with only a remote interest in Nietzsche knows is a rabbit-hole of sorts. In Nietzsche's *oeuvre,* one may detect at least three distinctively different views of truth. I examined each of these positions in chapters three and four. I will come to show that, given Nietzsche's metaphysical position above, he does not hold an *adequatio* idea of truth where propositions are true if they adequately reflect reality. Given that all there is, is a relation and that these relations are known from the inside as it were, or cross-perspectively; the traditional understanding of a true statement as one that mirrors reality is clearly rejected. Given this sense of truth, Nietzsche is clearly a "sophisticated deflationist" as opposed to a naïve deflationist, like Richard Rorty and Huw Price. However, of more importance is Nietzsche's later shift from truth to truthfulness. This divergence represents an important watershed in Nietzsche's thinking for he now recognizes, in *The Genealogy* and elsewhere, that an investigation into the nature of truth is necessarily coupled with a will willing to launch the analysis. Thus, any answer given to the question, "What is truth?" Is never complete because there is always something outside of the investigation, namely, the will engaged in the inquiry. This insight means that standard objections to deflationist accounts of truth will not apply in Nietzsche's case but indeed provoke a new thinking regarding the relationship between justification and truthfulness.

6.1 NIETZSCHE ON JUSTIFICATION

Regarding Nietzsche's stance on justification, I argue that Nietzsche is indeed a non-foundationalist. However, this fact neither entails that he is a contextualist, pragmatist, coherentist, or some hybrid combination thereof, as at least as one scholar seems to assume.[6] Arguing for any one position or all positions under this general coherentist-pragmatist-contextualist umbrella, is incoherent with much of Nietzsche's fully formulated position. I argue that Nietzsche is a foundherentist—the most accurate view of his epistemology is that it combines the merits of foundationalist and coherentist approaches to epistemic justification without absorbing each position's respective, problematic features. I will demonstrate this. Second, I will examine Nietzsche's remarks on perspectivism. Many scholars have taken perspectivism to be *Salva Veritate* with relativism, but this is not true.[7] The problem of perspectivism is only an issue if one equates non-foundationalism with coherentism. I provide a new solution to the perspectivist problem and in so doing provide a further means of legitimating the interpretation of Nietzsche's ontology that I have given above.

If Nietzsche's epistemic position is anathema to foundationalism, then the first logical question to ask is: "What is foundationalism?" Following Susan Haack, I argue that all foundationalist theories of epistemic justification hold two basic premises to be undeniably true:

(1) That some beliefs are epistemically secure, basic, and are not dependent on other beliefs for their security;

(2) Justification runs in one direction—from these basic beliefs to the upper tier beliefs. The justification of upper tier beliefs is derived from basic beliefs.[8]

Nietzsche rejects the first premise. He argues that no belief is epistemically secure. Every belief is revisable. Indeed, as the history of science has shown, no belief is ever completely justifiable. Nietzsche provides several different reasons for the rejection of premise one according to his epistemic and ontological commitments at various times, and we have already examined some of these. First, he argues that the world is not immediately given to us. Facts, Nietzsche famously declares in section 481 of *The Will to Power* "is precisely what there is not."[9] Examining this statement more closely we might think that this claim is self-referentially incoherent, and certainly, many critics and sympathizers of Nietzsche have interpreted the claim in this way, but further reflection reveals it is not necessarily nonsensical. The point I wish to make is subtle: I do not want to defend the claim that there are no facts, but to put into question, just as Nietzsche does, what a fact is. For Nietzsche, it is the idea of a *factum brutum* that poses significant problems and not, for example, the mundane facts that empirical disciplines utilize within Kuhnian normal science. Such "facts" are more like heuristic devices that serve pragmatic purposes as Nietzsche remarks in this regard referring to the immutable facts of chemistry: "Meanwhile, the formulas are true: for they are crude; for what is 9 parts oxygen to 11 parts hydrogen! This 9 to 11 ratio is totally impossible to achieve precisely; there is always an error in implementation, consequently a certain range within which the experiment succeeds."[10] Thus I do not wish to argue that facts do not exist independently of interpretation. This claim is much weaker than the position I defend but therefore much more defensible.

Although it is true that one could interpret section 481 of *The Will to Power* as a statement about the world or in common parlance a fact, one should be aware that this is only one interpretation of the phrase. The sentence may also be interpreted as a Rorschach test: how one interprets this sentence reveals the interpreter's intentions and agendas. Thus any time a claim is made an evaluation is also made and one cannot make value-free claims. It is this last point that I go to great lengths to articulate throughout the present book in multiple ways for it is this idea that really gets to the heart of Nietzsche's notion of will to power.

On some occasions, it would appear that Nietzsche would be in agreement with the second thesis of foundationalism (or perhaps a corrupted version thereof) namely, that of epistemic security. Nietzsche does seem to suggest that individuals justify beliefs from some inherent disposition or prejudice.[11] This prejudice cannot be dispensed with. But once more this idea is non-cognitive. In fact, it is more accurate to call it an affective disposition. It is this affective disposition that then gives rise to conscious deliberation and, ultimately, justification. But the use of the word "justification" is not meant in the traditional epistemic sense of this word. Justification here means something akin to rationalization. More will be said about the relation between the affects, reflection, and justification in the final pages of this section.

So if Nietzsche is not a foundationalist then how does he actually justify his interpretations of moral phenomenon such as guilt? In the second essay of *On the Genealogy of Morals*, Nietzsche seeks to demonstrate how guilt originated. It is clear that Nietzsche offers arguments for his interpretation and these arguments in turn are subtended by historical facts. However, what value would such an interpretation have if these same facts are themselves merely interpretations since Nietzsche does not believe in the epistemic security of any fact? How else can Nietzsche justify his position?

I argue that Nietzsche's basic epistemic schema for justification is foundherentist and not foundationalist in method. What is foundherentism? The foundherentist claims that belief requires three conditions to be fulfilled for it to be justified. First, the belief requires direct evidence. One cannot justify an empirical belief, for example, merely because it is consistent with a previously established belief system. However, the sensory evidence is never bare—it is already evidence and therefore infused with interpretation, understanding. Susan Haack, the founder of foundherentism, holds a double-aspect theory of justification. She makes a distinction between being in a state of believing and knowing what one believes. States of belief must be translated such that the propositional content of these conditions can be extracted and turned into what she calls "C-beliefs" (where C refers to content). So, for example, if I am about to drink a cup of coffee which is scalding hot and proceed to burn my tongue then I am in a state of believing that I am in pain. Now if I then extract the propositional content from this state I might extract the following: "My tongue is burnt. I am in pain because the coffee is too hot and the coffee, in turn, burnt my tongue." These C-beliefs are clearly factual claims about the world and therefore can serve an epistemic purpose. An S belief, on the other hand, can neither be justified nor be unjustified. The only epistemic role S-beliefs play is one of translation—the purpose of justification is to develop these belief states into propositions.[12]

The second aspect required for the justification of a belief relates to what Haack calls "C-reasons." To justify a belief, one should gather many sources of direct evidence and compare and contrast this evidence regarding the belief. Haack calls this stage the amassing and evaluating of C-reasons stage. C-reasons refer to the reasons I have for believing the content of my C- beliefs. If again I think that the coffee in my mug is too hot, I can corroborate this belief by looking to see if steam is emanating from the coffee. Alternatively, I may touch the mug of the coffee cup to feel how hot the coffee inside it might be.[13]

If the belief seems to be well-corroborated in this regard, then the subject moves onto the third aspect of justification which Haack calls the "comprehensive condition." The comprehensive condition requires that we compare all of the C-reasons we have for the C-belief that we are examining with our prior belief system. If this new belief is consistent with epistemically related beliefs which we also believe to be well-justified, then this new belief would also be justified. Stating all this as a primitive *explicandum*, Haack claims: "That A is more/less justified in believing in p depending how good his direct C-evidence is with respect to p."[14]

How does all this apply to Nietzsche? Consider Nietzsche's explanation for the creation of the "bad conscience" and its eventual development into guilt. In essay II of *The Genealogy*, Nietzsche traces the origin of guilt to what he calls the "bad conscience." After examining several competing explanatory hypotheses for the source of guilt, Nietzsche introduces the reader to his hypothesis. He argues that guilt may be traced to a primitive state of mental feeling that acted as a warning system for early human beings. Human beings, according to Nietzsche, were created by what he baptizes as the first warrior-artists—those who were responsible for constructing and then ruling the first civilizations.[15] These were brutal overlords who imposed equally terrible punishments for disobedience. As we already know, the will to power denotes the overflowing sense of power. It is much like a fast-moving river, always in flux but channeled to achieve the best possible power form at a particular time. However, if a river is somehow blocked such that it can no longer flow toward its goal, then its banks will eventually be overrun with water. This metaphor is analogous to how the soul was formed. The soul was formed after our natural instincts for war, adventure, and the freedom to roam were blocked by these blonde beasts of prey: These first rulers created the first laws, "five or six I shall nots" and enforced these laws with horrific punishments. As a result, power had to find new channels for its expression. One of these channels was the creation of the soul which in turn created the capacity for mental anguish or guilt in its fully developed form. "That will to self-tormenting" Nietzsche writes, " . . . that repressed cruelty of the animal-man made inward and scared back into himself, the creature imprisoned in the "state" so as to be tamed, who invented the bad conscience in order to hurt himself after the more natural vent for his desire to hurt had been blocked."[16]

Nietzsche provides compelling and direct C-evidence for his initial conjecture that guilt originated in the bad conscience, and the bad conscience itself was formed once the human animals' instincts for adventure, hunting, and war were turned inward. The human animal was bred to alter its nature: It went from a creature that hurts others to hurting itself. This propensity to cause pain and anguish to oneself was the result of the blockage of a once powerful and, Nietzsche thinks, healthy capacity to express will to power outwardly. However, since the ability to hurt cannot be turned it off it simply found a new channel of expression and turned inward. Guilt is a later development of the more primitive bad conscience as guilt allows the human being to torture itself more fully.

Nietzsche proceeds to amass more C- reasons to justify this initial C-belief. He shows that his hypothesis is well-corroborated by many biological, anthropological, and historical facts. For example, he demonstrates how the harsh punishments from the Twelve Tables of Rome, serve to provide further justification for his initial hypothesis.[17] The Twelve Tables prove that justice does not originate from a sense of fairness, but rather in a desire to hurt others. The Twelve Tables then points to the savage nature of human beings and therefore further buttresses Nietzsche's account of guilt.

Finally, Nietzsche shows that other considerations further justify these C-reasons. It is here where Haack's comprehensiveness condition comes into play. He demonstrates that the will to power, as a framework, can help to explain other conundrums of human behavior. For example, in essay three of his *The Genealogy,* Nietzsche shows how the will to power contributes in explaining the rise of the ascetic ideal. The ascetic is someone who is not motivated by pleasure but rather by pain. If this is an accurate picture of the psychology of the acetic, then it runs counter to what most human beings believe to be the real motivational source of human action: the pursuit of pleasure and the avoidance of pain. The ascetic, then, is a peculiar case. He or she seems to be motivated by discipline for the sake of discipline, self-suffering and self-inflicted pain and torture in the interests of self-suffering and self-torture. How might we explain the unusual psychology of the ascetic? Nietzsche shows that the dominant model of the psyche of his time, namely, utilitarian hedonism, is unable to account for this phenomenon.[18] All the hedonist could do is to beg the question: What the ascetic thinks is a pleasure is a pain for a "normal" individual and vice versa. Nietzsche provides an alternative hypothesis to explain this occurrence. He argues, convincingly, that pleasure seeking is simply a mode of a more basic drive in the human being, namely the pursuit of power. This hypothesis is corroborated by Nietzsche's genealogical analysis of the ascetic ideal in book three of *On the Genealogy of Morals*. Thus, Nietzsche's initial conjecture, regarding the origin of the bad conscience, is further substantiated by showing how a more comprehensive explanation for human behavior renders even Nietzsche's initial account, which is, of course, will to power, more coherent. Moreover, the epistemic warrant for this hypothesis can be analyzed and comprehended in foundherentist terms.

Foundherentism nicely solves some of the epistemic and justificatory problems that plagued the early Nietzsche. First, the foundherentist does not believe in a *factum brutum*—all sensation is theory laden. But this does not entail a skeptical position either. The foundherentist is harnessed to the world of relations which is the will to power, through one mode in particular: sensation. Therefore, sensation must play a necessary role when it comes to justification. However, sensations are necessarily tied to a theory, agenda, and narrative. It is at this juncture where a subject's C-reasons become so important. C-reasons may either put our immediate C-evidence for a belief into question or provide further support. Return to the hot coffee example. If I took some hallucinogenic drug before drinking the coffee in my cup, then obviously I am less justified in believing in the veracity of my sensations than when a drug-induced stupor does not unduly influence me. But we cannot draw from this example the conclusion that all perception is *mere* interpretation—there remains sensory experience that is particularly recalcitrant to some interpretations and not others. Again, for instance, I might have many reasons to believe that the coffee before me is not piping hot and yet for all this, I may still perceive the coffee as hot.

Even if the basic investigative and epistemic structure of Nietzschean genealogy is foundherentist, there is still much work to do. For Haack cleaves to traditional epistemic notions such as the correspondence theory of truth, a substantive and self-identical subject and many others. How then might the critic ask at this point, do we infuse foundherentism with the key Nietzschean ideas on the will to power as I developed them? I now spend the rest of this section showing how Nietzsche's primary ideas having to do with epistemology are consistent with a revamped, and, in my view, stronger foundherentist position.

The first step is to combine Haack's epistemic foundherentist schema above with the ontological perspectival theory of power I developed in chapter five. As was discovered, perspectives are not beliefs. They are not doxastic. Perspectives, rather, are non-doxastic environments of power. We do not have perspectives, as we might have beliefs, rather we are in them. Perspectives are merely the mode of relation that relate us to the world. But perspectives are not self-contained, distinct from others. Nor are they devoid of intention, at least where intention is minimally understood. All perspectives lust after power. Perspectives absorb other perspectives to yoke the latent power from them. Such an unquenchable lust even pertains to knowledge. To desire to know some "thing" is a willingness to control that very same thing. Knowledge is simply one mode of will to power.

However, this does not entail that we, as subjects, are distinct from our environments. It is not as though we are projecting our agendas, as subjects, onto the world in the hopes that we can control our environment. To argue in this way is to hold subject/object, realism/anti-realism dichotomies that Nietzsche surely rejects. So we must be able to make sense of the idea that all things are locked in a perpetual *agon* with all other things while also acknowledging that such things are not conscious in the sense that these very things project agendas, strategies, etc. onto a static world. The idea that I wish to promote is to understand strategies not as agendas which are placed on and then in the world, but as new relations which allow me to relate to the world, and to myself, in new ways.

Indeed, even the environment metaphor that I have been employing is problematic: to think of an environment is to think of some thing existing inside of it with some other thing existing on the outside. Moreover, conversely, to think of an environment is to think of oneself outside of it (I can pluck myself out of my current environment much as animals may be plucked out of their natural habitats). This notion, however, is inaccurate because it was discovered that all things are tied to each other *via* lines of force and, if this is the case then there is no longer a container called the "environment" which contains things. Rather, all things are inter and intraconnected precisely because each and every thing can affect every other. In this sense, there are only relations and no *relata*.

With this metaphysical recap in mind, I am now in a position to examine the epistemic problems of sections 3.3 and 3.5. The first of these was the error problem. The error problem held that if perspectives were non-doxastic then where and how does error arise? Now with a doxastic approach to perspectivism, this problem is rather easy to solve. The error can be accounted for by not having had sufficient information to make a claim about some state of affairs. We judge too hastily and therefore commit a mistake by claiming, for example, that an object has certain qualities when it does not. What's more, it is easy to account for how we make such a mistake. We make these mistakes because there is an objective standard by which we can use to measure our judgment against, namely, the object in question which exists independently of our minds.

However, the problem with a realist account of ontology and the simple correspondence theory of truth is that it is difficult to ascertain when we get it right: We cannot work our way out from the very environmental envelope that makes knowledge possible. If the mind is a mirror in the sense that we can only know that which our mind represents to us, and yet this mirror is itself produced *via* our evolutionary heritage, then we can never know if this mirror is indeed accurate. In fact, even foundherentism, as an epistemic theory, is susceptible to this charge of possible inaccuracy. It is for this very reason that Haack evinces that we can never have complete justification for P.[19]

The non-doxastic position, in contrast, guarantees "truth": Under a simple reading we have unmediated access to our environment since we are immersed in that very setting.[20] Indeed, more properly understood there is no "we" nor "us" at all. There is no definitive division between subject and object. The subject is just a series of relations. Moreover, there is nothing more than simply relations, which exist within, to, and between other things. These relations are nothing more than various modes of power. These things, in turn, are also relations, and therefore it does not make sense, on a global view of will to power, to speak of something being outside or inside an environment. However, if all this is true then how are mistakes possible? Certainly, a significant amount of mediation takes place between our belief system and the world. Delusional paranoids, for example, clearly do not have a grasp on reality and some can have very elaborate, intricate, and consistent belief systems. Moreover, these belief systems might prove to be very difficult to falsify. How do we account for these obviously false beliefs if there is no mediation required between the human being and his or her environment?

I argue that it is this very notion of "mediation" is the problem. Certainly, the idea of epistemic access has plagued philosophers since Plato. For Plato, the soul had to be like the Forms for the soul to perceive them.[21] Descartes, by contrast, required the criterion of clear and distinct ideas as well as the supposition of a perfect God to underwrite those judgments that could not be doubted.[22] Empiricists like Hume, on the other hand, sought to confer some special status to direct impressions—sensory experience expunged of any conceptual components. Sense impressions gave us direct and unvarnished access to the real world. We were led to make an error, so Hume thought when we attempted to make generalizations from these impressions.[23] Hegel's solution worked a little too well: All ideas were correct in the sense that they were correct for their time; they were nothing more than necessary stepping stones leading to the "World Mind" or Absolute Spirit.[24]

Indeed, even the logical positivists of the twentieth century did not seem to learn this lesson. They were also plagued with the problem of mediation because they accepted a revamped and more sophisticated version of the analytic/synthetic divide. Their solution was to guarantee the justification of sense experience by appealing to "protocol statements." Protocol statements were basic empirical statements that were devoid of metaphysical content and concepts. The positivists abhorred metaphysics and so ideal observation statements, so thought the positivists, should be sensory rich and metaphysically minimal. An example of a protocol statement might be: "Smith sees a red patch at 2:01 pm."[25] According to the positivists, statements could only be verified and therefore meaningful in one of two ways. Statements were either logically true, that is, they were mere tautologies or true *a posteriori* (according to empirical experience). Therefore, a scientific statement, such as Newton's third law of motion: "An object in motion tends to stay in motion" was verifiable and hence meaningful only insofar as it could be supported by protocol sentences.

However, true protocol statements do not exist. All empirical statements are already theory-ladened as both Karl Popper and N. R. Hanson definitively showed.[26] Empirical statements may only take on meaning if they are embedded in theory. All observation, after all, is theory directed: We are observing some event because we have a reason or purpose in doing so.

Thus, if mediation is the problem, then the solution to this troublesome idea is to examine that which is responsible for producing such mediation. Since there is no mediation between ourselves and the environment, according to the non-doxastic account that I delineate here, the problem is not that of epistemic access, in contradistinction to the position taken by most of the great philosophers in Western thought. The problem as construed by the history of philosophy is one of ascertaining whether the ideas we have of objects are accurate representations of those very objects in the world. The problem then has to do with the directedness of consciousness and the gap between mind and world. The problem, in other words, is one of fitness: Does this idea I have of the object fit with the very object of which the idea is merely a representation? What sort of access do I have to the object and how can I justify that this access is accurate?

But, what if the problem had to with the relationship between mind and mind? What if the problem had to do with the communication, so to speak, between two different components or parts within a subject? In other words, another way to approach the problem is not to focus on the gap between subject and world such that various bridges are constructed to ameliorate this spacing, but rather to bridge the spacing within the subject. This angle from which to examine the question leads to a further, more perplexing query: "What precisely is this gap within subjectivity of which I speak?"

Nietzsche provides us with an interpretation of this phenomenon of "subject spacing." The subject, as Nietzsche makes clear in section 19 of *Beyond Good and Evil,* is simply a collection of forces or "under-wills."[27] As already shown, Nietzsche believes that our very personality is constructed from various drives, and so when these drives disperse such that they become organized in new ways, then we are no longer the same person. For Nietzsche, the subject is not some substantive, static, concrete entity. The subject is more akin to a constitutional organization of competing forces. The "peace" of this constitution is held provided that it is to the advantage of all drives—all drives can strive for more power and are successful in achieving more power. When the constitutional structure is challenged, then the subject becomes more like a warring state.

To continue with the metaphor, the subject which becomes a true warring state will have many different and competing perspectives to things within the world. Without a unifying force or better perspective, working through these drives, directing them, such drives do not congeal to form an overarching power perspective. Thus the person appears "irrational," "erratic," "multiple," or simply "chaotic" or lacking an adequate grasp on reality but really, the person does not have an adequate grip on the competing drives within himself or herself.

According to Nietzsche, the entire notion of a static subject is nothing more than a dogma manufactured, in part, by those who would wish to hold us responsible for our actions so that we may be punished for them.[28] Therefore those philosophers who criticize attempts to naturalize philosophy, like Marian Thalos in her seminal work "Two Dogmas of Naturalized Epistemology," are correct to think that the very notion of subjecthood is one of the long-standing dogmas of naturalized epistemology. However, she does not and, perhaps, cannot explain why epistemologists have failed to question the nature and perhaps very existence of "S" in the so-called "primitive" epistemic *explicandum:* "When is S justified in believing P."[29] Nietzsche fills in this missing piece of the subject dogma puzzle: The subject is "ontologized" because it benefits some drive's agenda.

How does this model of subjectivity help us to explain error? First, unlike the representationalist story, we are not led to make a mistake, so this position goes, merely because we have insufficient evidence for our claim. It is also imprecise to say that we are led to error because we are basing judgments on evidence which turn out, in the end, to be false. Fundamentally, we are led to error or more aptly have recalcitrant experience because we are not virtuous enough. Why are we not virtuous enough? We are not virtuous enough because we are not merely cognitive creatures who objectively assess various forms of evidence to justify a belief. We are also and perhaps more fundamentally, affective creatures who have a stake and vested interest in what beliefs we form. Epistemic beliefs are undergirded by desire. There is no way to get around this. Indeed, the desire for objectivity, so Nietzsche contends, is just another mask of the will to power. We wish to justify our beliefs to others and even to ourselves, objectively, because doing so increases the likelihood that such beliefs will be true, or so we think, and we desperately wish to believe that we are in possession of the Truth. Truth has a premium value, and because it does so, it holds power. This trust and premium value given to Truth will be analyzed in more detail below.

Haack is in need of a corrective. Her basic epistemic *explicandum* is too "objective"; (where objective is being used in the Nietzschean and hence pejorative sense of the term) she forgets that subjects are not, primarily, knowing creatures, but feeling creatures. Therefore, her epistemic *explicandum* should read: "A is more less/more justified at time t depending on how good her virtuously derived C-evidence is with respect to p." The "break of truth access" as it were does not occur between the subject and the world but within the self. Our first task then should not be one of discovering the C-evidence for a belief, but rather how one feels about the belief's truthfulness. Instead of asking myself: "What evidence do I have to support this belief?" Instead, I should ask: "Is the belief one that I wish were true and if so why?" Alternatively, in contrast: "Am I afraid, on some level, that the belief could be true?" etc. If I do not undertake this affective analysis of belief, then it is entirely possible that I will miss key pieces of evidence that might serve to alter the initial justificatory assessment I gave to the belief.

To be clear, when I am discussing the notion of "fearing the truth of the belief" I am not referring to trivial beliefs like the temperature of the coffee in my mug. Such a belief has little if any emotional charge. No, what I am talking about are beliefs which have significant emotional resonance. I am referencing beliefs that form integral components of my belief system and, therefore of my character and personhood constitution. Such beliefs might include: God, the existence of free will, the intrinsic goodness of human beings, etc. I cannot have a truly objective relation, here meant as undetached and uninterested to these beliefs since such beliefs, if either true or false, would serve to alter my entire understanding of myself and the current relation I have to the world. In addition, such beliefs may be able to fail many justificatory tests and yet still be held true (or false) by the one who holds them—perhaps I try to continue to deceive myself into thinking that the justificatory tests in question were flawed in some way. Such beliefs cannot be detached from the desire to believe in them. It is this desire that continues to fuel the perceived "justification" of the idea. Error or more aptly put "insufficient-justification" is committed because we fail to examine all of the available C-reasons for the proposition. The connection between desire, reflection, feeling and character-forming beliefs, will be brought out in more detail in the next section.

It would seem, then, that some beliefs are more deeply embedded within a belief system than others. They are core beliefs. However, how do we account for the rather mundane mistakes we make every day, the skeptic might retort? Surely we must be able to provide an account of mistaken beliefs such as believing that the coffee in my mug is now too cold to drink. We can answer this charge by remembering that there is an affective component to judgment. We sometimes make a judgment too enthusiastically by simply following the lead of our emotions. To counter this, Nietzsche argues that we must reflect on the 'why' of our emotions: Why am I, at this present moment, feeling what I believe I am feeling? Certainly, our emotions are often the first indication of experiencing an "encounter" and such encounters are intrinsically meaningful and relevant to us when we experience a particularly strong emotion.

Richard Lazarus' work on the structure of emotions places what I have said above into sharper relief. Lazarus shows that emotions are appraisals: They are immediate indications of a relationship between a human being and his or her environment.[30] However, we can also be wrong about why we are feeling what we are currently feeling and even what we are truly feeling. For example, sometimes anger is misplaced: We attribute the cause of our anger to some undeserving target. But at other times, anger is wrongly felt: Anger can serve as a mask for feeling hurt. Thus even commonplace "purely epistemic" mistakes such as jumping to a conclusion or providing a hasty and ill-thought-out answer to a query can be accounted for given this model. We might claim that an individual who is guilty of these epistemic transgressions is attempting to remedy an unconscious insecurity by showing off. So mistakes of judgment, or so I argue, are not purely epistemic. They are not merely cognitive, if, by this term, we mean those categories which are divested of all emotion. Indeed, as Antonio Damasio has shown, all cognitive systems are already infused with emotion.[31]

Emotions are entry points into the relation we have to other things because feelings, according to Nietzsche, are expressions of drives and drives are perspectival. "Every drive is a kind of lust to rule; each one has its perspective that it would like to compel all the other drives to accept as a norm."[32] However, because emotions are not raw, in that they are infused with consciousness but according to Nietzsche, have in fact been perverted through the various practices of breeding within civilization, we sometimes misinterpret the information they are attempting to convey. It is precisely this spacing that we need to bridge. As Nietzsche remarks in this regard: "Only feelings not thoughts are inherited."[33] However, if feelings are inherited then they are not ours. Indeed they represent counter-selves for the self could have been organized according to the underlying drive of which the feeling is but a mere expression. Therefore, feelings must be interpreted and reinterpreted but according to a schema. I have suggested that this underlying schema is foundherentism. It is when we begin or fail to interpret emotions that we can be mistaken. Understanding the emotions we may experience as we start to investigate a deeply rooted belief which is acutely embedded within our belief system is the first step toward justifying our beliefs.

This account of justification, supplemented as it was by Haack's foundherentism gels well with Nietzsche's remarks in *The Will to Power*. Nietzsche claims that "It is in the nature of thinking that it thinks of and invents the unconditioned as an adjunct to the condition; just as it is though and invented the ego as an adjunct of multiplicity of its processes."[34] And further that, "the I or consciousness usually keeps the others closed."[35] "What man wants, what every smallest part of a living organism wants, is an increase in power."[36] Each of these drives lusts to rule and, accordingly, view the world as a relation from a unique power perspective. Thus, it is, for this reason, there are "many truths" because all power-centers interpret the set of relations from their agenda and thus when one considers that will to power is precisely one of these interpretations from a power center, one can consistently and coherently claim that there are just interpretations of interpretations. However, the more feelings we use to gather C-evidence, the more C-reasons we can bring to bear on a given proposition, the more complete our justification for said proposition will be and thus the more justified we are in holding the proposition.

This answer to the justification question also accommodates one of Nietzsche's most insightful yet perplexing passages on perspectivism to be found in his *oeuvre*. As noted in chapter two, it is in the third essay, section 12 of the *On the Genealogy of Morals*, where we find Nietzsche's clearest expression of perspectivism. It is here where he famously compares perspectives to affects and "eyes." Such comparisons have caused much puzzlement and for good reason: for Nietzsche mentions that, although we are restricted to having perspectives, the concept of perspective is not akin to perception. Perspective rather should be thought of as feeling, comportment, or attitude. Perspectives are like "eyes" in the sense that they reveal the myriad possible attunements we may have to things. If we combine this passage with the paragraph before it, Nietzsche's justificatory picture, as seen through the lens of foundherentism, comes into full view. Nietzsche writes: ". . . to want to see differently, is no small discipline and preparation for the intellect for its future 'objectivity'—the latter understood not as contemplation without interest which is a nonsensical absurdity but as the ability to control one's Pro and Con and to dispose of them, so that one knows how to employ a variety of perspectives and affective interpretations in the service of knowledge."[37] Many commentators have added their gloss to this passage. Scholars largely agree that what Nietzsche is advocating is that affects are like viewpoints. If we combine these points of view, as we might combine, say, the stances from which to view a physical object, then in an analogous fashion we would have a more comprehensive idea as to the qualities, agendas, and properties of the thing as a whole by using and combining different drives. What many scholars fail to do, however, is to consider, carefully in what way the collection of viewpoints or affective stances would amount to knowledge. There are two problems with this analysis: First, if the ego is just simply what we call the "head-drive" then how do we, as a substantive ego, occupy the thought-space or feeling space of another drive? To do that, we would need to adopt a new ego, if only temporarily. But that would entail that Nietzsche suggests we must go back and forth between the two egos. How is that possible? Second, if we view these affects as power-centers, then the perspective of one drive on the web of power relations that make up a thing would surely be incommensurable when viewed from the stance of another drive. The mere "heaping" of viewpoints would result in an incoherent mess of perspectives.

My theory nicely solves the above problems by showing that one must take the evidence from each emotive source and combine them to present a comprehensive and coherent narrative on the thing in question. By examining and controlling the C-evidence and C-reasons that each drive brings to bear on something and then, as Nietzsche directs us, use this evidence (or dispose of it but not on a whim but because it is unjustified), we can gain a better appreciation and more justified understanding of something. I develop this notion in far more detail in my book *Philosophical Genealogy*, which I will not go into at length here, but in the conclusion of that work, I offer a complete procedure of how the entertaining of perspectives from affective sources helps justify a genealogical inquiry.

6.2 NIETZSCHE ON TRUTH

What then of truth, we might ask? It seems there are several interesting questions that the above analysis provokes. How do we know when a well-justified position, when viewed through the lens of virtue foundherentism is true? What is truth? These and other questions, relevant as they are to the epistemic side of the question of truth problem, are the most difficult queries to answer in the Nietzschean secondary literature and subsequently would require an entire book on the subject to do them justice. However, it was discovered that Nietzsche uses truth in at least three senses. In this section, I wish to focus on the first rendering of truth, namely the metaphysical. This view of truth holds that a proposition is true just in case the proposition reflects reality as it truly is. Nietzsche rejects this view of truth (i.e., Truth) in many places. His argument is that one cannot view reality from outside of one's perspective: One cannot establish a non-relation relationship to reality as it truly is. Thus, since to grasp reality in itself is impossible; it makes no sense to speak about the distinction between appearance and reality. However, once we give up the distinction between appearance and reality, then we give up the metaphysical notion of truth, too.

Truth then is a kind of fiction according to Nietzsche believed in by different people for many reasons: some out of fear, others for pragmatic reasons and still others because it serves their self-interests. But clearly, all these reasons for accepting, adopting, and advocating Truth are done out of power: Truth can dispel one's fears, Truth can provide an investigator with a target to shoot for, and Truth can be wielded by those to persuade others to follow them. However, if Nietzsche is a fictionalist when it comes to Truth, then what kind of fictionalist is he?

One way out of this problem is to adopt a contemporary fictionalist position on Truth, of which there are many possible types. Richard Rorty's unique deflationist view of Truth is strikingly similar to some of the remarks on Truth Nietzsche makes in many of his works. Indeed, the resemblance between the two projects was not lost on Rorty who wrote that Nietzsche's project at times chimes with his own.[38] Christoph Cox in his work, *Nietzsche, Naturalism and Interpretation* recognizes these same similarities but goes one step further: He argues that Nietzsche's models about truth and justification are consistent with Rorty's pragmatic, philosophical approach. Cox's project is to explain and naturalize Nietzsche's position by using Rorty's very clear, and, unabashedly, pragmatic methodology.[39] I think Cox is right when it comes to Nietzsche's deflationist view of truth and therefore do not go to great lengths here to recapitulate Cox's powerful and convincing arguments to support his stance. However, as to the justificatory picture, Cox is wrong: Nietzsche would reject Rorty's "little" justificatory program. I reaffirm Nietzsche's affinities with Haack's position.

To begin, I wish to quote a passage that Cox himself uses to undergird his argument that Nietzsche is really a Rortian, although perhaps a rather muddled one. Rorty in "Science as Solidarity" writes, "There is nothing to be said about either truth or rationality apart from descriptions of the familiar procedures of justification which a given society—ours—uses in one or another area of inquiry."[40] Rorty's epistemic position is such that truth, the truth, or Truth (whatever nominalization of truths one wishes to use) are not necessary to make assertoric sentences. As a pragmatist, Rorty upholds the methodological rule of "no difference without a practical difference."[41] As Rorty explains: "Pragmatists think that if something makes no difference to practice, it should make no difference to philosophy. This conviction makes them suspicious of the distinction between justification and truth, for that distinction makes no difference to my decisions about what to do."[42] For Rorty, the best way to understand epistemic concepts such as truth, warrant, evidence, and so forth is to examine how these notions are used and therefore one must analyze the conditions for assertions. Assertoric discourse, of which scientific and other forms of inquiry are a species, is defined by the acceptance, challenging, and denying of claims. For this practice to occur, it is imperative that such claims be taken seriously—assertions must be expressed by a sincere speaker and, second, such claims are well supported *at least according to* what the speaker takes to be sufficient reasons, and strong evidence, etc. For Rorty the above two constraints are the only normative components assertions require; no other metaphysical, epistemic, or normative rule is needed.

What then of truth, we may ask? According to Rorty, the notion of Truth plays neither metaphysical, epistemic nor normative role when it comes to the practice of making assertions and denials. Truth has no metaphysical role to play because Truth does not exist outside of our procedures of justification and discursive practices in which we know our way around. Any notion where reality somehow existed beyond these procedures would be unknowable and hence of no practical purpose. Rorty proclaims that we must abandon, the third dogma of empiricism which holds that there remains a division between the schemes we use to organize the sensory world and the content of this world that exists somewhere beyond these arrangements.[43] The model is self-contradictory; if we cannot in principle know what the world is like then, we cannot claim that our perspectives view the world no matter how incompletely or inaccurately this may be—we would have no way to measure our schemas and no way of knowing what the schemas are mapping onto.

Turning now to the justificatory, Truth has no epistemic role to play because when we claim that some assertion is not true, we are not arguing that the speaker who as has made the assertion has not viewed the facts as they are because no one can see the facts as they truly are. All viewing takes place from a perspective and thus one cannot view facts from some completely objective ground. What the person is, in effect, saying, so holds Rorty is that the speaker is not justified; the reasons given to support some assertion are poor, or irrelevant, are inconsistent, are insufficient, or are not adequately weighted, etc. It is the notion of justification then which bears the epistemic and normative weight of assertoric discourse; Truth is not a load-bearing notion. Given that justification has an enormous load to bear it is prudent to examine Rorty's idea of justification in more detail.

Rorty makes clear, in *Contingency Irony Solidarity*, that justification, for him, is not uniform but varies from discipline to discipline. Rorty argues that the world, as we describe it, cannot be reduced to any particular model, idea, or theory. In fact, the idea of holding perspectives on reality where reality stands outside of these perspectives should be outright rejected. All there is, Rorty evinces, are a fixed number of "language games"—academic discourses and disciplines that determine the meaning of sentences and therefore of justified belief within that particular context. Rorty explains: "Uttering a sentence without a fixed place in a language game is, as the positivists rightly have said, to utter something which is neither true nor false—something which is not, in Ian Hacking's terms, "a truth-value candidate."[44] For Rorty, we simply should not view language as that of a jigsaw puzzle that we then try to fit together in a feeble attempt to unify both our language (and our knowledge) into one, grand super-vocabulary. This way of viewing justification would entail that no statement is ever truly justified because all statements would be true only according to some angle or perspective of "the truth." Holding this position would be disastrous because we would never be able to exorcise Descartes' ghost. Thus, according to Rorty, questions such as "What is the place of consciousness in a world of molecules?" or "What is the relation of language to thought?"[45] are ill-formed questions because they presuppose that the justificatory procedures accepted in one game hold for another. Rorty himself best summarizes the upshot of this approach: ". . . since truth is a property of sentences, since sentences are dependent for their existence upon vocabularies, and since vocabularies are made by human beings, so are truths."[46]

There are truths in physics, truths in history, and truths in geology but no Truth or the truth. As well the notion that there are truths, indexed as they are by a language game, should itself be deflated—truths refer to beliefs, positions, theories, etc. which are justified according to the discipline in which they are housed. Holding there is but one Truth, is to view the impossible for it would entail making the claim that such perspectives given as they are by the academic discipline in which they are couched, are limited but then what are they constrained by? Thinking of Truth instead of truths is to engage in the perverse practice of Platonic nominalization which entails thinking of goods in terms of the Good. However, neither nominalization, whether it is the Good, the Truth, or Beauty with a capital B, is particularly helpful and thus such notions remain vacuous when they are allowed to operate detached from the conditions that make them possible.[47]

Truth, given this model, is just a convenient fiction; there are no epistemic nor metaphysically interesting questions to be engendered on pondering the question "What is truth?" in a typical Socratic manner. Truth, according to this view is just a property language users use to confer a special status on some sentences. However, in fact, what is meant by Truth is intersubjective agreement, according to what a community deems to be warranted methods of inquiry and justification. The Truth is simply approval, but once more because we require approval and others seek approval by attempting to arrive at the truth then Truth has power.[48]

How can Nietzsche benefit from Rorty's incisive deflationary account of Truth? First, we can, as Rorty suggests, abandon the ontological, epistemic, and even normative role Truth plays in assertoric discourse. However, in turn, this means that we must also reject Rorty's "little" justificatory program. Nietzsche's genealogical program is one where he believes that all disciplines which attempt to investigate the nature of humanity or society are ripe for criticism. Nietzsche, by utilizing a genealogical methodology, tries to show that the contemporary disciplines and discourses of morality, philosophy, science, art, and the law may all be criticized because they are not honest, nor conscientious of their methods. If such disciplines are presented as absolute and construed to be entirely removed from their historical origins, then they are nothing but *lies*. What Nietzsche calls for is an approach that would explain and attempt *to eradicate* unjustified falsehoods in all of these disciplines and discourses. What Nietzsche calls for is a stricter method for arriving at more accurate, sounder theories, and hypotheses that extend across all disciplines and discourses. Thus, genealogy is not just on par with any other academic discipline. Rather, genealogy is a unique discipline that has the *right* to critique distinct areas of knowledge such as theology, the natural sciences, (including physics and biology) and of course philosophy because it is more epistemically rigorous and truthful than either of these sciences.[49]

All ideas and concepts are in the proper domain of genealogy. Academic discourses do not have the authority to "self-justify." Genealogies can do and must undermine the epistemic warrant of academic disciplines.

Thus, Nietzsche too would argue alongside Rorty that justification does the real work of Truth and that the necessity of metaphysical, epistemic, or even normative constructions of Truth are illusions. When Nietzsche puts forward sustained arguments against the utilitarians in the *Genealogy* or against the materialists in *Beyond Good and Evil* he demonstrates not that what they are saying is untrue but that it is unjustified.[50]

However, truthfulness does play a vital role in assertoric discourse for every empirical inquiry requires just that: an inquirer. As Nietzsche shows, the will to inquiry is just as important and indeed perhaps more important than the method and tools used for the investigation itself. I have argued that one must supplement foundherentism with a virtuous component where we take into consideration the affective attitude we feel about a particular proposition. We must be honest, and truthful about why we feel some evidence to warrant p and why some reasons and other kinds of evidence do not seem to warrant p. Only by examining the reasons *and feelings* we have for our reasons, would a subject resolve the "subject spacing" that at times renders his judgment less justified. However, there comes a point where the will to investigate is burnt out, and the subject asserts that he or she has now discovered "the truth" of some matter at hand. Really, Nietzsche would argue what is meant by "truth" here is simply complete justification—and we never arrive at a complete justification for a belief.

With this deflationist account of truth, coupled with Haack's "big picture" view of justification the old Pontius Pilate question, "What is Truth?" has been resolved or better dissolved. Truth has no epistemic load to bear with respect to assertoric discursive practices. Justification carries the real epistemic burden.

With all that said, is there some response from the metaphysical realist? Yes, yes there is. According to the realist any attempt to investigate the truth of Truth, as it were, ends up relying on a metaphysical and traditional understanding of truth as *adequatio* for the investigation. If we claim that truth is just a useful fiction following Richard Rorty or claim, following Huw Price, that truth is a normative rule that assertion-making creatures need to make sense of the claims others make, then we have provided a model of truth after all. Thus, it would then be reasonable to ask: "But is this model true?" If this question is a sensible one to ask then it is within the space of this gap—between the model expressed and the object the model attempts to capture—where the truth lies. The model can neither capture, reduce nor deflate truth—the chasm between model and truth, where truth is viewed as an object existing outside the very model that sought to capture it, has not been filled. Truth would then exist outside of the very model that attempts to define it and therefore remains undefined.

However, more than that, the metaphysician avers, the model fails to refer to its object, in this case, Truth. Thus, the model is in error and therefore not true! We remain stuck in a fictionalist construal of truth and therefore remain tied to using semantic notions such as truth and falsity as they are naively and metaphysically understood.

Here is where Nietzsche's will to power is necessary to deflate the incisiveness of this question. As demonstrated, objects are not singular things. They are bundles of relations. They are comprised of relations, and these relations are comprised of sub-relations and so on. It is also known that these relations exist in a state of agonic tension with their respective neighbors and thus dynamism is inherent to will to power. However, if all things are inherently dynamic, then it is impossible for any model, any concept, much less a model of truth to refer to anything! The very idea of a definite description denoting any object, group, etc. is not only impossible given will to power but breathtakingly incoherent.[51] Thus, to claim that Nietzsche's deflated model of truth is unable to refer to truth is to use a notion, namely reference, which no longer applies if one examines reality through the lens of will to power. Moreover, adopting will to power is not to adopt a model of how the world really works for this is now revealed to be an incoherent standpoint. It is, rather, to know the relationship one establishes to the world—now understood as a web of relations in dynamic and *agonic* reconfiguration and so formed according to an underlying ground form—from within the very channel of power itself.

We are now left with two final questions. First, "What is the relationship between foundherentism and truth and more accurately stated is a proposition justified by a virtue foundherentist approach truth-conducive insofar as it seems to give us the predictions we expect while concomitantly avoiding recalcitrant experience?" Second, "Is Haack's position consistent with Nietzschean naturalism?" I now spend the rest of this section taking up these concerns.

The answer to the first question, pace the reliabilist, is no because we cannot claim that virtue foundherentism is truth-conducive. If it no longer makes sense to think about the world in a *de re* sense, then the notion of conductivity goes out the window, too. All we may claim, at best, is that foundherentism is truth-indicative or given Rorty's deflationist reading, justificatory-indicative. Rephrasing Haack, I would argue that if any justificatory indication is possible for us (as human beings), then the satisfaction of the foundherentist criteria of justification is justificatory-indicative.[52]

The above answer is the only sensible one available for the question is not so much about justification as it is about meta-justification or ratification. The question is about how my virtue foundherentist construal of Haack's position is, in fact, justified. But notice that irrefutable reasons for ratification could never be proffered without overstepping our epistemological limits. All that may be offered is *what we believe* to be relevant reasons, evidence, logic, etc. for epistemic claims. We cannot, by hypothesis, provide conditions and criteria of ratification that lie outside of the very ways and means we employ for justifying propositions without using these very means and measures. Again, pulling from chapter five, there seem to be thought processes that are believed to be justified cross-perspectivally. We cannot ratify these thought processes from some aperspectival vantage point without falling into contradiction. Thus, foundherentism is self-justifying for if someone were to question the justification of foundherentism, we would ask this person: "Do you have good evidence for p?" "Is your evidence independently secure?" "Are your reasons for believing this evidence strong and warranted?" "Have you examined and taken into consideration all the relevant evidence when you formed your belief?" "Are your evidence and reasons comprehensive?" "Have you examined your feelings regarding the truth or falsity of foundherentism?" Moreover and finally, "Are these reasons the best you can muster, at this time, to at least provide some reassurance that my standards of evidence are not justificatory-indicative?"[53]

Regarding the second question, it is important to be clear that foundherentism is *not* a *strict* "method" for either scientific, social scientific, or genealogical investigation. Nor is foundherentism some epistemic schema that is peculiar to genealogy. Rather, as Haack makes clear in her profound and penetrating book, *Defending Science Within Reason*, all well-corroborated, predictively successful and highly warranted empirical inquiries are undergirded by a foundherentist schema. Indeed, one of the most impressive examples Haack uses to illustrate her argument (that all justified empirical inquiry, scientific, historical, or otherwise are just individual species of the "long arm of reason") is the discovery of the double helix structure of DNA of Watson and Crick in 1953. On commenting on Watson and Crick's 1967 paper (where the scientists explain how they discovered the double helix structure of DNA) Haack notes:

> Just about all the essential ingredients of my analysis of the concepts of evidence and warrant are found in this example: degrees of warrant, shifting over time; confirmation, increment of warrant, as new evidence comes in; sharing of evidential resources; positive evidence and negative; observational evidence and reasons working together; the role of special instruments and techniques of observation; the ramifying structure of evidence; supportiveness, independent security, and comprehensiveness as determinants of evidential quality; the intimate connection of supportiveness with explanatory integration, and hence its sensitivity to the identification of kinds.[54]

Haack continues building her argument, concretely, by demonstrating how other well-established scientific theories, social science studies and detective work, are congruent with the three basic criteria of foundherentism.[55]

Haack advocates for an innatist epistemic position in that the justification of a proposition is conditioned by what human beings *intuitively understand* when thinking about the justificatory concepts (e.g., "well supported," "secure," "evidence," "related," and "comprehensive"). Nevertheless, this "innate" epistemic position is not *a priori*. Haack's innatism is not metaphysical, and neither is Nietzsche's. It is entirely consistent to say that our schema for justification is just "turtles all the way down" in that our reasoning, evidence collecting, and logical argumentation are products of natural and social forces such as evolution and breeding. However, having said that, we can always learn more about our cognitive capacities, biological endowments, cultural conditioning, and our perceptual faculties *via* empirical inquiry. Moreover, we can also "learn" and continue to relearn the difference between what is "valid" as opposed to "invalid," and what is fallacious as opposed to cogent reasoning, might entail. However, in the arena of empirical inquiry, or in the domain of logic, to be justified, necessitates that we rely on an evidential and internalist theory of justification namely, foundherentism.[56] Thus, even epistemology, Haack maintains, can be revised according to new discoveries in empirical fields, but these discoveries themselves are warranted provided that they are underpinned by a foundherentist model of justification.

As a final point, we must also remember that scientific discoveries, as well as genealogical investigations, are more the result of the unquantifiable genius, imagination, and even despair than any single method or epistemological schema. Speaking of despair and perhaps desperation, Werner Heisenberg wrote in the 1920s that quantum physics was in such difficulties that "we (the community of physicists) reached a state of despair." However, as Haack notes, it was out of this very state of despair that came a change of attitude and method.[57] It should also be remembered that it was Nietzsche's same state of despair and Paul Ree's book, *The Origins of Moral Sensations and Psychological Observations*, that allowed him to focus his energies on developing his philosophical genealogy.[58] So, although empirical kinds of investigation, like genealogy, rely on foundherentist methods of research and justification, this does not diminish the role the emotions might play (whether positive or negative as in the case of despair) in scientific inquiry. The question concerning what prompted the *initial* conjecture or insight leading to a highly warranted empirical investigation can only be answered, as noted physicist, Percy Bridgman writes: by "doing one's damnedest with one's mind, no holds barred."[59]

To conclude this section, I would like to answer the Socratic question: What is Truth? from a modified Nietzschean-Rortian-Haackian approach. It was discovered that truth is an attempt to fixate: it is an attempt to arrest becoming. More precisely, truth is an attempt to eternalize, nominalize, and ontologize the dynamism that is the will to power. But more than this, truth is an attempt to renarrate something and to renarrate something is to constellate it. It is to bring some idea into a preestablished agenda with the aim of using this idea to advance the agenda at hand. Truth, then, in Nietzsche's final analysis, is an attempt to control, a valuation, an effort to seize power. However, to arrest something, to try to control it, to constellate it, is to perform an action: truth then presupposes a will to truth, a will to complete justification. However, what is this will to be truthful? Is such an act of willing ours to will? What allows us to fixate on a single object to will? To answer these questions, I turn to Nietzsche's ethics where I focus on the seemingly cognitive and affective capacities that allow us to fixate on some state of affairs to will.

NOTES

1. For a sample list see: Richard Schacht, *Nietzsche* (London: Routledge, 1983). Alexander Nehamas, *Nietzsche: Life as Literature* (Cambridge Mass: Harvard University Press, 1985). Wolfgang, Muller-Lauter, *Nietzsche: His Philosophy of Contradictions and the Contradictions of His Philosophy*, Trans. David J. Parent (University

of Illinois, Press: 1985). Babbette Babich, *Nietzsche's Philosophy of Science: Reflecting Science on the Ground of Art and Life* (Albany NY: SUNY, 1994). Christoph Cox, *Nietzsche, Naturalism and Interpretation* (Berkeley California: University of California Press, 1999).

2. See Ken Gemes, "Nietzsche's Critique of Truth," *Philosophy and Phenomenological Research* Vol. 52 (1992), 47–65. George Stack, "Nietzsche and Perspectival Interpretation," *Philosophy Today* 25 (1981), 221–241. A sample list would include the following: Arthur Danto's *Nietzsche as Philosopher*. Tracy Strong's, *Friedrich Nietzsche and the Politics of Transfiguration* expanded edition (Berkeley, Los Angeles, London: University of California Press, 1978). Paul de Man's *Allegories of Reading* (New Haven: Yale University Press, 1979). Alan Schrift's *Nietzsche and the Question of Interpretation* (New York: Routledge, 1990).

3. Nietzsche, *Beyond Good and Evil*, section 22 in *Basic Writings of Nietzsche*.

4. Nietzsche, Beyond Good and Evil, section 43 in *Basic Writings of Nietzsche*.

5. See Jurgen Habermas' chapter on Nietzsche in *The Philosophical Discourse of Modernity,* Trans. Fredrick Lawrence (Cambridge, MA: MIT Press, 1985).

6. See Christoph Cox's, *Nietzsche, Naturalism and Interpretation* (University of California Press, 1999), 217. Cox writes: "In the end, neither utility, coherence, correspondence, nor any other single criterion serves for Nietzsche as the determinant of truth. Rather, the truth of a statement or belief is the more or less stable result of its having been relativized to a particular theory or interpretation that itself has been found viable according to at least some of the most rigorous criteria of justification available."

7. For a clear introduction to the relativist critique of perspectivism, see Nehamas' article entitled "Nietzsche" in *A Companion to Epistemology,* 305.

8. See Susan Haack's *Evidence and Inquiry: Towards Reconstruction in Epistemology* (Blackwell 1993), 16–17.

9. Nietzsche, *The Will to Power*, section 481.

10. Nietzsche, KGW, Vol. 2, 397.

11. See Nietzsche, *Beyond Good and Evil,* Trans. Holingdale, section 289: "Every philosophy is a foreground philosophy—that is a hermit's judgment: 'there is something arbitrary in the fact that *he* stopped, looked back, looked around here, that he stopped digging and laid his spade aside *here*— there is also something suspicious about it.'"

12. Susan Haack, *Evidence and Inquiry*, chapter 4 Foundherentism Articulated.

13. Haack, *Evidence and Inquiry*, chapter 4 Foundherentism Articulated.

14. Susan Haack, *Evidence and Inquiry*, 74.

15. Nietzsche, *On the Genealogy of Morals*, Essay II, section 22, 528 and GM: II: 16. Nietzsche calls this process the internalization of man.

16. Nietzsche*, On the Genealogy of Morals*, Trans. Kaufmann and Holingdale, Essay II, section 22, 92.

17. Nietzsche, *On the Genealogy of Morals,* Essay II, section 5.

18. See the third essay of Nietzsche's *On the Genealogy of Morals*: "What Is the Meaning of Ascetic Ideals?" See Ivan Soll's "Nietzsche on Cruelty, Asceticism and

the Failure of Hedonism" in *Nietzsche, Genealogy, History* 168–192 and especially, the section Pain that Is Pleasure: The Paradox of Ascetcism.

19. See Susan Haack, *Evidence and Inquiry,* chapter 10 and especially page 221.

20. As I will demonstate later, truth in the *adequatio* sense, is no longer required once it is deflated. I will make this clearer below.

21. See Plato, Phaedo, 78d-80A in *Great Dialogues of Plato*, Trans. W.H.D. Rouse, (New York: Signet Classics), 575–577.

22. See Rene Descartes, *Meditations on First Philosophy*, Mediations Two and Three.

23. David Hume, *An Enquiry Concerning Human Understanding* in *Classics of Western Philosophy,* edited by Stephen Cahn (Indianapolis: Indianna, Hackett Publishers, 1977), section IV, Part 1.

24. In G.W.F. Hegel's *The Phenomenology of Spirit*, Trans. A.V. Miller and J.N. Findlay (Oxford: Oxford University Press, 1979). Hegel argues that the history of humankind is a development and evolution of Absolute Spirit or *Geist* coming to self-realization and knowledge concerning not only its essential Being but also its very historical development and purpose.

25. Otto Neurath, "On Protocol Statements" (1932) in *Otto Neurath's Philosophical Papers*, 1913–1946, edited by R.S. Cohen and M. Neurath (Dordrfecht: Reidal, 1983).

26. See N.R. Hanson, *Patterns of Discovery* (Cambridge University Press, 1958).

27. Nietzsche, *Beyond Good and Evil*, section 19.

28. See chapter three of the present work.

29. Mariam Thalos, "Two Dogmas of Naturalized Epistemology," *Dialectica*, Vol. 53 Issue 2 (1999): 111–138.

30. See Richard Lazarus, "Progress on a Cognitive-Motivational-Relational Theory of Emotion," *American Psychologist* 46:8 (1991), 819–834.

31. See Antonio Damasio, *The Feeling of What Happens* (New York: Harcourt, 1999).

32. Nietzsche, *The Will to Power*, section 481.

33. Nietzsche, *Daybreak*, section 30.

34. Nietzsche, *The Will to Power*, section 574.

35. Nietzsche, KGW, VII, 2, 112.

36. Nietzsche, *The Will to Power*, section 702.

37. Nietzsche, *On the Genealogy of Morals*, III, 12, 555.

38. Richard Rorty, *Objectivity, Relativism, Truth, Philosophical Papers Volume 1*(Cambridge: Cambridge University Press, 1991), 23.

39. Indeed, Cox, in footnote 65 on page 60 states as much: "Here, Nietzsche is in agreement with Richard Rorty." See Christoph Cox's, *Nietzsche, Naturalism and Interpretation.*

40. Richard Rorty, "Science as Solidarity" in *Dismantling Truth*, edited by Hilary Lawson and Lisa Appignanesi (New York: St. Martin's, 1989), 11.

41. See Huw Price, "Truth as Convenient Friction" *in Naturalism and Normativity*, edited by De Caro and Macarthur (New York: Columbia University Press, 2010), 229–252, 229.

170　　　　　　　　　　　　　　*Chapter 6*

42. Richard Rorty, "Is Truth a Goal of Enquiry? Donald Davidson versus Crispin Wright" in Richard Rorty, *Truth and Progress, Philosophical Papers,* Vol. 3 (New York: Cambridge University Press, 1998), 19.

43. The labeling of the third dogma is often called scheme/content dualism. See Donald Davidson, "A Coherence Theory of Truth and Knowledge" in *Truth and Interpretation Perspectives on the Philosophy of Donald Davidson* (Basil Blackwell, 1986), 307–319.

44. Richard Rorty, *Contingency, Irony, Solidarity* (Cambridge: Cambridge University Press, 1989), 18.

45. Rorty, *Contingency, Irony, Solidarity,* 11–12.

46. Rorty, *Contingency, Irony, Solidarity,* 21.

47. See Rorty's reply to Price's paper, "Truth as Convenient Friction," "Rorty Further Remarks" (Feb. 2005) in *Naturalism and Normativity,* 255.

48. See Huw Price, "Truth as Convenient Friction," in *Naturalism and Normativity,* 241.

49. What mankind has so far considered seriously have not been realities but mere imaginings—more strictly speaking, lies prompted by the bad instincts of natures that were harmful in the most profound sense—all concepts "God," "soul," "virtue," "sin," "beyond," "truth," "eternal life." Nietzsche, *Ecce Homo,* in *Basic Writings of Nietzsche,* 712. Also see *Twilight of the Idols* III: 3, and the entire book three of *The Genealogy* where Nietzsche argues that scientists are sick and degenerate because they remain captive to the ascetic ideal.

50. Utilitarian accounts are unwarranted from an external vantage point because there are better-warranted theories such as genealogy. Genealogy is better grounded in terms of historical facts. Utilitarian theories, in contrast, gaze haphazardly into the blue and are not documentary gray *(On the Genealogy of Morals,* preface, 7). From an internal vantage point genealogy is more justified than utilitarianism because utilitarianism is either not universally true (it cannot explain all types of human behavior) or inconsistent when it comes to explaining the ascetic ideal.

51. See Keith Donnellan, "Reference and Definite Descriptions," in *Philosophical Review* 75 (1966), 281–304.

52. "If any truth indication is possible for us (as human beings) then the satisfaction of the foundherentist criteria of knowledge is truth-indicative." See Haack, *Evidence and Inquiry,* 222.

53. Haack, *Evidence and Inquiry,* 221.

54. Susan Haack, *Defending Science Within Reason,* 81.

55. See especially Haack's chapter on "The Long Arm of Common Sense: Instead of a Theory of Scientific Method," 57–93, in *Defending Science Within Reason.*

56. Susan Haack in her first major work *Deviant Logic* (Cambridge University Press, 1974) argues quite persuasively that rules of inference in standard symbolic logic may be invalid at a later time (as Russell did in fact find an invalid mode of inference in Frege's logical system). This further corroborates foundherentism even in the sphere of analytic truths since no logical law may be immune from revision: though such a revision cannot be predicated on the synthetic *a posteriori.*

57. Susan Haack, *Defending Science Within Reason,* 345.
58. See Nietzsche, *On the Genealogy of Morals*, Preface, sections 5–7.
59. Percy Bridgman, *Reflections of a Physicist* (New York: Philosophical Library, 1955), 551.

Chapter 7

Homo Natura
Nietzsche's Naturalized Morality

This chapter examines Nietzsche's ethics. It would not be hyperbole to claim that this is perhaps the most difficult aspect of Nietzsche's philosophy to comprehend. I do not pretend to answer all of the many questions in the secondary literature regarding Nietzsche's fully developed ethical stance in what follows, but only wish, rather, to examine the "how" of Nietzsche's ethics: How can we act ethically? (where ethically here is minimally construed to mean freely acting toward a self-defined goal). Another way to put this is to state that while some commentators have concentrated on the normative guidelines, principles, and goals of Nietzsche's ethics, I intend to distillate on the ascetic practices of self that allow us to enact these principles and correspondingly reach the goals identified as worthy by these same principles.[1]

Many works, for example, have fleshed out the goals, principles, and behavior of "free spirits," "*Ubermenchen*," "choice individuals," "strong types," and other cognate terms that describe Nietzsche's respective names to represent ideal beings who live beyond good and evil.[2] I will not focus on this aspect of Nietzsche's ethics. Instead, I emphasize those mechanisms which allow us to arrive at our ethical goals with an aim to showing how Nietzsche's advocacy for "subject-alteration" and "value transvaluation," broadly construed, is coherent. Shoulds and oughts imply capacity after all, and ability is the *sine qua non* for all ethical positions. So the task at hand is to understand how we might put ethical principles into practice or, at the very least, mark a path to demonstrate that such goals can be reached.

Nietzsche's ethical position is hard to understand because he has an unusual conception of agency. Nietzsche argues that the notion of a static agent is an incorrect inference that is drawn from observing some action. Some action is witnessed, and it is then inferred that something is responsible for committing the action. However, Nietzsche claims, we are only justified in judging the action. Such judging takes place along the continuum of life-affirming or life-denying values. We have already seen the problems with such an expressivist view of agency in sections 3.4 and 3.5.3.

Despite all of this, Nietzsche clearly holds that a subject may change his or her behavior.[3] The entire point of his moral philosophy, in a sense, is to show how and why morals have become constructed. The most basic answer to this story has to do with power. Morality is actually the story of some set of values trumping those of another. Moreover, since all values presuppose evaluators, then all evaluation takes place with an agenda in mind.

However, this very brief reconstruction of Nietzsche's position hides an inherent contradiction: All evaluation is predicated on the existence of evaluators who are relatively stable entities in that they have definite, calculable agendas. However, if this is true, then we do have actors acting on their evaluations. In point of fact, a stronger claim may be produced: Actions would only be meaningful if the agenda behind the action were known. Agendas are construed by agents who develop strategies to fulfill what they desire. Agendas without agents would seem to make little sense.

This interpretation clearly contradicts Nietzsche's expressivist view of agency. Nietzsche would need to hold a thick view of agency where agents are capable of formulating and acting on strategies to render his account of power coherent. Realizing this inconsistency, some Nietzscheans have argued for a deterministic approach to agency. If the agent is an illusion, in the sense that he is not some static entity, but a bundle of drives, then it must be the drives themselves that are doing the evaluation.[4] Thus we can claim that morality is simply a reflection of a drive's value and also argue that there is no substantive agency behind the evaluation. Drives would have strategies, but there would be no hidden strategist behind these drives. Such a position would be perfectly consistent with the claims made above. An added advantage is that it would accord with much behavior that most philosophers would take to be perfectly naturalized. The project of naturalism, at least as construed by De Caro, Richardson, the Churchlands, and others is to reduce or eliminate any vestige of mind. It is a difficult task as I have noted and may appear deeply incoherent when applied to Nietzsche's ethical philosophy, however, the following example will hopefully make this position more palatable.

Take the high rate of infanticide in lion prides. When a male lion vanquishes the most dominant male of a pride of lions, the first thing he often does is to kill the sons of his vanquished foe.[5] The evaluation is clear: "Such cubs are not valued because they belong to my former rival." The goal for the lion is to reproduce his genes and not to protect the genes of his opponent by raising cubs that are not his own. Such an evaluation, is, of course, not cognized: The lion is simply acting in accordance with the hidden goal of natural selection. By analogy, commentators in the secondary literature have argued that the goals of power are often unknown to the subject who puts them into practice. The subject is much like the male lion in this regard: His actions are only truly explicable from the perspective of will to power. Quoting another famous Nietzschean, we might say that: "The subject is not the *vis a vis* of power but one of its prime effects."[6]

The great difficulty with the above analogy, though, is that it leaves very little wiggle room for the possibility of moral change and, as such, is inconsistent with another well-developed notion of Nietzsche's moral philosophy. The expression of value if we wish to call the lion's action that is clearly non-reflective is made from instinct: He can no more change his behavior to kill the sons of his rivals as he may choose to become a herbivore. In contrast, we, as human beings, have the capacity to change our behavior, indeed perhaps radically so. It would seem then that Nietzsche would need to account for this commonplace, yet profound, and in some cases, life-altering phenomenon and likewise, so too, would his defenders.

One way to respond to this objection while defending the deterministic line of interpretation is to claim that all instincts, even powerful ones, can be tamed through discipline. Take the example of a lion and his tamer. The lion's instinct to kill and eat his tamer can be redirected through consistent disciplining and training. What's more this line of interpretation, which suggests that powerful natural instincts may be redirected and reinterpreted by cultural constraints, is well-corroborated throughout Nietzsche's *oeuvre*. Nietzsche argues that most of our instincts have already been redirected through generations of breeding. Such breeding has taken place well below our conscious reflection such that it is difficult if not impossible to decipher whether one can differentiate what drive has been culturally inculcated and which is natural. In *The Will to Power* section 684 Nietzsche writes: "Everything that escapes the human hand and breeding, turns almost immediately back again into its natural condition. The type remains constant one cannot *denatuter la nature*."[7] However, another important aspect to add to this discussion, which is often not noted, is to recognize that Nietzsche also holds that we, as agents, can train our behavior for our betterment. We can morally improve. In section 109 of *Daybreak*, Nietzsche notes that there are at least six different ways to combat the mastery of a singular drive.[8]

Brian Leiter also discusses the phenomenon of moral change in relation to Nietzsche's philosophy in his remarkable book, *Nietzsche on Morality*. Leiter argues that *On the Genealogy of Morals* possesses real causal powers in that readers of the book who also happen to belong to the physiologically strong type will no longer be chained to what Leiter refers to as Morality in a Pejorative Sense (MPS).[9] However, Leiter does not go into enough detail explaining what these causal powers might be nor what is acting and what is being acted upon. Indeed, part of the problem with Leiter's account, as demonstrated in chapter two, is that he maintains such a sharp division between weak and strong types. The problem in the maintenance of this distinction is that if the strong are entirely different from the weak, then it seems doubtful that MPS would come to infect the strong in the first place. Nietzsche's point, of course, is that all human beings have been corrupted, so to speak, by Christian morality. No one is safe from MPS, and yet, Nietzsche declares, some of us do have the power to free ourselves from this debilitating morality.

So the difficulty I am faced with is one of establishing a model of agency that is non-static and yet non-metaphysical. More fully worked out, such an idea of agency will be causally efficacious and will be the necessary component needed to explain how we may act toward moral improvement. Also, reflection, construed in rather broad terms, will have to be that faculty which at least is partially responsible for procuring agential change. Second, this capacity to change one's character will have to be one that can be understood without invoking some supernatural postulates. To address these two related concerns, I will argue that reflection is a special development of will to power that is underwritten on what Colin Mcginn calls "selective cognition." I will show how self-reflection as a historical improvement on "selective cognition" can be naturalized.

It might be advisable to return to how the very notion of agency is constructed in the first place, to determine what Nietzsche's conception of agency entails. Nietzsche argues that agency is formed when drives are blocked. Drives for hunting, warfare, sex, etc. normally express themselves outwardly. However, when they are forced to turn inward, they proceed to carve out an agent. However, if this is true, then some animals are clearly agents, at least in a very minimal sense of the word. For clearly any animal that belongs to a higher mammal social group will have distinct drives that are blocked. Nietzsche's genealogical account of the origin of agency, which ends with the bad conscience, clearly does not go back far enough.[10] Any herd or pack animal will have a clear understanding of his or her place within a group's hierarchy. Those who occupy the bottom rungs of the ladder have specific roles to play that are prescribed to them because of their position in the group. The very low status of such animals obviously constrains their drives.

The constraint of the sexual drive is most apparent among males who compete with other males to mate. Any casual watcher of nature shows which depict the contest of rams, lions or most notably gorillas for the right to sexual pairing sees what happens to the male who loses.[11] The defeated male often goes off into a corner to brood. He acknowledges his loss in some sense of this word and therefore his status of "second banana" in the group. However, this does not always happen with the human animal. As Nietzsche shows such troubling emotions like frustration and defeat are themselves reflected upon. These reflections turn into brooding. Brooding leads to *resentiment* (resentment), and *resentiment* leads to a reinterpretation of defeat. Moreover, a reinterpretation of defeat sometimes leads to the creation of new values.[12]

The distinctiveness of human beings has often been equated with their apperception or self-awareness.[13] This claim has increasingly come under fire as more becomes known about higher apes. There is strong evidence to suggest that chimpanzees are self-aware; they possess self-conscious awareness.[14] We might think of self-conscious awareness as the ability to stand back and to be aware that one is distinct from the world. Some higher apes seem to have this capability because they can recognize their reflection in mirrors. Recognition of oneself in a mirror is thought to demonstrate that such a creature recognizes itself as a being-in-the-world.[15]

If chimpanzees are self-conscious then how did this capacity come about? Indeed, how did intelligence, as a capacity to understand, to recognize, develop? Colin Mcginn in *Prehension: The Hand and the Emergence of Humanity* argues that the development of the hand in conjunction with a larger brain led to what he calls Intelligence, a catch-all notion for Mcginn which includes culture, tool-use, advanced cognitive development and so forth.[16] What is perhaps most interesting about Mcginn's book, at least for my purposes, is his conception regarding a particular aspect to thinking that we seem to possess and understand only too well. He calls this aspect, "selective cognition," Mcginn writes: "By this I mean the ability of thought to concern a single object in abstraction from surrounding objects: to pick one object out and focus on that object to the exclusion of others."[17] This trait is a bit of mixed bag: We have the ability, as humans, to concentrate on some idea such that we ignore everything else. This ability has tremendous advantages in that it allows us to think all the ins and outs, all the nuances of an idea without getting distracted by having other thoughts or feelings. However, it is also detrimental in that we can obsess over some idea, too.

What McGinn does is to provide a speculative evolutionary tracing of this trait. He argues that since we quite clearly can cognitively select a notion from a multitude of ideas within the confines of thought, then this ability cannot be the result of a saltation, a leap of evolution. Nor, of course, can it be of supernatural interference, but rather must be a long-standing device that creatures well before us used to survive. The trait was passed down because it was successful: Those who were able to select cognitively survived and passed on the genes responsible for the phenotypical trait which then served as the seeds that later germinated the neural circuitry for the faculty.

The question, of course, is "How are we able to trace this notion to some physical characteristic?" We cannot trace it to an earlier form of self-consciousness because then we are clearly caught within the mental, and this is all too easy. Arguing that chimpanzees are self-aware too, only pushes the question back: "How did chimpanzees become self-aware?" "How did the necessary condition for self-awareness, namely cognitive selection, develop in them?" What McGinn shows is that the trait must be a further advancement by some physical adaptation. His account argues that it is the hand that helps us to grasp tools and that the notion of grasping is part of our conceptual thinking regarding being able to grasp ideas. In effect, the continual development of the hand, such as the elongation of the thumb, helped us to survive in an increasingly hostile world once we were cast out of the arboreal forest. Grasping and cognitive selection are the same thing: they both *envelope* some thing and make it part of our being. They reinterpret said thing under a new form. "Thus the essence of life," Nietzsche reminds us, "its *will to power* is ignored; one overlooks the essential priority of the spontaneous, aggressive, expansive, form-giving forces that give new interpretations and directions."[18]

However, before the development of the hand, there must have been a proto-capacity of envelopment. McGinn now fills in the missing evolutionary chains linking cognitive selection with the mind, to grasping with the hand, to biting with the mouth. The mouth is a means of taking in what is foreign to it. It is a primitive means of appropriation and absorption and envelopment. Gripping with the mouth, whether the animal that grips is a human, chimpanzee, dog, or fish, is a means of selectivity albeit a primitive one. It was this proto-power of selectivity which, over the course of millions of years, led to the development of cognitive selection.[19]

Whether McGinn is right about all this is not the point of this analysis. What he points out is that if the theory of Neo-Darwinism is true, then there must be vestigial remnants of the most important aspects of mind already contained in earlier species. These properties along of course with the genes that turn them "on" survived because they had clear survival value.

Returning to the question of self-consciousness then, it is clear that such a trait cannot be the true test of being human. As the above discussion demonstrates, the actual difference between mankind and even chimpanzees, does not have to do with self-conscious awareness but rather with the ability to reflect on one's character, one's very personhood, and all this might entail—behavior, thoughts, feelings, etc. with the purpose of changing, perhaps fundamentally, this very personhood. It is this ability of self-reflection or so I would argue which marks another evolutionary development of selective cognition. Only it is we as subjects, as representing a totality, as such, that we focus on. As the philosopher Julia Kristeva once stated: "a subject is a process in crisis" and I think this is a pithy way to put what it is I am trying to communicate.[20] I will call this sort of reflection, character reflection. I argue that it is this power of character reflection which not only is distinctly human but is irreducible. It is impossible to define character by claiming that it is merely a *collection* of drives or instincts. The difference between the human being and the animal then has to do with our ability, as humans, to reflect on our drives so that we may direct (or redirect them as the case may be).

Again, if we think of animal mating contests, the loser in such battles acknowledges the rules of the game and recognizes that he or she has lost. While it is always possible that the loser might eventually gain the upper hand, the rules for how this might happen are well established. It may be through brute strength or through an accumulation of allies, but the point is that there is no essential reevaluation taking place here. This is not the case for the human being. According to Nietzsche the ancestors of the priestly class, the shamans, sorcerers, and soothsayers, the philosophical type, changed the rules of the game of power. They realized that they could not compete against the warrior caste in terms of strength and instead relied on confusion which led to fear. How did they instill fear in their fellow tribesmen? Nietzsche believes it was through self-inflicted torture. Walking on hot coals, self-mutilation, painful ascetic practices testing physical endurance and concentration, etc. all of these practices were merely ways to trick the warriors into fearing this new class of humans, the religious type. Nietzsche writes: "As men of frightful ages, they did this by using frightful means: cruelty towards themselves, inventive self-castigation—this was the principal means these power-hungry hermits and innovators of ideas required to overcome the gods and traditions in themselves so as to *believe* in their own innovations" (Nietzsche's italics).[21] The warriors became afraid of such human beings because to them it only made sense to inflict wounds onto an enemy: not oneself.[22] The priestly caste soon became a mystery to the noble types and, over time, the nobles themselves became infected with priestly values.

What allowed for this radical reevaluation? The answer at bottom is power. But power works in a twofold way. First there is an intuitive sense as to what will lead to the warrior's undoing. Foucault expresses this notion best in his treatment of Nietzsche's *Genealogy*: "Nietzsche Genealogy History." He there writes "that the battle between competitors never occurs on the same battlefield but rather in the interstice."[23] The priestly caste had an intuitive sense as to how to outflank their opponents, the warriors. Indeed, it is precisely this aspect of will to power which makes it interesting: Things are co-opted for the sake of another group's power. As Nietzsche claims "life is crooked" meaning that in some cases the power of a group is absorbed through a reinterpretation of that group and the group whose power is being co-opted is unaware of what is happening.[24] In sum, Nietzsche suggests that the noble warrior caste engaged in a war which they could not anticipate. They were oblivious because the war did not exist on the physical plane; a plane they knew all too well. The war was waged from below; from the squinting ground of *resentiment*. The will to power evolved creating a new arena, namely, the "spiritual" in which to wage battle. "The priest must be the natural opponent and despiser of all rude, stormy unbridled, hard, violent beast of prey health and might . . . He will not be spared war with the beasts of prey, a war of cunning (of the spirit) rather than one of force . . . "[25]

But there is a second aspect to this, too. The second aspect of power has to do with a willingness to go along with the new construction of power. There is a peculiar lassitude that allows for one group to be used by another. The accumulation of power by a group occurs not because there is some overbearing force which subdues something else into total submission. If this were true, then power would be very clumsy indeed. Power is subtle and seductive. Power entices. Nietzsche suggests that there is a willingness for some weaker thing to serve a strong entity if, through serving, the weaker individual has an opportunity to subdue as well. This notion might very well explain the toady phenomenon. A toady does not serve a bully against his will, but rather takes some delight in such serving.

So if reflection is irreducible, then the next question seems to be immediately forthcoming: "What does the human reflect on?" The answer is an emotion, a feeling. Feeling a new emotion is the first indication that something is "happening" within our environment, from our perspective. We see this in the animal world. For example, it is common for herd animals to display fear when a predator enters into their space. The ability to sense danger by "feeling afraid" has a clear survival advantage for such animals. The animal, if it is a mammal, then engages in a flight or fight response. This reaction mechanism has served animals and early humans well.

For the human being, however, our emotions are infused with reflection. If we visited a zoo and a lion broke free from its pen and stood there before us, it is fair to say that we would be justified in feeling afraid. However, we would not just feel fear we would know that we are in a state of fear. It is this knowledge which in part distinguishes humans from non-human animals. To be sure, I am not claiming that instincts have no role to play when it comes to decision making. What I object to is the interpretation of the instincts which holds that they are pure or primal. The instincts like the fight or flight responses are always infused with a cognitive dimension.

Human beings spend lots of time reflecting. I would argue that human beings reflect primarily on feelings. They cognitively select to focus on feelings they are experiencing and on what they believe the causes of these feelings to be. We not only feel anger, for example, but we usually understand why we feel angry: we often identify a source for our anger. Sometimes we are mistaken as to what or who is making us angry, but this further corroborates my position as will be shown shortly. Thus an emotion, at least for the human being, is comprised of three elements: the feeling or affect, the understanding that we are in a state of feeling this way, and the tacit inkling that someone or something is responsible for making us feel this way.

Reflection, as a capacity, allows us to grasp the state of a feeling. Reflection permits us to construct narratives for the feeling, to identify sources for the feeling, and to think of strategies for coping with future occurrences of the feeling. Feelings, then, provide the initial impetus for reflection. Reflection leads to action or inaction, and we act or fail to act by how we wish to be as human beings. We might think of feeling as analogous to a car battery: Feelings power the engine of reflection. Without some initial feelings, the driving force behind action will not start. However, reflection is not reducible to feeling.

We can flesh all this out in more detail by returning to a rather curious passage in the *The Genealogy* that explains the relationship and formation between the inner and outer worlds: the world of reflection, imagination and thinking in general, and the world of sensation. Much has been written on Nietzsche's analysis of the development of the bad conscience in *The Genealogy*. Very little, however, has been written on what Nietzsche means when he suggests that the division between the world and the human being was once as thin as a cell membrane.[26] Many interpretations may be drawn from this rich passage. The first is purely cognitive: It is impossible to discern what the world might be like independently of our cognitive capacities. We can never get to the essences of things because we cannot decipher what are merely our thoughts being projected onto the world, from what exists independently outside of our bubble of consciousness. This interpretation would sketch the introduction of the concept of "human" in the world in a rather skeptical light: Since one cannot have direct access to anything outside of consciousness, one is forever trapped within one's feelings and thoughts. However, one does not have any way to test whether these thoughts and feelings are accurate reflections, and therefore there is a rift between the human being and nature. We are, in some sense, non-natural creatures forever caught in the trap of discovering our essences which, although they appear foreign to us, we are nonetheless responsible for creating.

Foucault and Habermas both agree that the clearest expression of this rift within nature between the world and the human being can be found in the work of Kant. As Foucault explains in *The Order of Things*, Kant's philosophy creates something called the transcendental-empirical doublet or "man." Man, Foucault maintains, is a creation of the eighteenth century. Man is the being responsible for ordering the world as it is and is, therefore, the transcendental source for the uniformity and orderliness of nature and yet it is from this very ordering of nature that we, as human beings, seek meaning through understanding what we are as empirical things in the world. Foucault believes that such a starting position is irrevocably incoherent because we strive to get ontological traction on some impermanent, arbitrary ground: the ground itself is nothing more than a sand dune of history.[27] Habermas in a less pessimistic manner demonstrates that Kant sets into motion the turn to Romanticism since the Romantics tried to understand how the subject was responsible for ordering nature while being a product of nature. As long as we are held captive by the notion that we must start from the position of "the philosophy of subjectivity," so argues Habermas, then we will never solve the diremption in nature: the split between subject/object and community/nature.[28]

How might we overcome these difficult and troubling concerns? Some time ago, David Couzens Hoy wrote an interesting paper that investigated "philosophies of the corner."[29] Corner philosophical positions are skeptical philosophies—such as Hume's and Nietzsche's—where any purported truths about the world are inscrutable. We cannot be sure about the "concrete of the world," but it is likely that cause and effect are simply superstitions or projections of our imagination stemming from, in Nietzsche's view, our insecurities. In the paper, "Nietzsche, Hume and the Genealogical Method," Hoy demonstrates that such corner philosophies rest on a fundamental mistake. He notes that just because we cannot extricate ourselves from a cognitive and even affective corner (either because of our peculiar evolutionary heritage or by language) does not entail that truth, justification or even hope is forever out of our collective grasp.[30]

However, instead of conceiving the human predicament from right angles, perspectives that we inherently cannot see behind, Hoy evinces that one should look at our epistemic and ethical limits, as akin to the boundaries of a circle. Thinking of such limitations in this way allows us to travel beyond the restrictions of hard "epistemic angles" where the only possible conclusion we may reach is that of skepticism and, perhaps ethically one of nihilism and to embrace a more open, inviting, and communal model of philosophy. In effect, we are led to hermeneutic concentric circles of self and other understanding. Rethinking this "epistemic problem of the corner" as that of a hermeneutic circle, allows us to escape from a seemingly inexorably skeptical position. Being in such a corner means that we are forever trapped, bound to our peculiar angle on the universe where we are confident neither that our ideas correspond to objects in the world nor that our self-descriptions are truly accurate depictions of who we are. However, the world is simply a text. There is nothing outside of it: Words are not merely signs of some object but that everything is interpretation through and through. The old problems regarding whether our interpretations line up with the world disappear because there is no longer a clear separation between the reader and the world. To quote Hoy, "there is no mental-physical dichotomy, as well as no problem about the gap between our knowledge and the given."[31]

While Hoy has something here with his circular metaphor, there remains a fundamental problem with Hoy's solution: it is too cerebral. The problem with Hoy's construal of what we might call a hermeneutics of action and subjectivity is that he has failed to identify what precisely we mean by "our" corner. When Nietzsche refers to our corner in *The Gay Science,* he is referring to a species-specific relationship to the world. More appropriately we have come to discover that he is referring to an interrelationship between relations: A mode of relation that allows us to relate to other relations. Nietzsche seeks to understand our unique mode of relating. He aims to understand how we relate to the world, to each other and ourselves. In brief, Nietzsche wants to answer the age-old question: "Who are we?" so that we can respond to the ethical question: "How did we become who we are and how might we change?" Nietzsche's notion of "our," then, is a fully fleshed out and ultra-thick concept. It denotes our obvious capacities to reason, to reflect on ourselves as persons, but it also denotes all those things that we have little immediate control over such as our ability to feel anguish and, especially, guilt. Ours also refers to our species capacity to deceive ourselves and, perhaps most importantly, our facility to lust after power in new ways. These capabilities are "ours" too. However, in another sense, such capacities present themselves as alien forces. What's more, these are the structures and capabilities that we cannot necessarily remove or even do without. We do not possess ownership of them in the sense that we possess ownership of a car where we are detached from the object of property. I am clearly not my car. If I grow tired of my car I can sell it and get another one or choose an alternative means of transportation altogether.

However, the "our" in this case is different. To say "our corner" in Nietzsche's sense is to say, "this is where we have been put." Much like a child who is relegated to a mere corner of the room against her or his will, in the same way, to think of "my corner" in this manner, is to recognize that we cannot fully get behind our capacities. Just as the child might not have the power to leave her or his corner because there is something more powerful restraining her or him, in the same way, we cannot change our capacities by exercising some conscious act of will. They are ours in the sense that they were given to us, but we had no choice in their ownership. Indeed, looking at "our" from another sense it might fairly be claimed that we cannot own them at all.

Thus, to recast Nietzsche's initial metaphor, as Hoy does, clearly does not solve the problem because there are substantive anchor weights, like the emotions, that we cannot cast off. Such moors determine where we can and cannot go: what we can and cannot reinterpret. It is for this reason that Nietzsche stresses in the very first line of the preface of *The Genealogy*, "We are unknown to ourselves, we men of knowledge and with good reason. We have never sought ourselves—how could it happen that we should ever find ourselves?"[32] Nietzsche's task is to discover who we are to know how to think, act, and even feel differently. Moreover, it is feeling that carves out our subjectivity. Nietzsche's answer then to the question: "Why are we unknown to ourselves?" is that "men of knowledge" have not delved into what makes reflection possible, namely, feeling. Projecting interpretation after interpretation to see which of these interpretations is more feasible, as Hoy suggests we do, is most unhelpful because we are no closer to understanding the true engine behind our actions nor of how we come to form a relationship with ourselves. It is the production of new interpretations that are not anchored to who or what we truly are which leads Nietzsche to shudder at the possibility of an endless horizon of interpretations untethered to what truly grounds and propels action: emotion.

Still, is there not something that we might salvage from Hoy's metaphor? My reconstruction of Hoy's metaphor is as follows: think of the self as an enclosure, but as an enclosure with extendable and permeable boundaries, like an animal cell membrane. An animal cell is its own factory in that it uses energy and expunges waste. Its perimeter is never fixed: It is constantly changing shape according to what it confronts and what confronts it in its environment. Sometimes it extends its pseudopod to absorb other essential amino acids to feed, but sometimes it is pressed in upon. When we feel that certain things press upon us, that is the self; we say that we are gripped by a powerful feeling. Such powerful feelings tend to come from the outside: They are not merely produced by us. Certainly, we might produce feelings of anger within the self, for example, by brooding on some prior incident but such an incident, if it is to have any reflective fuel, must itself afflict and affect us directly. For example, we at first feel hurt by some action taken by some person whom we thought was a trusted friend. However, this initial feeling of hurt may turn to anger depending on the course of our reflection. We have the capacity to reflect on our emotions. We can determine what such emotions mean to us within our "membrane." They can be restrictive in that they can impact on the shape and contours of the space within the cell. Indeed, such feelings can be so penetrating that they rupture the self causing us to lose any sense of cohesion. However, such feelings can also allow us to recast the interior of our lives in our fashion. We can reflect on these feelings such that we use them to motivate us toward new and untold interpretations of the self.

In sum, the goal of Nietzsche's naturalism is not to stay enclosed within the circle of man as Hoy suggests nor is it to reduce the uniqueness of humanity to some reductive physical place of existence. The actual goal is, as Nietzsche writes in section 230 of *Beyond Good and Evil*, ". . . to translate man back into nature; to master the many vain and fanciful interpretations and secondary meanings which have been hitherto scribbled, scrawled, and daubed over that eternal basic text *homo natura* . . ."[33] However, as I hoped to have shown, even this goal, if realized, would reveal an incomplete project: for nature must be translated back into man. Will to power naturalizes both man and nature.

In summation, selective cognition explains the how of ethics: "How is it possible to take ethical action?" "How can we change our behavior?" Selective cognition allows us to reflect on our actions and feelings with the aim of developing strategies to change these behaviors. How do we know that selective cognition has this power? Because it has been selected for: the primal notion of envelopment, of engulfment, of taking something in that is not our own, has a long evolutionary history and natural selection selects those traits that have proven survival advantage. By cognizing a particular thing, idea, or aspect of personality, we can construct ways to engage with it and thereby constellate it into a pattern of our choosing. However, this power works in the other direction too: It allows a warrior-artist to fixate on the human being and change its character within limits. Cognitive reflection is a dual-edged sword: It makes it possible to improve ourselves by giving us the power to totalize our personhood, but by the same token it gives someone else the ability to recast our subjectivity such that we become nothing more than a tool or creative project for some alien agent. I call the first side of cognitive selection the "freedom side" and the second side "the coercive."

Along the freedom axis of cognitive selection, Nietzsche discusses this power in his famous section 290 of *The Gay Science*. Nietzsche does not deny the existence of what he calls first-order nature—properties of our character which are immutable. However, he also argues that all individuals possess second-order properties that can be changed and rearranged into a style of the subject's choosing.[34] Indeed, Nietzsche suggests that we should think of our character as a form of "style." In analogous fashion, Nietzsche thinks that humans are also free to arrange their attributes in a style within limits. Nietzsche's argument is that we do not have a preordained *telos*, as human beings, readymade because of our biological endowments a la Aristotle but that this does not mean that we are formless pieces of clay which may be freely molded into a model of our own or others choosing.

On the coercive side, we see that torture became the means for the formation of civilization and the creation of humankind. The warrior-artists developed terrible punishments for those who broke the first five or six I will nots of civilization. The initial development of particular forms of punishment was no easy task: it required a deep understanding of the body. Selective cognition, once again, as an ancient vestigial form of mind, allows one to mark out a particular trait and analyze it such that it is then redeveloped, reinterpreted, and redeployed. In any case, it is this ability to cognize selectively that makes such reinterpretation by ourselves or others possible.

With all this stated I now wish to tackle the last question: "How do we go about using our latent power of self-reflection to recast the interiority of our lives?" I argue that this question is best answered by examining Nietzsche's naturalized method of moral investigation, namely genealogy.

NOTES

1. In Michel Foucault's "On the Genealogy of Ethics, An Overview of a Work in Progress" in *The Foucault Reader*, Trans. Paul Rabinow (New York: Pantheon Books, 1990), 340–373, he provides a very novel and useful model for understanding ethical behavior. He argues that we can divide all fully developed ethical theories into four categories: the ethical substance; the mode of subjection; the mode self-forming activity; and the telos. I am particularly interested in Nietzsche's mode of subjection and self-forming activity. In other words, I am interested in how we go about recognizing, as subjects, the need to change our behavior and what practices we perform in order to change it.

2. For a sample listing of books which examine Nietzsche's moral philosophy, see Brian Leiter's *Nietzsche on Morality* (London: Routledge, 2002). Edgar Sleinis' *Nietzsche's Revaluation of Values: A Study of Strategies* (Urbana: University of Illinois Press, 1994). And of course the classic: Walter Kaufmann, *Nietzsche: Philosopher, Psychologist, Antichrist*, 4th edition (Princeton University Press, 1974). Also see Jacob Gollum's interesting article, "Can one really become a Free Spirit Par Excellence or an *Ubermensch*" in *Journal Of Nietzsche Studies* 32:1 (2006), 22–40. Gollum argues that there is another type beyond that of the *Ubermensch*, a Free Spirit Par Excellence.

3. Nietzsche, *The Gay Science*, section 290 and *On the Genealogy of Morals*, preface, section 3.

4. See, for example, Daniel Ahern's *Nietzsche as Cultural Physician* and Ruedigger Hermann Grimm, *Nietzsche's Theory of Knowledge* (New York: De Gruyter, 1977) for standard views on this position. Perhaps the clearest articulation of this view is to be found in his *Nietzsche on Morality*. Leiter writes: "A 'person' is the arena in which the struggle of drives (type-facts) is played out; how they play out determines what he believes, what he values, what he becomes," Leiter, 100.

5. See Craig Packer and Anne E. Pusey, "Adaptations of Female Lions to Infanticide by Incoming Males," *The American Naturalist* 121:5 (1983), 716–728.

6. Michel Foucault, "Two Lectures," in *Power/Knowledge, Selected Interviews and Other Writings*, edited by Colin Gordon (New York: Pantheon Books, 1980), 98.

7. Nietzsche, *The Will to Power*, section 684.

8. Nietzsche, *Daybreak*, section 109.

9. Brian Leiter, *Nietzsche on Morality* (London: Routledge), 177–179.

10. Nietzsche's starting point for the bad conscience begins with our "semi-animal" status: when proto-homo sapiens became bipedal. It was at this stage that "the entire inner world, originally as thin as if it were stretched between two membranes, expanded and extended itself, acquired depth, breadth, and height, in the same measure as outward discharge was *inhibited*" (Nietzsche's italics). *On the Genealogy of Morals*, Trans. Kaufmann and Holingdale, GMII: 16, 84. I will suggest that a genealogy can go even further back into our collective prehistory.

11. See Bercovitch, F.B., "Social stratification, social strategies, and reproductive success in primates," *Ethology and Sociobiology* 12 (1991), 315–333.

12. Even this is not entirely correct as many animals use feints and deceptions to win contests which appear on the surface to be purely tests of strength. See Murmatsu,

Daisuke and Koga, Tsuneroi, "Fighting with an unreliable weapon: opponent choice and risk avoidance in fiddler crab contests," *Behavioral Ecology and Sociobiology* 70:5 (May 2016), 713–724. "Current signaling theories predict that animal signals are generally honest, but each signaling system allows some admixture of deception. Male fiddler crabs fight aggressively through the use of their greatly enlarged major claw, which grows on the left or right side. Some males have fragile regenerated claws (regenerated males) and others have robust original claws (original males), but crabs cannot visually discriminate between the two types." What Murmatsua and Koga show is that the regenerated males will engage in bluffing tactics: they will appear ultra-aggressive so as to avoid fighting altogether. However, if they are physically confronted they surrender immediately.

13. "A person is a being who has a sense of self, has a notion of the future and the past, can hold values, and make choices; in short, can adopt life-plans. At least, a person must be the kind of being who is in principle capable of all this, however damaged these capacities may be in practice." Charles Taylor, "The Concept of a Person," *Philosophical Papers Volume 1* (Cambridge: Cambridge University Press, 1985), 97. Harry G. Frankfurt, "Freedom of the Will and the Concept of a Person," *The Journal of Philosophy* 68:1 (January 14, 1971), 5–7.

14. See Jane Goodall's convincing essay, "The Sentience of Chimpanzees and Other Animals" in *Animal Ethics and Trade: The Challenge of Sentience,* edited by Jacky Turner and Joyce D'Silva (London: EarthScan, 2006), 3–12.

15. See G.G. Gallup's "Chimpanzees: Self-Recognition," *Science* 167 (1970). For an updated treatment of Gallup's work see Julian Paul Keenan, *The Face in the Mirror: How Do We Know Who We Are* (New York: Harper Collins, 2003).

16. Colin Mcginn, *Prehension: The Hand and the Emergence of Humanity* (Cambridge, MA: MIT Press, 2015), 143.

17. McGinn, 76.

18. Nietzsche, *On the Genealogy of Morals*, GM: II 12, 515.

19. See McGinn's chapter, "Selective Cognition and the Mouth," 75–87.

20. For more on Kristeva's notion of subjectivity, see Kelly Oliver's *Subjectivity Without Subjects: From Abject Fathers to Desiring Mothers* (Lanham, MD: Rowman and Littlefield Publishers, 1998), 77–80.

21. Nietzsche, *On the Genealogy of Morals*, Trans. Kaufmann and Holingdale, GM III: 10, 115.

22. Nietzsche, *On the Genealogy of Morals*, I:7, 469.

23. See Michel Foucault, "Nietzsche, Genealogy History," in *Language, Counter-Memory, Practice: Selected Interviews and Essays*, edited by D.F. Bouchard (Ithaca: Cornell University Press, 1977), 139–164, 150.

24. Why Nietzsche asks, in Essay One, section 7 of *On the Genealogy of Morals*, are the priests the most evil enemies? "Because they are the most impotent." This impotence causes this caste to seek out black subterranean arts of revenge against the nobles (see section 8). They intuitively understand that they cannot vanquish the nobles on the sacred grounds of mortal combat.

25. Nietzsche, *On the Genealogy of Morals*, III: 15. See also Daniel W Conway, "How We Became What We Are: Tracking the Beasts of Prey," in Nietzsche's *On the*

Genealogy of Morals: Critical Essays, edited by Christa Davis Acampora (Lanham, MD: Rowman and Littlefield, 2006), 305–320.

26. Nietzsche, *On the Genealogy of Morals*, Essay II, section 16.

27. See Michel Foucault, *The Order of Things*, chapter one "Man's Doubles" Trans. A. Sheridan (London: Tavistock and New York: Pantheon, 1973).

28. See Habermas, *The Philosophical Discourse of Modernity*, chapter 11.

29. Hoy is referring to the well-known passage from the section 374 of *The Gay Science*, "Our New Infinity": "We cannot see round our own corner: it is a hopeless piece of curiosity to want to know what could exist for other species of intellect and perspective . . . But I think that today we are at least far from the ludicrous immodesty of decreeing from our corner that perspectives are *permissible* only from out of this corner. The world has rather once again become for us 'infinite': insofar as we cannot reject the possibility that it *contains in itself infinite interpretations*." Quoted from *A Nietzsche Reader*, Trans. R.J. Holingdale (London: England, Penguin Books), 69.

30. David Couzens Hoy, "Nietzsche, Hume and the Genealogical Method" in *Nietzsche, Genealogy, Morality: Essays on Nietzsche's On the Genealogy of Morals,* edited by Richard Schact (University of California Press, 1994), 251–269.

31. Hoy, "Nietzsche, Hume and the Genealogical Method," 259.

32. Nietzsche, *On the Genealogy of Morals*, Preface, section one, 451.

33. Nietzsche, *Beyond Good and Evil*, Trans. Holingdale, section 230.

34. Nietzsche, *The Gay Science*, section 290: "Here a large amount of second nature has been added, here a piece of original nature removed." Quoted from *A Nietzsche Reader*, Trans. Holingdale, 237.

Conclusion
Genealogy

Genealogy is a historical and philosophical method that Nietzsche developed upon reading Paul Ree's book on morality.[1] Genealogy, is, in its most basic form, an empirical investigation that studies value. To be even more precise, genealogies expose how specific values within a given culture have come to have value. Thus genealogy is a study of the process of valuation itself; that is to say, it is the study of both why and how we, as humans, value values. There is, therefore, a three-pronged analysis of values within any genealogical investigation. First, Nietzsche examines the values of a given culture as an expression of power. Specific values like honesty and chastity, receive value because there is some group that values them. A group will come to place value on some ethical principle because of the principle's perceived value to the group. The principal aspirations of genealogy are to understand why collections of humans, of all stripes (e.g., groups, classes, castes, cultures, etc.) value the values they do and how such groups came to exist through the valuation of particular values.

According to Nietzsche, groups come to value particular values over others for either one of two reasons: (1) The values of a group grow organically from the group's true nature and therefore are accurate expressions of the group's true power-character. When this is the case, then the group's values are deemed active and strong by Nietzsche. For example, nobles, according to Nietzsche, value freedom and war because such propensities for these activities come naturally to them.[2] Their values are outwardly expressed and so is their will to power. (2) The group does not actively adopt values but only adopts those values which are oppositional to those of another group. In this case, Nietzsche declares, the values are reactive and denote a group that is weak. For example, the slave revolt in morality occurred when the slaves inverted noble values. However, the slaves do not realize that their values are parasitic on ideals of human excellence. Human history according to Nietzsche might be viewed as a battle between noble and slave values or in Nietzsche's terms: Rome versus Judaea.[3] Nietzsche believes that this struggle is now won and that the tension that once existed between noble and slave values is no longer existent.

Nietzsche's second principal task then in *The Genealogy* is to understand the extent of this slave moral victory. Certainly, much of the territory that human beings call the soul has been conquered by slavish values like guilt—a life-stultifying capacity that causes the human being to inflict self-harm. The modern penchant for participating in all forms of asceticism is yet another victory for slave morality. But, for Nietzsche, discipline is neither necessarily reactive nor self-harmful. The warrior caste disciplined themselves in the ancient forms of warfare and hunting. Both practices, moreover, required much time and training to perfect. Nietzsche's issue with discipline in the modern era, though, has to do with its lack of direction. Discipline has now become an end in itself. Hard work is a value that is intensely valuable, but it does not seem to matter whether such work produces any discernible goal. This commitment to hard work for the sake of reaffirming the idea that one is a hard worker is an anathema to noble values. To be well-skilled in the arts of war one must have the proper intention and produce the right result.

Nietzsche is not merely interested in surveying the conquests of slave morality. Rather he desires to see how he might reinterpret these victories for his benefit. The third aspect of a genealogical investigation is, therefore, curative. Slave morals have produced much suffering, but Nietzsche is not primarily interested in reducing suffering. Rather the true goal for Nietzsche's reevaluation of all values is for greater freedom.

However, Nietzsche's conception of liberty is one where an individual becomes self-determined. The end point of a genealogical inquiry, the cure it encourages, is to produce the Sovereign Individual:

> If, on the other hand, we place ourselves at the end of the enormous process, where the tree finally produces fruit, where society and its morality of custom finally brings to light that to which it was only the means: then we find as the ripest fruit on its tree the sovereign individual, the individual resembling only himself, free again from the morality of custom, autonomous and supermoral . . . in short the human being with his own independent long will, the human being who is permitted to promise and in him . . . a true consciousness power and freedom, a feeling of the completion of man himself.[4]

Nietzsche is not interested in returning to an ancient warrior code of conduct; there is no going back to what we might call the "blonde beast of prey."

Nietzsche's task is to see if there are some redeeming elements regarding the victory of morality and to take these moral fundaments and fashion a new code of ethics by which to live. It is the sovereign individual, or so I would argue who collects the reward of a long, brave genealogical journey. As Nietzsche declares: "For cheerfulness or in my language Gay Science, is a reward, the reward of a long brave industrious and subterranean seriousness of which not everyone is capable."[5] *Gaya Scienza* is learning to live joyfully with one's knowledge of the self, as currently constructed, with the purpose of going beyond this construction. Genealogy is the way in which we come to this knowledge. Genealogy is necessarily methodological and substantive; it is genealogy, I would argue, that best exemplifies Nietzsche's naturalism.

How does genealogy work? We can get a sense of Nietzsche's genealogy by understanding its three anchor weights. These anchor weights are the three aspects of will to power I examined above. Genealogy is a study of ontology. It is a study of epistemology, and it is a study of ethics.

As noted in chapter five, Nietzsche's ontology can be best described as an organizationist-contellationist position. All entities are comprised of bundles of forces. However, bundles are organized in two ways. Bundles have a "contractual form" that arranges an internal relation between units of power in the bundle. However, bundles are also organized according to how other things (but actually other bundles) perceive them. The latent power of such bundles is then used for the sake of this perceiver bundles' perspective.

If this is true of all things, then it must also be true of the human being. We, then, are bundles. The purpose of a genealogical inquiry is to understand how we have become so organized. Bundles are organized according to naturalistic arrangements, or as Aydin calls them "ground forms." One such ground form appears to be what Nietzsche calls "chains of nutrition" or what we may call DNA. However, such forms may yet be constellated by some other thing. Thus, Nietzsche attempts to understand how this half-human, half-animal creature became men and women, that is, fearful, guilt-ridden, life-denying creatures. The answer as argued in *The Genealogy* is threefold: through the transmission of priestly values and likewise through a breeding program that taught us to value otherworldly things in contrast to this worldly values; through emotional formatting, that is, guilt; and through the adoption of truthfulness coupled to a rigorous yet ascetic scientific methodology. The human being is a confluence of these three sources.

Once we understand how we, as subjects, were produced, we then have the unenviable task of reconstructing ourselves. Character reflection, as a further development and refinement of cognitive selection, provides us with this twofold ability to totalize the self with the goal of overcoming the drives, breeding, and other causal factors that made us who we are. We can get a sense of how and why we act and, by doing so, can learn the practice of acting differently.

How do we go about learning about ourselves? I would argue that the answer is yet another twofold process. The first is epistemological. Nietzsche demonstrates that learning about biology, and cognitive capacities are critical; it is important to understand what we have to work with. However, these facts themselves are always indexed to a perspective. More accurately they are given weight only insofar as we have given them value. All facts are already shot through with power and perspective. Justification is already agenda driven, too. So too, it is important to understand the origins of civilization and why and how specific values have come to have the premium value that they currently have. This point is important because to transform ourselves we must take a critical look at the values which we believe to be valuable. According to Nietzsche, the most valuable value we have is truthfulness. No other coupling to belief will suffice.

Thus Nietzsche must provide a more convincing narrative for the origin of morals than the one traditionally proffered. The only way to do this is to provide a more justified account. Nietzsche, I would argue, undergirds his three accounts in *The Genealogy* with a virtue foundherentist epistemic position. All three essays of *The Genealogy* serve as supports for Nietzsche's overall thesis: The actual engine of human action is power. But power is something that all of us can wield.

The second part of this process concerns the roles of the emotions. Nietzsche realizes that a mere cerebral history of how our current moral system was produced is not enough. Feelings impel beliefs and beliefs in turn drive action. However, feelings, Nietzsche shows, are not completely separate from beliefs. Beliefs can serve to change feelings. We change our feelings along with the desires inspired by them, by reflecting on our emotions. Emotions tell us something about the world and ourselves. They are near-immediate appraisals of our current environmental and mental conditioning. However, because there is epistemic content to emotion, we can assess this information, reflect on it, strategize to change it, constellate it and, if necessary, reconstellate it reinterpreting a supposed "defect," as Nietzsche suggests in section 290 of *The Gay Science*, into a virtue.

NOTES

1. See Nietzsche's commentary on Paul Ree's book in section 7 of the preface *On the Genealogy of Morals*.
2. Nietzsche, *On the Genealogy of Morals*, I: 11, "The noble man . . . conceives the basic concept of 'good' in advance and spontaneously out of himself and only creates for himself an idea of 'bad'!"

3. Nietzsche, *On the Genealogy of Morals*, I:16.
4. Nietzsche, *On the Genealogy of Morals*, GM II: 2, Trans. Clark, 36.
5. Nietzsche, *On the Genealogy of Morals*, GM: preface, 7, 457.

Bibliography

PRIMARY SOURCES (NIETZSCHE)

Nietzsche, Friedrich. *Werke: Kritische Gesamtausgabe*. 22 vols. ed(s)., Giorgio Colli and Mazzino Montinari. Berlin: Walter de Gruyter, 1967–84.

Nietzsche, Friedrich. *Kritische Studienausgabe*. ed(s)., Giorgio Colli and Mazzino Montinari. Berlin: Walter de Gruyter, 1967–88.

TRANSLATIONS OF NIETZSCHE'S PUBLISHED WORKS

Beyond Good and Evil in *Basic Writings of Nietzsche*. Trans. Walter Kaufmann. Intro. Peter Gay. New York: Random House, 2000.

Beyond Good and Evil. Trans. R.J. Holingdale. Intro. Michael Tanner. London, Penguin Books, 2003.

The Birth of Tragedy. Trans. Walter Kaufmann. New York: Vintage Books, 1967.

Human all too Human. Trans. R.J. Holingdale. Intro. Richard Schact. Cambridge University Press: 1996.

The Gay Science. Trans. Walter Kaufmann. New York: Vintage Books, 1974.

On the Genealogy of Morals: A Polemic. Trans. Walter Kaufmann and R.J. Holingdale. New York: Vintage Books, 1989.

On the Genealogy of Morals in *Basic Writings of Nietzsche*. Trans. Walter Kaufmann. Intro Peter Gay New York: Random House, 2000.

On The Genealogy of Morals: A Polemic. Trans. Maudemarie Clark and Alan Swensen. Intro. Maudemarie Clark. Indianapolis, IN: Hackett Publishing ,1998.

Thus Spoke Zarathustra. Trans. by R.J. Holingdale. Harmondsworth, Middlesex: Penguin, 1975.

Twilight of the Idols/The Anti-Christ. Trans. R.J. Hollingdale. Harmondsworth, Middlesex: Penguin, 1972.

Untimely Meditations. Trans. R.J. Hollingdale. Intro. J.P. Stern. Cambridge: Cambridge University Press, 1983.

"The Will to Power." In *The Will to Power*, trans. Walter Kaufmann and R. J. Hollingdale, with an introduction by Walter Kaufmann. New York: Vintage, 1968.

"The Will to Power." In *The Complete Works of Friedrich Nietzsche*, ed. Oscar Levy. *The Will to Power An Attempted Transvaluation of All Values*. Trans. Anthony M. Ludovici. Volumes I and II. New York: Russell and Russell, Inc, 1964.

Nietzsche, Contra Wagner in *The Portable Nietzsche*, Trans. and ed. Walter Kaufmann. London: Penguin Classics, 1977.

A Nietzsche Reader, selected and translated with an introduction by R.J. Holingdale, London: Penguin Books 1977.

SECONDARY WORKS

Abbey, Ruth. *Nietzsche's Middle Period*. New York: Oxford University Press, 2000.

Alcoff, Linda Martin. *Real Know: New Versions of the Coherence Theory of Truth*. Ithaca, NY: Cornell University Press, 1996.

Ardrey, Robert. *The African Genesis: A Personal Investigation into the Animal Origins and Nature of Man*. New York: Dell Publishing, 1961.

Ahern, Daniel. *Nietzsche as Cultural Physician*. Pennsylvania: Pennsylvania University State Press, 1995. *St. Anselm, Anselm of Canterbury: The Major Works, Monologion, Prosologion and Why God Became Man*. ed(s)., Brian Davies and G.R. Evans. Oxford University Press: 1998

Aristotle. *The Nicomachean Ethics*. Trans. David Ross. Oxford: Oxford University Press, 1925.

Aristotle, *Basic Works of Aristotle*, ed. Richard McKeon. New York: Random House, 1942.

Aydin, Ciano. "Nietzsche on Will to Power Toward an Organization-Struggle Model." *Journal of Nietzsche Studies*, 33:1, 2007, 25–48.

Ayer, A.J. *Foundations of Empirical Knowledge*. London: MacMillan, 1940. Ayer, A.J. *Language, Truth and Logic*, 2nd edition. London: Gollancz, 1946.

Babich, Babette, E. *Nietzsche's Philosophy of Science: Reflecting Science on the Ground of Art and Life*. Albany, NY: SUNY, 1994.

Baumeister, Roy, Catanese, Kathleen and Wallace, Harry. "Conquest by Force: A Narcissistic Reactance Theory of Rape and Sexual Coercion." *Review of General Psychology*, 6:1, March 2002, 92–135.

Behe, Michael. *Darwin's Blackbox: The Biochemical Challenge to Evolution*. New York: Free Press, 1996.

Beschta Robert and Ripple, William. "Trophic Cascade Effects in Yellowstone: The First 15 Years After Wolf Reintroduction," *Biological Conservation*, 145:1, January 2012, 205–213.

Beschta, Robert and Ripple, William. "The Role of Large Predators in Maintaining Riparian Plat Communities and River Morphology." *Geomorphology*, 157–158, July 2012, 88–99.

Bird, Alexander. "Natural Kinds" in *The Stanford Encyclopedia of Philosophy* http://plato.stanford.edu/entries/natural-kinds/.

Blondel, Eric. *Nietzsche: The Body and Culture. Philosophy as a philological Genealogy.* Trans. Sean Hand. Stanford, California: Stanford University Press, 1991.

Blondel, Eric. The Question of Genealogy." In *Nietzsche, Genealogy, Morality: Essays on Nietzsche's Genealogy of Morals.* (Hereafter *NGM*). ed. Richard Schacht. Berkeley. California: California University Press, 1994.

Boekhoven, Jeroen, W. *Genealogies of Shamanism: Struggles for Power, Charisma and Authority,* New York: Barkhuis, 2011.

Boas, M. "The Establishment of the Mechanical Philosophy." *Osiris* 10, 1952.

Boscovich, Roger. *A Theory of Natural Philosophy,* ed(s)., J.M. Child. Chicago: Open Court, 1922.

Botha, Catharine F. "Reconsidering the will to power in Heidegger's Nietzsche," *South African Journal of Philosophy,* 35:1, 2016, 111–120.

Bridgman, Percy. *Reflections of a Physicist.* New York: Philosophical Library, 1955.

Brown, Richard, S.G. "Nihilism: "Thus Speaks Physiology" in *Nietzsche and the Rhetoric of Nihilism: Essays on Interpretation, Language and Politics.* ed(s)., Tom Darby, Bela Egyed and Ben Jones. Ottawa: Carleton University Press, 1989.

Brown, Richard, S.G. "Nietzsche: That Profound Physiologist." Aldershot: Ashgate Press, 2004.

Bubner, Rudiger. *Modern German Philosophy.* Trans. Eric Matthews. Cambridge University Press, 1981.

Butterfield, Herbert. *The Whig Interpretation of History.* London: G. Bell and Sons, Ltd., 1963.

Campbell, Neil. *Biology.* Menlo Park California, Benjamin and Cummings, 1991

Cartwright, Nancy. *The Dappled World: A Study of the Boundaries of Science.* Cambridge, UK: Cambridge University Press, 1999.

Chalmers, D.J. *The Conscious Mind: In Search of a Fundamental Theory.* Oxford University Press, 1996.

Churchland, P.M. "Eliminative Materialism and the Propositional Attitudes." *Journal of Philosophy* 78, 67–90, 1981.

Churchland, Paul. *Matter and Consciousness.* Cambridge, M.A.: MIT Press, 1983.

Churchland, Paul. *Neurophilosophy: Toward a Unified Science of the Mind/Brain.* Cambridge, MA: MIT Press, 1986.

Clarke, Maudemarie. *Nietzsche on Truth and Philosophy.* Cambridge, U.K.: Cambridge University Press, 1990.

Conant, James Bryant. *The Overthrow of Phlogiston Theory: The Chemical Revolution of 1775– 1789.* Cambridge MA: Harvard University Press, 1950.

Conway, Daniel, W. "Genealogy and the Critical Method" in *NGM*, 318–334, 1994.

Conway, Daniel, W. "How we became What we are: Tracking the Beasts of Prey in *Nietzsche's On The Genealogy of Morals: Critical Essays,* ed. Christa Davis Acampora. Lanham: Maryland: Rowman and Littlefield, 2006, 305–320.

Cox, Christoph. *Nietzsche, Naturalism and Interpretation.* Berkeley California: University of California Press, 1999.

Craw, R.C. "Margins of cladistics: Identity, differences and place in the emergence of phylogenetic systematics." *Trees of life: Essays in the Philosophy of Biology,* ed. Griffiths. P.E. Dordrecht: Kluwer Academic, 1992, 65–107.

Bibliography

Damasio, Antonio. *The Feeling of What Happens,* New York: Harcourt, 1999.

Dancy, Jonathan and Sosa Ernest. *A Companion to Epistemology.* Cornwall, UK: Blackwell Publishers, 1992.

Danto, Arthur. *Nietzsche as Philosopher.* New York: Columbia University Press, 1980.

Darwin, Charles. *On the Origin of the Species by Means of Natural Selection.* London: Murray, 1859.

Davidson, Donald. "A Coherence Theory of Truth and Knowledge" in *Truth and Interpretation Perspectives on the Philosophy of Donald Davidson.* Basil Blackwell, 1986, 307–319.

De Caro, Mario and MacArthur, David, eds. *Naturalism in Question.* Cambridge, MA: Harvard University Press, 2004.

De Caro Mario. "Is Freedom Really A Mystery?" De Caro and Macarthur eds, *Naturalism in Question*. 188–200.

De Caro, Mario and MacArthur, David, eds. *Naturalism and Normativity.* New York: Columbia University Press, 2010.

Deleuze, Gilles. *Nietzsche and Philosophy.* Trans. Hugh Tomlinson. New York: Columbia University Press, 1983.

Dennett, Daniel C. *Darwin's Dangerous Idea: Evolution and the Meanings of Life.* New York: Simon and Schuster, 1995.

Descartes, Rene. *Meditations and Other Metaphysical Writings*, Trans. Desmond Clarke. London: Penguin Bookk, 2003.

Dewey, John. *The Theory of Emotion* in Robert C. Solomon's, *What is an Emotion: Classic and Contemporary Readings.* Oxford: Oxford University Press, 2003.

Donnellan, Keith. "Reference and Definite Descriptions," in *Philosophical Review* 75, 281–304, 1966.

Emanuele, et. Al. "Raised Plasma Nerve Growth factor Levels associated with Early-Stage Romantic Love." *Psychoneuroendocrinology* 288–94, (April 31, 2006).

Emden, Christian. *Nietzsche's Naturalism: Philosophy and the Life Sciences in the Nineteenth Century.* Cambridge University Press, 2014.

Ellis, George, F.R. "On the Nature of Emergent Reality" in *The Re-emergence of Emergence: The Emergentist Hypothesis from Science to Religion,* ed(s)., Philip Clayton and Paul Davies. Oxford University Press, 2006, 79–109.

Ernster and Schatz, "Mitochrondria: A Historical Review," *The Journal of Cell Biology* 91, 227–255.

Field, Hartry. *How to do Science Without Number: A Defence of Nominalism.* Princeton: Princeton University Press, 1980.

Feigl, H. "The 'Mental' and the 'Physical'" in: *Minnesota Studies in the Philosophy of Science*, II, 370–497. J.J.C. Smart, "Sensations and Brain Processes" in: *Philosophical Review* 68, 141–156.

Feyerabend, Paul. "An attempt at a Realistic Interpretation of Experience."*Proceedings of the Aristotelian Society* 58, 1958.

Feyerabend, Paul. *Against Method: Outline of An Anarchistic Theory of Knowledge.* New York: Verso Books, 1975.

Fine, Kit. "What is Metaphysics?" in *Contemporary Aristotelian Metaphysics.* ed. Tuomas E. Tahko. Cambridge University Press, 2012, 8–25.

Fodor, Jerry. "Special Sciences or the Disunity of Science as a Working Hypothesis." *Synthese* 28, 1974, 97–115.
Foucault, Michel. *The Order of Things*, Trans. A. Sheridan. New York: Pantheon Books, 1973.
Foucault, Michel. "Nietzsche, Genealogy History" *in Language, Counter-Memory Practice*. ed. D. Bouchard. Ithaca, NY: Cornell University Press, 1977.
Foucault, Michel. "Two Lectures" in *Power/Knowledge, Selected Interviews and Other Writings, 1972–1977*. Trans. and ed. Colin Gordon. New York: Pantheon Books, 1980.
Foucault, Michel. *The History of Sexuality Volume II: The Use of Pleasure*. Trans. R. Hurley. New York: Random House, 1985.
Foucault, Michel. *The Foucault Reader*. ed. Paul Rabinow. New York: Pantheon Books, 1990.
Frankena, W.J. "The Naturalistic Fallacy, *Mind*, 48, 1939, 464–77.
Frankfurt, Harry, G. "Freedom of the Will and the Concept of a Person," The Journal of Philosophy, 68:1, January 1971.
Fukuyama, Francis. *The End of History and the Last Man*. New York: The Free Press, 1992.
Gallup, G.G. "Chimpanzees: Self-Recognition," *Science*, 167, 1970.
Gemes, Ken. "Nietzsche's Critique of Truth." *Philosophy and Phenomenological Research*, 52, 1992, 47–65.
Gibb, Sophie. "The Causal Closure Principle.," *Philosophical Quarterly*, 65:261, April 2015, 626–647.
Goldman, Alvin, I."A Causal Theory of Knowing." *The Journal of Philosophy*, 64, 1967, 357–372.
Goldman, Alvin, I. *Epistemology and Cognition*. Cambridge, Mass: Harvard University Press, 1986.
Goldman, Alvin, I. "Reliabilism." In *A Companion to Epistemology*. ed(s). Johnathan Dancy and Ernest Sosa. Cornwall, UK: Blackwell Publishers, 1992.
Granier, Jean. *Le probleme de la Verite dans la Philosophie de Nietzsche*. Paris: Seuil, 1966.
Granier, Jean. "Nietzsche's Conception of Chaos." Trans. David B. Allison. In *The New Nietzsche: Contemporary Styles of Interpretation*. Ed. David B. Allison Cambridge Mass: MIT Press, 1977.
Gettier, Edmund. "Is Justified True Belief Knowledge?" *Analysis*, 23, 1963, 121–123.
Gibson, J.J. *The Ecological Approach to Visual Perception*. Boston: Houghton Mifflin, 1979.
Goodall, Jane. "The Sentience of Chimpanzees and Other Animals" in *Animal Ethics and Trade: The Challenge of Sentience*, ed. Jacky Turner and Joyce D'Silva. London: EarthScan, 2006, 3–12.
Grimm, Rudiger. *Nietzsche's Theory of Knowledge*. Berlin: Walter de Gruyter, 1977.
Guthrie, W.K.C. *A History of Greek Philosophy, Volume 1, The Early Presocratics and the Pythagoreans*. Cambridge UK: Cambridge University Press, 1962.
Guyer, Paul. *Kant*. London: Routledge, 2006. Haack, Susan. "Theories of Knowledge: An Analytic Framework." *Proceedings of the Aristotelian Society* 83, (1983):143–157.

Haack, Susan. *Evidence and Inquiry, Towards Reconstruction in Epistemology.* Oxford: Blackwell Publishers, 1995.

Haack, Susan. "Precis of *Evidence and Inquiry*: Towards Reconstruction in Epistemology." *Philosophy and Phenomenological Research* LVI:3, September, 1996, 611–615.

Haack, Susan. "Reply to Commentators." *Philosophy and Phenomenological Research* 56:3 September, 1996, 641–656.

Haack, Susan. *The Intellectual journey of an Eminent Logician-Philosopher.*

Haack, Susan. *Defending Science Within Reason: Between Scientism and Cynicism.* Amherst, New York: Prometheus Books, 2003.

Haack, Susan. "The Ideal of Intellectual Integrity in Life and Literature." *New Literary History*, 36, 2005, 359–373.

Habermas, Jurgen. *The Philosophical Discourse of Modernity*, Trans. Frederick Lawrence. Cambridge, MA: MIT Press, 1985.

Hacking, Ian. *The Social Construction of What?* Cambridge Mass: Harvard University Press, 1997.

Hales, Steven and Welshon, Rex. *Nietzsche's Perspectivism.* Urbana, Illinois: University of Illinois Press, 2000.

Hanson, N.R. *Patterns of Discovery.* Cambridge UK: Cambridge University Press, 1958.

Hatcher, R. "Insight and Self-Observation." *Journal of the American Psychoanalytic Association* 21, 337–398.

Hegel, G.W.F. *The Phenomenology of Spirit.* Trans. A.V. Miller, J.N. Findlay Oxford: Oxford University Press, 1979.

Heidegger, Martin. *Nietzsche, Volume 3: The Will to Power as Knowledge and as Metaphysics.* Trans. Joan Stambaugh, David Farrell Krell and Frank A. Capuzzi. New York: Harper and Row 1987.

Heil, John. *The Universe as We Find It.* New York: Oxford University Press, 2012.

von. Helmholz, Hermann. *Hermann von Helmholtz. Epistemological Writings. The Paul Hertz/Moritz Schlick Centenary Edition of 1921*, Trans. Malcom Lowe. ed. Robert Cohen and Yehuda Elkana. Dordrecht: D. Reidel, 1977.

Henze, Martin et. al. "Evolutionary biology: essence of mitochondria." *Nature* 426, 2003, 127–8.

Higgins, Kathleen, Marie. "On the Genealogy of Morals—Nietzsche's Gift." *In NGM*. Hinman, Lawrence. "Nietzsche, Metaphor and Truth." *Philosophy and Phenomenological Research* (1982): 179–198.

Hinman, Lawrence. "Can a Form of Life Be Wrong." *Philosophy,* 58:225, July 1983, 339–355.

Holton, Richard. *Willing, Wanting, Waiting.* Oxford: Oxford University Press, 2009.

Houlgate, Stephen. "Kant, Nietzsche and the 'Thing in Itself." *Nietzsche-Studien* 1993, 22.

Hoy, David, Couzens. "Nietzsche, Foucault and the Genealogical Method." In *NGM.*

Hume, David. *An Enquiry Concerning Human Understanding in Classics of Western Philosophy,* ed. Stephen Cahn. Indianapolis: Hackett, 1977.

Hurka, Thomas. *Perfectionism.* Oxford: Oxford University Press, 1996.

Jackson, F. *From Metaphysics to Ethics: A Defense of Conceptual Analysis.* Oxford Clarendon Press, 1998.

Janaway, Christopher. "Nietzsche's Illustration of the Art of Exegesis," *European Journal of Philosophy*, 5, 1997, 251–68.
Janaway, Christopher. "Naturalism and Genealogy." In *Blackwell's Companions to Philosophy: A Companion to Nietzsche.* ed. Keith Ansell Pearson. Blackwell Publishers, 2006, 337–353.
Janaway, Christopher. *Beyond Selflessness: Reading Nietzsche's Genealogy.* Oxford: Oxford University Press, 2007).
Janaway, Christoper. *Nietzsche, Naturalism and Normativity.* ed. Christopher Janaway and Simon Robertson. Oxford: Oxford University Press, 2012.
Jervis, Robert. *Why Intelligence Fails Lessons from the Iranian Revolution and the Iraq War.* Ithaca, NY: Cornell University Press, 2010.
Katsafanas, Paul. *Agency and the Foundations of Ethics, Nietzschean Constitutivism.* New York: Oxford University Press, 2013.
Kaufmann, Walter. *Nietzsche: Philosopher, Psychiatrist, Anti-Christ.* Cleveland: The World Publishing Company, 1956
Keenan, Julian, Paul. *The Face in the Mirror: How Do We Know Who We Are:* New York: Harper Collins, 2003.
Kenny, Anthony. *Five Ways*: St. Thomas Aquinas. London: Routledge Press, 2003.
Kim, Jaegwon. *Physicalism or Something Near Enough.* Princeton New Jersey: Princeton University Press, 2005.
Kirk, G.S., Raven J.E. and Schofield, M. *The Presocratic Philosophers*, 2nd Edition. Cambridge, UK: Cambridge University Press, 1983.
Klein, Wayne. *Nietzsche and the Promise of Philosophy.* Albany, NY: State University of New York Press, 1997.
Koffman, Sarah. *Nietzsche et la Metaphor.* Paris: Payot, 1972.
Kornblith, Hilary. *Naturalizing Epistemology.* Cambridge, MA: MIT Press, 1994.
Kuhn, Thomas, S. *The Structure of Scientific Revolutions,* 2nd Enlarged Edition. Chicago: University of Chicago Press, 1970.
Laplace, Pierre, *A Philosophical Essay on Probabilities*, 6th Edition (1840), trans. F.W. Truscott and F.L. Emory. New York: Cosimo Classics, 2007.
Lakatos, Imre. *The Methodology of Scientific Research Programs, Philosophical Papers* Volume 1. Cambridge, UK: Cambridge University Press, 1978.
Lazaraus, Richard. "Appraisal: The Minimal Cognitive Prerequisites of Emotion" in *What is an Emotion.* ed. Robert C. Solomon. 125–131.
Lehrer, Keith. "The Coherence Theory of Knowledge." *Philosophical Topics*, 14, 1986, 5–25.
Leiter, Brian. "Perspectivism in the Genealogy of Morals." In *NGM.* Leiter, Brian. *Nietzsche on Morality.* London: Routledge, 2002.
Leiter, Brian. "Nietzsche's Theory of the Will." *Philosopher's Imprint*, 7:7 2007.
Lightbody, Brian. *Philosophical Genealogy: An Epistemological Reconstruction of Nietzsche and Foucault's Genealogical Method, Volumes 1 and 2.* New York: Peter Lang Publishers, 2010 and 2011.
Lightbody, Brian. *The Problem of Naturalism: Analytic Perspectives, Continental Virtues.* Lanham, Maryland, Lexington Books, 2013.
Lightbody, Brian. *Dispersing the Clouds of Temptation.* Eugene: Oregon, Pickwick Press, 2015.

Lingis, Alphonso. "The Will to Power" in *The New Nietzsche*, ed. David B. Allison, Cambridge Mass: MIT Press, 1977.

Lingis, Alphonso. *Excess Eros and Culture*. New York: State University of New York Press, 1984.

Long, Thomas. "Nietzsche's Philosophy of Medicine." *Nietzsche Studien* Band 19, (1990): 112–128.

Lowe, E.J. "Causal Closure Principle and Emergentism," *Philosophy* 75 (2000): 571–85.

MacIntyre, Alasdair. "Genealogies and Subversions." In *Nietzsche, Genealogy, History*. Magnus, Bernd. *Nietzsche's Existential Imperative*. Bloomington: Indiana University Press, 1978.

Magnus, Bernd. "The Use and Abuse of The Will to Power." In *Reading Nietzsche*. ed(s). R.C. Solomon and K.M. Higgins. Oxford: Oxford University Press, 1988.

Man, Paul de. *Allegories of Reading*. New Haven: Yale University Press, 1979.

Marshall, Hobbs and Cooper. "Stream Hydrology Limits Recovery of Riparian Ecosystems after Wolf Introduction," *Proceedings of the Royal Society B-Biological Sciences*, April 2013 280, 1756.

McDermott, Tingley, Cowden, Frazzetto, and Johnson "Monoamine Oxdase A predicts Behavioral Aggression Following Provocation." *Proceedings of the National Academy of Sciences*, 106:7, 2008, 2118–2123.

Mcginn, Colin. *Prehension: The Hand and the Emergence of Humanity*. Cambridge MA: MIT Press, 2015

McIntyre, Alex. "Communion in Joy: Will to Power and Eternal Return in Grand Politics." *Nietzsche-Studien*, 25, 1996, 24–41.

Mele, Alfred. *Effective Intentions, The Power of Conscious Will*. Oxford: Oxford University Press, 2009.

Migotti, Mark. "Slave Morality, Socrates, and the Bushmen: A Critical Introduction to *On the Genealogy of Morals*, Essay I" in *Nietzsche's on the Genealogy of Morals: Critical Essays*. Lanham, MD: Rowman and Littlefield, 2006, 109–131.

Montmarquet, James, A. *Epistemic Virtue and Doxastic Responsibility*. Lanham, MD: Rowman and Littlefield Publishers Inc 1993.

Moore, G.E. *Principia Ethica*. Cambridge, UK: Cambridge University Press, 1903.

Moore, Gregory. *Nietzsche, Biology, Metaphor*. Cambridge, UK: Cambridge University Press, 2002.

Muller-Lauter, Wolfgang. *Nietzsche: His Philosophy of Contradictions and the Contradictions of his Philosophy*. Trans. David J. Parent. University of Illinois Press, 1999.

Nagel, Thomas. *The View from Nowhere*. Oxford: Oxford University Press, 1986.

Nehamas, Alexander. *Nietzsche: Life as Literature*. Cambridge Mass: Harvard University Press: 1985.

Nehamas, Alexander. "Nietzsche." In *A Companion to Epistemology*. London: Blackwell Publishers, 1992.

Neurath, Otto, Von. 'Protocol Sentences' (Protokollsatze). Trans. A.J. Ayer. In *Logical Positivism*. New York: Free Press, 1959.

O'Connor, Timothy. "Emergent Properties." *American Philosophical Quarterly*, 31, 1994, 91–104

Oliver, Kelley. *Subjectivity Without Subjects: From Abject Fathers to Desiring Mothers* Lanham; MD, Rowman and Littlefield, Publishers, 1998.
Owen, David. *Nietzsche's Genealogy of Morality.* Montreal: McGill-Queen's University Press 2007.
Papineau, David. "Mind the Gap," *Philosophical Perspectives*, 32:12, 373–388, 1998.
Pepper, S. "Emergence" *Journal of Philosophy* 23 (1926): 241–245.
Pasley, Malcolm. "Nietzsche's Use of Medical Terms." In *Nietzsche: Imagery and Thought.* ed. Malcom Pasley. Berkley, California: California University Press, 1978.
Plato, *Plato: Five Dialogues*: *Euthyphro, Apology, Crito, Meno Phaedo*, Trans. G.M.A. Grube. Indianapolis, IN: Hackett Publishing Company, 1981.
Plato, *Phaedo* in *Great Dialogues of Plato,* Trans. W.H.D. Rouse. New York: Signet Classics, 1984.
Plato. *The Theaetetus.* In *The Collected Dialogues of Plato.* ed. Edith Hamilton and Huntington Cairns. Trans. F.M. Cornford. New Jersey: Princeton Press, 1963.
Pollock, John L. *Contemporary Theories of Knowledge.* Totowa: Rowman, 1986.
Popper, Karl. *The Logic of Scientific Discovery.* New York: Harper and Row Publishers, 1959.
Porter, James I. "Nietzsche's Theory of the Will to Power," in *A Companion to Nietzsche.* ed. Keith Ansell Pearson. UK: Blackwell Publishers, 2006, 548–565.
Povinelli, Daniel, J.*Folk Physics for Apes: The Chimpanzee's Theory of How the World Works.* Oxford University Press, 2003.
Price, Huw. "Truth as Convenient Friction" *in Naturalism and Normativity*, ed(s)., De Caro and Macarthur. New York: Columbia University Press, 2010, 229–252.
Proctor, Nobel, S. *Manual of Ornithology: Avian Structure and Function.* New Haven: Yale University Press, 1993.
Putnam, Hilary. *Realism and Reason: Philosophical Papers, Volume III.* Cambridge, UK: Cambridge University Press, 1983.
Putnam, Hilary. *Representation and Reality.* Cambridge, Mass: MIT Press, 1996.
Putnam, Hilary. *The Many Faces of Realism, The Paul Carns Lectures.* New York: Carus Publishing, 1988.
Quine, W.V.O. "Two Dogmas of Empiricism." In *From a Logical Point of View.* Cambridge, MA: Harvard University Press, 1953.
Quine, W.V.O. *Word and Object.* Cambridge, Mass: MIT Press, 1960. Quine, W.V.O. and Ullian, J. *The Web of Belief.* 2nd Edition. New York: Random House, 1978.
Reginster, Bernard. *The Affirmation of Life: Nietzsche on the Overcoming of Nihilism.* Harvard University Press, 2006
Richardson, John. *Nietzsche's System.* Oxford: Oxford University Press, 1996.
Richardson, John. *Nietzsche's New Darwinism.* Oxford: Oxford University Press, 2004.
Ritchie, Jack. *Understanding Naturalism.* Stocksfield, UK: Acumen Press, 2008.
Robinson, T.M. *Heraclitus: Fragments, A Text and Commentary.* Toronto: University of Toronto Press, 1987.
Rorty, Richard. *Objectivity, Relativism, Truth, Philosophical Papers Volume I.* Cambridge, UK: Cambridge University Press, 1991.
Rorty, Richard. *Contingency, Irony, Solidarity* Cambridge, UK: Cambridge University Press, 1989.

Rorty, Richard. "Science as Solidarity" in *Dismantling Truth*, ed. Hilary Lawson and Lisa Appignanesi. New York: St. Martin's, 1989.

Rorty, Richard. "Is Truth a Goal of Enquiry? Donald Davidson versus Crispin Wright" in *Richard Rorty, Truth and Progress, Philosophical Papers*, Volume 3, New York: Cambridge University Press, 1998.

Rorty, Richard. "Rorty's Reply to Price's Paper, "Truth as Convenient Friction," "Rorty Further Remarks" (February 2005) in *Naturalism and Normativity*, 255.

Ruse, Michael. "The Biological Sciences Can Act as a Ground for Ethics" in *Contemporary Debates in the Philosophy of Biology*. New York: Wiley-Blackwell, 2010.

Schacht, Richard. *Nietzsche*. London: Routledge, 1983 Schacht, Richard. "Nietzsche's Naturalism." *The Journal of Nietzsche Studies*, 43:2, Autumn 2012, 185–212.

Schafnner, Kenneth. *Nineteenth Century Aether Theories*. Oxford: Pergamon Press, 1972.

Schrift, Alan. *Nietzsche and the Question of Interpretation*. New York: Routledge, 1990.

Sellars, Wilfrid. "Empiricism and Philosophy of Mind" in *Minnesota Studies in Philosophy of Science*. Minneapolis, MN: University of Minnesota Press, 1956, 253–329.

Sellars, Wilfred. "Empiricism and the Philosophy of Mind." In *Science, Perception and Reality*. New York: The Humanities Press, 1963.

Smart, JJC. "Sensations and Brain Processes." *Philosophical Review* 68,141–156.

Soll, Ivan. "Nietzsche, On Cruelty, Asceticism, and the Failure of Hedonism." In *NGM*.

Sosa, Ernest. "The Raft and the Pyramid." *Midwest Studies in Philosophy*, v. 1980.

Sosa, Ernest. *Knowledge in Perspective: Selected Essays in Epistemology*. New York: Cambridge University Press, 1991.

Stack, George. "Nietzsche's Critique of Things in Themselves." *Dialogos* 36: 1980.

Stack, George. "Nietzsche and Perspectival Interpretation." *Philosophy Today*, 25, 1981.

Stevenson, C.L. The Emotive Meanings of Ethical Terms (1937) in *Ethics: History Theory and Contemporary Issues*, ed. Steven Cahn and Peter Markie. New York: Oxford University Press, 2015 6th edition. 514–524.

Storey, David, E. *Naturalizing Heidegger: His Confrontation with Nietzsche, His Contributions to Environmental Philosophy*. SUNY Press, 2015.

Strong, Tracy. *Friedrich Nietzsche and the Politics of Transfiguration:* Expanded Edition. Berkeley, California: University of California Press, 1978.

Stroud, Barry. "The Charm of Naturalism" in *Naturalism in Question*, 21–36.

Taylor, Charles. "The Concept of a Person," Philosophical Papers. Volume 1. Cambridge: Cambridge University Press, 1985

Thalos, Mariam. "Two Dogmas of Naturalized Epistemology." *Dialectica* 53:2, 1999, 111–138.

Wan, Chikwook. "Overdetermination, Counterfactuals and Mental Causation" *Philosophical Review*, 123:2, 2014, 205–229.

Wegner, Daniel. *The Illusion of Conscious Will*. Cambridge, MA: MIT Press, 2002.

White, Richard. "The Return of the Master. An Interpretation of Nietzsche's Genealogy of Morals." In *NGM*.

Wilcox, John, T. *Truth and Value in Nietzsche*. Ann Arbor Michigan: University of Michigan Press, 1974.

Williams, Bernard. "Nietzsche's Minimalist Moral Psychology." In *NGM*. Williams, Bernard. *Truth and Truthfulness: An Essay in Genealogy*. Princeton and Oxford: Princeton University Press, 2002.

Williams, Linda. *Nietzsche's Mirror, The World as Will to Power*. Lexington MD: Rowman and Littlefield, 2000.

Wittgenstein, Ludwig. *Philosophical Investigations*. Ed(s). G.E.M. Anscombe and R. Rhees.Trans. G.E.M. Anscombe. Oxford: Blackwell, 1959.

Zagzebski, Linda, Trinkaus. *Virtues of the Mind: An Inquiry into the Nature of Virtues and the Ethical Foundations of Knowledge*. New York : Cambridge University Press, 1996.

Index

Abbey, Ruth, 9
akrasia (weakness of will), 73–74
Aristotle, 56–57, 74, 83n2, 185

bad conscience, 71, 78, 98–99, 137–38,
    149–51, 176, 181, 186n10
Boscovich, Roger, 58, 83n8
bundle theory:
    agregationist/conjunctivist position,
        127–30;
    constellationist position, 130–32;
    organizationist/internalist position,
        132–33;
    synthesis of constellationist and
        organizationist, position, 133–35

Causality:
    powers model, 19, 138;
    productive model, 14–18
Churchlands Paul and Patricia, 7–8
conflict model of self, 71–73

deflationism, 11, 19, 25, 55n67, 122

eidecity, xii–xvii
eliminativism, 25, 77
emergentism, XVII, 15, 136–37
epistemic meritorious problem,
    (EMP), 33

error problem of perspectivism, 80–81,
    150–56
eternal return/recurrence, 103–10
ethical naturalism, 1, 74
Euthyphro, 4

Fine, Kit, xiii–xvii
Foucault, Michel, 37, 51n46,
    51n49, 69–70, 86n47, 179,
    181, 186n1
foundherentism, 147–51;
    virtue, ix, 159, 165

ground, xii–xvii, xviiin9
ground forms (of will to power), 68,
    136, 164, 191

Heidegger, Martin, xi, xii, xiv, xviiin1,
    2, 9, 1 20n2
homunculus fallacy, 60
Hume, David, 3, 12 21n8, 33, 61,
    153, 182
hypokeimenon (view of substance), 76,
    78

Intentions, 94–95

Janaway, Christopher, xviiin 8, 20n2,
    43–45

Kant, Immanuel, 11, 75–76, 80, 181–82

Leiter, Brian, 24n55, 32–45, 80, 87n66, 103, 109, 117, 175–76, 186n4

mediation (Problem of), 153–54
mirror test, 89, 103–13
Moore, G.E., 4, 11
morality in a pejorative sense (MPS), 40, 42, 103, 175
multiple realization argument, 94

natural kind of thing, 97, 134
natural selection, 6, 20n5, 52n55, 62–64, 89, 97, 99–102, 118, 126, 185
nature as container, 75–76
nerve growth factor, 7

optimist epistemology hypothesis, 117
overdeterminism, 16

philosophical genealogy, 37–39
phlogiston, 27
purity claim, 34
Putnam, Hilary, 30
philosophies of the corner, 182

Quine, W.V.O., 8–10

resentiment, 177–79

Schacht, Richard, 45–47
selective cognition, 176–78
Sellars, Wilfrid, 17, 24n51, 26–28, 43
Stevenson, C.L, 11–13
subject spacing, 155
supernaturalism, 3

trophic cascade effects, 101, 121n44
true viewers/ subsumers, 128
type-facts, 33

will to power expression valence, 105

About the Author

Brian Lightbody is associate professor of philosophy at Brock University, located in Saint Catharines, Ontario, Canada. He has published numerous articles and book chapters on such thinkers as Foucault, Nietzsche, Haack, Ellul, Sartre, Heidegger, Marcuse, and Husserl. He has authored four monographs: *Philosophical Genealogy: An Epistemological Reconstruction of Nietzsche and Foucault's Genealogical Method* (2 vols.), *The Problem of Naturalism: Analytic Perspectives, Continental Virtues*, and *Dispersing the Clouds of Temptation: Turning Away from Weakness of Will and Turning Towards the Sun*.